TEACHER LEADER STORIES

The Power of CASE METHODS

Judy Swanson
Kimberly Elliott
Jeanne Harmon
Foreword by **Barbara Miller**

CORWIN
A SAGE Company

FOR INFORMATION:

Corwin
A SAGE Company
2455 Teller Road
Thousand Oaks, California 91320
(800) 233-9936
Fax: (800) 417-2466
www.corwin.com

SAGE Ltd.
1 Oliver's Yard
55 City Road
London EC1Y 1SP
United Kingdom

SAGE India Pvt. Ltd.
B 1/I 1 Mohan Cooperative Industrial Area
Mathura Road, New Delhi 110 044
India

SAGE Asia-Pacific Pte. Ltd.
33 Pekin Street #02-01
Far East Square
Singapore 048763

Acquisitions Editor: Dan Alpert
Associate Editor: Megan Bedell
Editorial Assistant: Sarah Bartlett
Production Editor: Cassandra Margaret Seibel
Copy Editors: Codi Bowman, Cate Huisman
Typesetter: C&M Digitals (P) Ltd.
Proofreader: Jennifer Gritt
Indexer: Wendy Allex
Cover Designer: Scott Van Atta
Permissions Editor: Karen Ehrmann

Photo of Elliott on page xiii: Mark W. Vallone, Photographer

Printed in the United States of America

Library of Congress Cataloging-in-Publication Data

Swanson, Judy.

Teacher leader stories : the power of case methods / Judy Swanson, Kimberly Elliott, Jeanne Harmon.

p. cm.
Includes bibliographical references and index.

ISBN 978-1-4129-9523-8 (pbk. : alk. paper)

1. School management and organization—United States—Case studies. 2. Educational leadership—United States—Case studies. 3. Problem solving—United States—Case studies. 4. Decision making—United States—Case studies. I. Elliott, Kimberly Anna, 1964- II. Harmon, Jeanne. III. Title.

LB2805.S84 2011
371.200973—dc22   2011000033

This book is printed on acid-free paper

11 12 13 14 15 10 9 8 7 6 5 4 3 2 1

Contents

Foreword

Barbara Miller, Education Development Center

Teacher leaders—educators who take on leadership responsibilities meant to improve practice in their schools and beyond—are an important force in reforming K–12 education. The impact of their work is beginning to be understood, yet the resources to help them develop and refine their leadership practices are still few and far between.

This book is one of those needed resources. It offers rich and thoughtful cases of teacher leaders' practices and the dilemmas they must address as well as a clear process for teacher leaders to write cases to make meaning of their experience so that others can benefit. This volume can be used productively by teacher leaders themselves and by those who design and facilitate professional development for teacher leaders.

These cases—and the process for developing cases such as these— reveal the introspection that teacher leaders often bring to their work. Reading these cases and, more important, discussing and reflecting on the cases with others, is like peering over the shoulder of a teacher leader to see the practice, hear the questions, witness the successes, and acknowledge the challenges. Having that up-close-and-personal vantage point invites those working with these cases to be similarly reflective and committed to figuring out the answers to the hard, yet important, questions posed in each case.

These cases speak to the following fundamental issues that teacher leaders encounter in their work, whether that work is in the classroom; at the district level; or on a state, regional, or national stage:

- Building support among administrators
- Dealing with resistance
- Establishing and maintaining credibility
- Developing new expertise
- Defining roles and responsibilities

By situating these issues in real-life contexts, the cases offer insight and vivid detail to develop an understanding of what makes an issue problematic and how it might be addressed to enhance teacher leader practice.

There is a real and pressing need for this book, because the wisdom of experience of teacher leaders is an important knowledge source that should be available to other teacher leaders. The teacher leaders who authored the 16 cases in this book don't claim to have all the answers or to be experts; rather, they frame the dilemmas they faced in ways that open opportunities to learn from their actions, they reflect on their decisions and questions, and they identify lessons that cross from a teacher leader's case into one's own context.

Beyond the cases themselves, this book offers a facilitation guide for each case with questions, activities, and suggestions for constructing a meaningful professional learning experience. There are guidelines for engaging in case analysis, many tips teacher leaders can employ as they work with these cases, and a clear process for how cases like these might be written by teacher leaders. This book, then, is both a user's guide for teacher leaders to learn from and develop cases of practice as well as a volume of cases reflecting the wisdom of these 16 teacher leaders. It is one of the very resources that are needed to help teacher leaders develop and refine their leadership practice in support of improving K–12 education.

Preface

The Center for Strengthening the Teaching Profession (CSTP) is an independent, nonprofit organization dedicated to building a strong, supported, and effective teaching force for Washington's students. CSTP believes teacher leaders with the right combination of skills, knowledge, vision, and opportunities can and do improve teaching quality, increase student learning, and enhance the profession.

CSTP offers opportunities for teacher leaders to develop skills in speaking and writing regarding professional issues, identifies opportunities for experienced teachers to participate in policy discussions, and supports accomplished teachers as they expand their knowledge and skills to be successful leaders for and among their colleagues.

CSTP's case-writing retreats are an important aspect of its leadership development work. Over the course of four summers, the writers who produced this book's cases worked intensively in small groups—discussing their cases, writing and rewriting drafts, and critiquing one another's work. The result is an array of compelling cases covering a broad range of leadership experiences that will help all teacher leaders grow.

Acknowledgments

We are deeply grateful to the teacher-authors for trusting us when we claimed this challenging venture into a new genre of writing would be rewarding. We were continually impressed with the honesty and deep reflection they brought to the task and their willingness to open their professional lives to the rest of us. Many thanks to Washington educators Sarah Applegate, Matthew Colley, Molly Daley, Christy Glick Diefendorf, Christopher Drajem, Terese Emry, Debra Rose Howell, Diane Kane, Claudia McBride, Joanna Michelson, Jane Oczkewicz, Irene Smith, and Krista Swenson, as well as to those who chose to remain anonymous.

The Stuart Foundation funded much of the cost of the summer case-writing retreats as well as the development of the supporting text in this book. CSTP is grateful for the foundation's investment in this contribution to the field.

We are forever indebted to Dan Alpert at Corwin who was enthusiastic about this project from the beginning and helped shape our lump of clay into a polished vessel.

And finally, we dedicate this book to Lee and Judy Shulman. Lee issued the original challenge to us to get teacher leaders writing about the dilemmas they face, and Judy taught us how to do it.

Enjoy,

Judy Swanson, Research for Quality Schools
Kimberly Elliott, The Word Mechanic
Jeanne Harmon, Center for Strengthening the Teaching Profession

PUBLISHER'S ACKNOWLEDGMENTS

Corwin gratefully acknowledges the contributions of the following reviewers:

Bertha L. Brown, Codirector
Professional Development Services/Teacher Leadership Program
Houston Independent School District
Hattie Mae White Educational Center
Houston, TX

Nancy Brumer, Staff Developer
Guilderland Schools
Guilderland, NY

Tammy Evans, Director
Professional Development
Bradenton, FL

Stephanie R. Moss, Director
Curriculum and Instruction
Houston Independent School District
Houston, TX

About the Authors

Judy Swanson, PhD leads a nonprofit research and evaluation firm, Research for Quality Schools, in Seattle, Washington. For 20 years, she has conducted research in urban schools throughout the United States. Her expertise and recent research have focused on teacher leadership, professional development for instructional improvement, and teacher development at all stages of a teacher's career. She has worked with the Center for Strengthening the Teaching Profession (CSTP) to develop and facilitate case-writing retreats for teacher leaders since 2003.

She received her PhD in educational psychology at Stanford University. She may be reached at jswanson@4qualityschools.org.

For 19 years, **Kimberly Elliott** has written about P–16 education reform issues, raised funds to support innovative health and education projects, and developed curriculum materials. As The Word Mechanic, she currently helps clients such as the Center for Strengthening the Teaching Profession (CSTP), Education Development Center (EDC), and the National Association for the Education of Young Children (NAEYC) create resources that promote changes in teacher practice and in educational systems to enhance student learning. She began her career at Wheelock College, where she helped advance the professional and leadership development of early childhood teachers. She has special expertise in writing for the web, and she has contributed to online learning environments such as the *Success at the Core* professional development toolkit developed by EDC and Vulcan Productions. A published author, she produces training guides, reports, articles, policy briefs, and white papers for educators and policymakers and has edited books published by Jossey-Bass, Rowman & Littlefield, and Heinemann. She may be reached at info@thewordmechanic.com (www.thewordmechanic.com).

 **Jeanne Harmon** is the founding executive director for the Center for Strengthening the Teaching Profession (CTSP), an independent nonprofit organization focused on improving teaching quality in Washington State. Before launching CSTP in 2003, she managed the public-private partnership that created Washington's statewide system of support for National Board Certification for teachers. CSTP develops leadership skills and promotes leadership opportunities for the state's 5,200 National Board Certified Teachers as well as hundreds of mentors and instructional coaches and other accomplished teachers across Washington. Previously, Jeanne taught elementary and middle school in Central Kitsap School District (Silverdale, Washington), directed technology and professional development efforts there, and spent five years in the Northeast coordinating services to a network of 70 schools committed to math and science reform. She may be reached at jeanne@cstp-wa.org. (Learn more about CSTP at www.cstp-wa.org.)

Introduction

Every day, moment by moment and decision by decision, thousands of teacher leaders nationwide are working to improve the quality of education. As they fill an ever-expanding array of roles—mentors, coaches, curriculum reformers, advocates, and staff developers—in their schools and districts, their leadership development journeys are most often a process of trial and error. Teacher leadership is defined in many ways (see Chapter 1). It does not come with a user's manual, and few teacher leaders receive specialized training and support for their new roles. Instead, they must learn how to guide changes in learning environments while negotiating a complex obstacle course of district politics, interpersonal conflicts, and reform initiatives. Although the journey of each teacher leader is different, all must find strategies to cope with unfamiliar situations with few tools and resources. In the following montage, excerpts from 3 of the 16 cases that appear in this book demonstrate that even highly skilled, perceptive educators find their new roles inevitably lead them back to school—fumbling for answers and questioning themselves.

Mrs. G., I need your help *now*. I tried the science lesson and the kids just destroyed it!" I try to listen to Ryan as he explains to me everything the students have done wrong. He is having this conversation in front of his students in the middle of class. *What has gone wrong? Has all of my work been a waste of time?* (When Do I Tell? Chapter 3)

Mark interrupts, "Again, I am not comfortable with this idea of accountability and visits." This spark ignites other voices. . . ."I don't feel we have enough time to plan this right now." "What if we only offer positive feedback first?" "What about first-year teachers? Can we be excused?" *I don't know how to respond to this snarled web of worries and fears.* (Filling a Leadership Vacuum, Chapter 4)

One of the few colleagues who knew about my decision to apply quickly grabbed me. "Steve told the whole staff you applied to the district office. . . . He also joked we should shun you like the Amish do when a member of the community chooses to leave." *I didn't even know if I had the job yet, but I already felt like I violated the trust of the community.* (Where Do I Stand? Leadership in a Culture of Us and Them, Chapter 4)

Consensus is growing that successful school improvement will require strategies that foster leadership at all levels of the system (Elmore, 2000; Fullan, Hill, & Crevola, 2006; Lambert, 2003; Spillane, 2006). As teacher leaders, like the ones spotlighted in the previous montage, are called on to lead school improvement efforts, there is increasing recognition that they need meaningful learning opportunities to develop leadership skills. All of the teacher leaders who contributed their stories to this volume used a powerful form of professional development—case methods—to reflect on and learn from key turning points in their journeys into leadership. Learning from case methods is powerful because of the inherent qualities cases offer:

• *Compelling narrative accounts:* The cases explore real, and really troubling, events. These stories of leadership in the making—and often leadership under fire—actively engage readers in the authors' experiences and provide insight into the many faces and phases of teacher leadership. By writing these accounts, the authors themselves gained a deeper understanding of teacher leadership and the problematic events that led them to write their cases.

• *Readily identifiable conflicts and contexts:* The cases present a broad range of leadership dilemmas that arise frequently across diverse roles and settings. From special educators to librarians to district literacy coaches to beginning teacher mentors, all of the case authors explore the rough and often murky terrain of teacher leadership. Among the 16 cases, at least 1 has special meaning for every teacher leader and educator.

• *Unsolved problems and unanswered questions:* The cases do not end tidily. The authors do not wrap up the conflict in the last several paragraphs and present a solution. Instead, all 16 cases end in the midst of a quandary, challenging readers to think about what they would do in the same circumstances. In doing so, they provoke deep thinking and discussions about the factors that contributed to the dilemma and how to solve it from multiple points of view.

WHO THIS BOOK IS FOR

We imagine that this book may be of use to many educators—including school and district leaders—who are interested in learning more about teacher leadership, looking for ways to support teacher leaders, or seeking effective professional development models. However, we wrote this book with two specific groups of educators in mind: (1) staff development professionals and (2) teacher leaders.

Staff Development Professionals

With this book, we want to encourage all of those charged with designing and facilitating professional development for teacher leaders—curriculum directors, instructional leaders, staff development consultants, and education professors—to explore the powerful ways in which case writing and collaborative case analysis foster teacher leadership. We hope that you will be motivated to undertake leading case-writing seminars in your settings and inspire teacher leaders to write their leadership cases. Be forewarned: Case writing requires a significant investment. However, the rewards are great. According to the writers whose cases are published here, there are many reasons to take on this challenging work. As Naumes and Naumes (1999) note, writing a case is essentially an action research project with a sample of one. It's a rare opportunity for teacher leaders to engage in introspection, to examine a troubling or painful experience they want to understand, with the support of empathetic colleagues.

We focus on using case methods with teacher leaders because there is a critical need to provide teachers who move into leadership roles with opportunities to develop their leadership skills. However, case analysis can be a productive experience for any group that has a stake in fostering teacher leadership. For example, analyzing cases can be a very effective form of professional development for administrators by helping school and district administrators understand the challenges that teacher leaders face and stimulating conversations about what they can do to support the work of teacher leaders. Engaging mixed audiences of administrators and teacher leaders in case analysis can create a shared understanding of the benefits that can result from working together, as well as help both groups appreciate the challenges and pressures that are pervasive in each other's work.

Teacher Leaders

If you are a teacher leader, you will find that the cases in this book are thought provoking. Some of the cases will be familiar and resonate with your experiences; other cases will give you a glimpse into teacher leadership journeys that are quite different from yours. As you see from our comments to staff development professionals, and as you follow our approach through this book, working with a group is *the* best way to engage in the process. The power of case methods is the learning that comes from collaboratively engaging in discussions, asking probing questions, challenging assumptions, and considering alternate points of view. For that reason, we urge you to not just read and analyze the cases in this book on your own. You will benefit more from case analysis if you have a group—or at least one colleague—to talk to about your questions and ideas. If you lack a facilitator, try to organize your own grassroots teacher leader case-analysis/writing retreat. Throughout Chapter 2, we have provided tips and suggestions to help you do so. Or perhaps you can find an online study partner who will be willing to work through the cases (virtually) with you.

If you must work through these cases by yourself, try journaling your questions and reactions—in addition to answering the discussion questions—to examine how these cases relate to your experiences as a teacher leader. Exploring the challenges encountered in these cases will stimulate you to reflect on your leadership dilemmas. Capturing those reflections in a writer's notebook is a great way to nourish your writing and leadership work, and it will encourage you to pay close attention to all aspects of your practice. Collect your thoughts, feelings, and uncertainties about your leadership trials, triumphs, and tribulations as you experience them. Later on, you may find a seed for sprouting a powerful case of your own.

OVERVIEW: HOW TO USE CASE ANALYSIS AND WRITING

The starting place to engage in case methods is case analysis—that's where all of the teacher leaders whose stories appear in this book began. To make meaning of their experiences, they read, discussed, and debated the cases of others. The rich group discussions that form the core of the case analysis process allow all of those who participate in the process to learn from the experiences of others who have pioneered leadership roles. These conversations stimulate participants to analyze the similarities and differences they find in their own leadership dilemmas. The discussions also reveal the skills that teachers need to become effective leaders. This might mean deepening their content knowledge, helping them develop facilitation skills, supporting them in gaining mastery of conflict resolution techniques or building relationships, refining their coaching or mentoring strategies, or assisting them in comprehending and navigating political forces that surround their work.

The next step is to learn to facilitate case discussions. We contend that learning to facilitate adult learning is an essential leadership skill, so we want to encourage all education leaders, regardless of role, to learn to facilitate group case analysis. The facilitator's job is to make the work easier by creating a structure to help groups work together constructively. By breaking the learning down into a series of manageable steps, the facilitator improves the group's ability to analyze problems and extends what the group can accomplish far beyond what an individual can do alone. The facilitator also helps the group reflect on and articulate their observations and the implications of their learning for their professional practice. Whether or not you assume a formal facilitator role, learning to use facilitation skills will help you to be a more effective problem solver and contributor to group work. The best way to learn to facilitate is to give it a try (see Chapters 2 and 6 for suggestions on how to get started).

Finally, the case-writing process sharpens teacher leaders' abilities to probe their leadership dilemmas, to identify the real issues, to analyze the dynamics of events, and to examine the consequences of their actions. Engaging in group writing helps teacher leaders gain insight into their leadership practices, as well as the leadership practices and challenges of peers, and it forces teacher leaders to examine the perspectives of other stakeholders involved in a reform effort. The product—their finished cases—contributes to the profession by giving others the chance to learn from their experiences. Further, completing a well-crafted case affirms the teacher leaders' abilities to communicate the expertise they have to offer.

ORGANIZATION OF THE BOOK

The book is organized to accomplish three objectives. First, it introduces research that documents the need to develop quality professional learning opportunities for teacher leaders and the potential for using case methods to fulfill that need. Next, it guides you through the processes of case analysis and case writing. Finally, the facilitation guides and the discussion questions that accompany each of the 16 teacher leadership cases offer ideas to help you get the most out of your work with the cases. Although we present a strong rationale for using case methods to provide teachers with the training and support they need to succeed, the reflections of the 16 case authors throughout this book provide the most persuasive argument for engaging in case writing; it provides a rich, substantive professional learning experience for teacher leaders.

Chapter 1 explains why there is a need for a resource like this on teacher leadership. It provides background information about case analysis and case writing and discusses how you can use case methods to create a profound professional development experience. It also documents the supports teachers need to grow as leaders. We conclude the chapter by presenting the evidence we've gathered that demonstrates that case methods are a powerful way to build understanding of the vital role that teacher leaders play at all levels of the education system, the many demands they face, and the support they need to fulfill their promise.

In Chapter 2, we look at the "hows" of case methods and offer hands-on protocols to guide you in using case writing and case analysis. As we walk through a case-writing seminar, we describe steps for learning about the genre, introduce how to facilitate case analysis, and suggest strategies to help you organize a collaborative writing process to produce compelling cases about teacher leadership.

The 16 cases in this book represent a broad range of leadership dilemmas that arise in diverse settings. They are factual accounts of actual events. The characters and events in these cases are real, but the names, genders, and titles may have been changed to protect their identity. The cases are organized in three sections according to the context of teachers' leadership work.

Chapter 3 presents the first set of cases. The cases in this chapter recount experiences of teacher leaders who are still in the classroom and have taken on additional leadership roles. Dilemmas arise as they simultaneously straddle the roles of teacher and leader.

The cases in Chapter 4 describe the issues teachers encounter when they leave the classroom to assume leadership roles at the district level. These teacher leaders often play a key role as liaisons between the central office and schools, interpreting policies and practices and attempting to finesse their implementation across a range of schools, each with a unique culture.

Chapter 5 contains a set of cases about the challenges teachers face when they take on leadership roles at the state, regional, or national level. Many of the dilemmas they experience are difficult to anticipate as they pioneer groundbreaking work.

Chapter 6 provides case-by-case facilitation guides to support you as you learn to facilitate case analysis. Each guide describes how to structure your discussions with teacher leaders, administrators, and district leaders and gives you ideas to help you meet the needs of your audience.

Finally, additional materials to support your work appear in the Resources. In Resource A you will find an annotated list of recommended websites, books, and other writings to support your experimentation with case methods. Resource B provides an extensive list of definitions of teacher leadership gleaned from the literature. Resource C presents the Center for Strengthening the Teaching Profession's (CSTP's) Teacher Leadership Skills Framework (Resource C1), Teacher Leader Self-Assessment (Resource C2), and a four-part tool titled School and District Capacity to Support Teacher Leadership (Resource C3).

In Resources D and E, we provide sample agendas for case-writing retreats. We encourage you to be creative in your use of all these materials and the cases in this book to lead thoughtful explorations into the challenging work of teacher leadership.

1 The Value of Case Methods

Promoting Reflection on the Precarious Real World of Leadership

WHY USE CASE METHODS TO SUPPORT TEACHER LEADERS?

While the case method of teaching and learning has become a standard in medical, legal, and business education, it is not yet a common approach in the field of education, although its use has grown in the last two decades. More than 10 years ago, Lee Shulman (1996) advocated for developing a case literature of teaching so that cases could help teachers "chunk" or organize their experiences into units they could analyze and use as a resource for disciplined reflection. The sampling of casebooks listed in Figure 1.1 reveals that significant progress has been made toward Shulman's goal. Casebooks have been developed for a number of the needs that arise during a teacher's career.

However, as Miller et al. (2000) noted in *Teacher Leadership in Mathematics and Science: Casebook and Facilitator's Guide,* in the realm of teacher leadership case literature, the options are limited to the domains of math and science. In the foreword to that volume, Susan Loucks-Horsley observes, "Well-crafted materials for use with teacher leaders are few and far between" (p. v). Sadly, this is still the case—quality professional development tools for teacher leaders are still in short supply. With the tremendous expansion of teacher leadership in the last decade (Smylie, 2008), a

Figure 1.1 The Growing Catalog of Casebooks in Education

Casebook Topics	References
Preservice teachers	Greenwood & Parkay, 1989 Kowalski, Weaver, & Hensen, 1990 Shulman & Colbert, 1988 Merseth, 1991 Shulman, 1992
Mentoring new teachers	Shulman & Colbert, 1987
Teaching mathematics	Goldenstein, Barnett-Clarke, & Jackson, 1994 Merseth, 2003 Smith, Silver, & Stein, 2005a Smith, Silver, & Stein, 2005b Stein, Smith, Henningsen, & Silver, 2000
Teaching English	Small & Strzepek, 1988
Teaching science	Miller, Moon, & Elko, 2000 Tippins, Koballa, & Payne, 2002
Instructional approaches	Shulman, Lotan, & Whitcomb, 1998 Shulman, Whittaker, & Lew, 2002
Teacher decision making	Greenwood & Parkay, 1989
Education administration	Childress, Elmore, Grossman, & Johnson, 2007 Merseth, 1997
Teacher leadership in math and science	Miller et al., 2000 Morse, 2009

broader examination of teacher leadership is called for, and case methods are particularly well suited to expanding professional learning for teacher leaders who are often isolated as "one of a kind" in an individual school.

Focus on Dilemma-Based Cases: Leadership Challenges Under the Microscope

Case methods make for compelling learning because "cases recount, as objectively and meticulously as possible, real events or problems so that the reader relives the complexities, ambiguities, and uncertainties confronted by the original participants in the case" (Golich, Boyer, Franko, & Lamy, 2000, p. 1). Cases tell vivid stories, which make for robust learning, because "good stories move us. They touch us, they teach us, and they cause us to remember" (Kouzes & Posner, 1999, p. 25). Yet, Lee Shulman (1986) reminds us that not all stories are cases. He notes that, "To call something a case is to make a theoretical claim—to argue—that it is a 'case of something,' or to argue that it is an instance of a larger class" (p. 11).Thus, a case represents a type of dilemma[1] or problem that arises with some frequency. The dilemmas themselves and the factors that contribute to their complexity provide the grist for focusing discussions, debates, and collaborative learning.

By definition, dilemmas are ill-defined, complicated, and stressful situations that require leaders to make difficult choices. Because leaders can rarely solve dilemmas by applying existing knowledge (Chrislip, 2002; Heifitz, 1994), they must engage in thoughtful dialogue, careful analysis, new learning, and collaborative problem solving. Analysis of dilemma-based cases simulates this real-life decision-making process, which allows teacher leaders to practice the arts of compromise and *satisficing* (Simon, 1957)—accepting a choice that is not optimal, but good enough to satisfy most constituents.

> My group was quite diverse in the kinds of jobs that people had and I remember thinking that teacher leadership can be so many different things. And I also remember that I was struck that almost every one was in an area that was not the focus of the national reform agenda of either literacy or math. Teacher leadership was happening in places where policy wasn't paying attention. These teachers were trying to define what they do because the system wasn't supporting their work in the same way districts were in math and literacy.
>
> **Case Author**

Dilemma-based cases have three additional important characteristics. First, they are not meant to lead to one "right" solution (Childress et al., 2007; Miller et al., 2000). That means that the teacher leaders who analyze the cases must raise questions, critique assumptions, and consider multiple perspectives to analyze the complex circumstances in each case. This process can expose conflicting perspectives that push participants to reflect on their beliefs, which often produces changes in their thinking (Levin, 1999). Second, dilemma-based cases that focus on complex challenges in leadership can help teacher leaders develop greater appreciation for the nuanced contributions of situational factors, personalities, or power dynamics (Sykes & Bird, 1992) that facilitate or inhibit change—excellent preparation for their work within school, district, and state and national reform efforts. When you engage teacher leaders *and* building and district administrators together in case discussions, you create opportunities for them to align their expectations—an important step toward the creation of

---

[1]The cases in this book are dilemma-based cases as conceptualized by Harrington, Quinn-Leering, and Hodson (1996).

coherent policies and practices throughout a district that advance teacher leadership.

Third, dilemma-based cases allow teacher leaders to follow the actions, thoughts, and decision-making processes of real teachers who faced real problems in real settings. Miller and Kantrov (1998) provide a nice image of cases as providing both windows and mirrors. They offer a window into the experiences and ideas of the educators in the case as well as a mirror that reflects the beliefs and attitudes of those who engage in collaborative conversations about the case. In the process, new knowledge and awareness is built. Most important, participants learn a way of thinking that fosters reflective practice. Developing these analytical skills helps build teacher leaders' confidence and competence as leaders and their ability to make informed decisions.

HOW DO CASE METHODS PROMOTE TEACHER LEADERS' PROFESSIONAL GROWTH?

Research on professional development helps us understand why case methods yield powerful learning. There is a growing consensus in the research literature about the critical features of effective professional development that produce changes in practice (Desimone, 2009). When supported by skilled facilitation, both case writing and case analysis include all five of these essential features:

• *Content focus.* Learning activities focus on developing content knowledge and an understanding of how individuals learn that content (i.e., pedagogical content knowledge) (Carpenter, Fennema, Peterson, Chiang, & Loef, 1989; Cohen & Hill, 2001; Garet, Porter, Desimone, Birman, & Yoon, 2001; Kennedy, 1998).

• *Active learning.* Participants must be actively engaged in making meaning of their experiences and new practices (Garet et al., 2001; Penuel, Fishman, Yamaguchi, & Gallagher, 2007).

• *Duration.* Intellectual and pedagogical change requires professional development to be of sufficient duration—at least 30 to 100 contact hours over several months to a year (Garet et al., 2001; Wenglinsky, 2000).

• *Collective participation.* Collegial learning is critical for interaction and discourse that helps internalize learning and its transfer into practice (McLaughlin & Talbert, 2006).

• *Coherence.* When learning is consistent with teachers' knowledge and beliefs (Elmore & Burney, 1997), and consistent with school, district, and state reforms and policies (Elmore, 2002; Fullan, 1993; Guskey, 1994), professional development is more likely to produce changes in practice.

The *content focus* is to deepen understanding of teacher leadership and how one learns to lead. Analyzing and discussing cases, and certainly writing cases, requires *active learning;* participants must deeply engage with the issues and with one another to make sense of dilemmas embedded in a case. The Center for Strengthening the Teaching Profession's (CSTP) approach to case writing is of significant *duration.* Case writers commit to participate in writing retreats and continue to write and revise with online support until the case is ready for publication, a process that, on average, takes three to six months. As one case author pointed out, *collective participation*—the conversations and analysis that writers take part in as they work and learn with colleagues—strengthens the learning:

> Having the case writers work in a group and talk as a group about the things that they were struggling with and to have everybody listen was key. It gave everyone the opportunity to not only tell their story, but also to explore more deeply and analytically their own experiences and the difficulties they wrestled with much more effectively than they could have done on their own.

Finally, when case writers come together, they also discover that although the particulars of their experiences may be unique, others have encountered similar issues in their leadership work. This realization creates *coherence* for the teacher leaders as they recognize that their shared experiences are shaped by similar school and district policies. This discovery will not in itself solve leadership challenges, but it affirms for the writers that the issues are legitimate and it provides a starting place for seeking solutions.

WHY INVEST IN TEACHER LEADERS' GROWTH?

During the standards movement in the late 1990s, Swanson's interest in teacher leadership grew out of the following observation:

> When visiting schools I was often struck by the depth of knowledge and skill of a few exceptional teacher leaders. Their students were doing amazing work and their colleagues looked to them as models. I wanted to understand what made these teachers stand out. I found that even the teachers themselves found leadership to be an elusive quality, one that was difficult to define in the form of

a collection of skills and abilities. Not only was it a challenge for these teachers to identify what they knew and did as leaders, it was also difficult for them to articulate how they had become leaders. One of the teachers explained, "It is hard to be reflective about arriving at a place we had not really intended to go." In most cases, these teachers were leaders by chance and they had to piece together their own course of professional learning. (2001, p. 158)

As the focus of school reform shifted from the standards movement to increased accountability for student achievement, teacher leadership gained new prominence (Mangin & Stoelinga, 2008; York-Barr & Duke, 2004). Nationwide, school districts wanted to capitalize on teachers' specialized knowledge to assist with developing curriculum and leading professional development, as well as improving school climate, culture, and classroom instruction. Formal leadership positions (e.g., mentors, lead teachers, coaches) have been designed to play strategic roles in district-wide school reform efforts. Portin and his colleagues at the University of Washington (Portin et al., 2009) found that teacher leaders often act as a bridge between the classroom and district or state expectations for instruction. Federal initiatives have also contributed to the proliferation of teacher leadership positions (e.g., instructional coaches for Reading First and math/science partnerships).

Despite this expansion of teacher leadership roles, the education field has not established an agreed-upon definition of teacher leadership or set clear guidelines for professional practice (see Resource B). Even when titles are identical, roles and responsibilities are rarely the same. Lack of recognition and support for teacher leaders also continues to be an issue. Although many states acknowledge the expertise and leadership of National Board Certified Teachers (NBCTs) with either additional financial compensation or credit toward specialized endorsements, only a few states (e.g., Louisiana, Georgia, and Illinois) have instituted endorsements to reward teachers who take on leadership roles outside their classrooms (Olson, 2007).

Most often, when exceptional teachers move into leadership positions, administrators assume they have the necessary leadership skills for these roles—whether or not they have had previous training or experience relevant to the new expectations (Katzenmeyer & Moller, 2009). In a 2003 survey of teacher leaders conducted by the Center for Teacher Leadership at the Virginia Commonwealth University School of Education, 82% of respondents reported that they had not received any training (Dozier, 2007). The experiences of many of the teacher leaders represented in this book underscore the accuracy of these findings.

What Do Teacher Leaders Need?

Smylie (2008, p. ix) reports that the number of books, articles, and technical reports on teacher leadership has increased by nearly 50% during the past 10 years. Yet we still have much to learn about the nuances of how teacher leaders take on influential roles and how districts can best support their work (Lieberman & Friedrich, 2007). Current studies indicate that teacher leaders have substantial needs for institutional support, professional development, and professional learning communities if schools are to maximize their contributions.

Institutional support. Johnson and Donaldson (2007) found that without institutional support, many teacher leaders have to develop their own coping strategies. Without administrators who understand the cultural norms, anticipate the potential obstacles, and help broker relationships with staff, teacher leaders often struggle to establish legitimacy. Smylie and Hart (2000) also contend that the research is clear that principals play a critical role in the development of teacher leaders. Principals can create structures and time for teachers to collaborate and foster productive social relations and a culture of critical reflection. When there is coherent alignment between district priorities, school reform agendas, and teacher leaders' assignments, teachers are less resistant to working with teacher leaders, especially when the focus is on instruction and student learning (Stoelinga, 2008). Yet there is evidence that while most agree that principal support is critical, the demands of running a school often take precedence, leaving little time to actively promote teacher leadership (York-Barr & Duke, 2004), and when district support is lacking—if teacher leaders do not receive training, if norms of private practice perpetuate, and if the district does not allot sufficient time to professional development—teacher leaders' efforts to improve teachers' practices have little effect (Lord, Cress, & Miller, 2008).

Professional development. We've come a long way in recent years using the talents of many "accidental" teacher leaders who have been thrust into or find themselves in leadership roles without any training. However, the growing reliance on teachers to lead instructional improvement suggests a need to be more intentional about preparing future teacher leaders. Unlike teachers' classroom knowledge, which one can categorize into two broad domains of subject matter and pedagogy (Leinhardt & Green, 1986), in the case of teacher leadership, the knowledge base is difficult to codify (Fullan, 1999; Katzenmeyer & Moller, 2009; York-Barr & Duke, 2004). Subject matter knowledge remains central, as teacher leaders' expertise makes them influential among their peers. A few recent studies suggest that extensive content knowledge is a prerequisite to becoming a teacher leader (Lord et al., 2008; Mangin, 2008; Spillane, Hallett, & Diamond, 2003). High levels of teaching capacity can influence teachers' receptivity to working with teacher leaders (Manno & Firestone, 2008). But what additional skills and expertise do teacher leaders want and need to be effective?

First and foremost, teacher leaders want to build their capacity to influence change. This requires an array of skills, including facilitation skills and the ability to work with adult learners as well as to provide the kind of "hard feedback" necessary to stimulate continuous improvement (Lord et al., 2008). Further, the 2003 Center for Teacher Leadership survey revealed that teacher leaders identified training to become more effective in the policy area as their greatest need (Dozier, 2007).

What are the best ways for them to gain these skills and expertise? Reeves (2008) demonstrated that learning from peers' professional practices—as in case-analysis and case-writing processes, in which teacher leaders share practical experience and engage in disciplined analysis with accomplished colleagues—and action research are more likely to influence teachers than research articles or university coursework. In a review of the existing teacher leadership literature, he also concluded that although research on teacher leadership is growing and contains many compelling anecdotes, there is little systematic research that provides educators with the practical information they seek about how to fulfill their responsibilities as leaders or how to overcome the obstacles they encounter in their work (Reeves, 2008). Further, although the demand for the services of teacher leaders has generated a proliferation of graduate programs (MA, EdD, and certificate programs) in teacher leadership, these programs often serve as stepping-stones to administration. Thus, they are not always relevant to teachers who want to maintain their focus on instruction.

Learning communities. While one might view a move into leadership as an opportunity to reduce the isolation of one's classroom, in many contexts the move can actually result in increased isolation. Teachers often view their colleagues who leave "the trenches" as quasi-administrators, no longer members of the teaching ranks. For this very reason, it's not uncommon for potential teacher leaders to be reluctant to take on formal leadership roles; doing so goes against the traditional norms of autonomy, egalitarianism, and seniority in teaching.

To counter this loss of a supportive community, teacher leaders have a very real need to connect with their peers. Yet in our work with teacher leaders, we found that opportunities to learn with and from the experience of others who have, like them, tried to navigate the unpredictable path of teacher leadership, are largely absent. Few school schedules provide the time and structure for meaningful reflection on professional practice. It is even more unusual for these opportunities to occur for teachers across schools and districts. Professional learning communities that meet regularly to critically examine practice, provide opportunities to obtain feedback, and reflect on progress are needed to enable teacher leaders to deepen their work with individual teachers and promote change at a wider level (Lord et al., 2008; York-Barr & Duke, 2004). Case methods can be an effective way to create learning communities that focus on helping teacher leaders gain the skills and expertise they need most.

THE EFFICACY OF CASE WRITING: FINDINGS FROM CSTP'S SEMINARS

CSTP invested in case writing to fulfill two major objectives. The first was to develop a set of teacher leadership cases that we could use to raise awareness of the challenges teacher leaders face and the need for greater support. The second was to design a powerful professional development experience—a case-writing process—for teacher leaders. Creating a writing seminar for teacher leaders, and pilot testing their leadership cases with groups of educators around Washington State and at leadership conferences, achieved the first objective. Staff developers successfully used the cases in workshops at state and national education conferences, in university classes, and with individual schools, school districts, and teacher leader networks. After each session—and across all of these diverse audiences—the staff developers reported high levels of engagement as participants found the opportunity to delve into probing discussions of common challenges thought provoking and worthwhile.

To learn whether the case-writing process contributed to teacher leaders' growth, we asked the teacher leaders who participated in the seminars to reflect on what they learned from the experience. Below, we detail the four major benefits they described: (1) rising to a challenge that demands strong leadership skills, (2) collaborating with colleagues, (3) gaining confidence, and (4) finding new ways to exercise leadership.

> [Case writing] doesn't necessarily show you the solution to the dilemmas you are facing, but it might enable you to see a path. The benefit is that if you are struggling with something as a leader you have a structured way of analyzing it, with the support of a facilitator and other teacher leaders. It could actually help you figure some things out.
>
> **Case Author**

Rising to a Challenge That Demands Strong Leadership Skills

All of the teacher leaders found the writing seminar made them stretch. Teacher leaders found the process asked them to tap into many of the skills needed by effective leaders: engaging in honest self-assessment, admitting uncertainty and fallibility, persevering through distressing situations, questioning norms of school culture that did not serve students, and setting fear aside to be able to take risks.

Writing is hard work, because it is a "struggle of thought, feeling, and imagination to find the words to express oneself clearly enough for others to understand the complex mix of sentiments" (National Writing Project & Nagin, 2006, p. 9). More specifically, in case writing, it can be excruciating to articulate, publicly share—even in a small group, and evaluate texts based on situations in which one felt at a loss, ineffective, wronged, or a host of other unpleasant sensations. During the seminar, experienced teacher leaders often find themselves vulnerable and in the uncomfortable position of viewing events from different perspectives and writing about questions that have no answers.

> After writing my case, I learned that as a leader there is a point that I have to step forward and say this isn't working; this is damaging to the kids. It helped me realize that as a leader—even though that's an uncomfortable place to be, I need to do that. You don't want that situation to occur, but it does. And it gave me permission to cross what some people consider to be an ethical line to tell someone that hey, this person shouldn't be in the classroom. It taught me that I need to say it and that I need to not wait so long. That was really valuable.
>
> **Case Author**

For any writer, when writing about personal experiences, it is difficult to present events objectively or fairly represent another's point of view. Yet the effectiveness of a teacher leader's case—and the ability of a teacher leader to make wise decisions, in fact—is a direct reflection of how well he or she has thoroughly analyzed and understood his or her behavior. Through case writing, participants cultivate the habit of revisiting and reassessing their actions as teacher leaders. A participant described this process as an essential way to get to the truth of the matter:

> When you relive [a dilemma] in your mind you have a tendency to put in extra scenarios. I think having to put it on paper made me be very honest. It made me go back and look at all of the steps I had jumped over and made some assumptions about why things were taking place. It forced me to really look at it step by step.

For many participants, brevity was as great a challenge as honesty. A tight page restriction made the already tough writing task even harder and forced teacher leaders to dig down to the essence of their cases. Many teacher leaders wrestled with this restriction, even as they found it prompted them to reflect deeply on their leadership dilemmas. In the words of one, "Deciding what was essential for people to know, in the service of making it more universal, was very hard."

Collaborating With Colleagues

Despite the challenges, all seminar participants agreed that what made the case-writing work doable and rewarding was the support of colleagues who shared their passion and possessed great empathy for their situation. Leadership can be very lonely work. The collegial experience of the case-writing process, with its emphasis on frank, open communication, respectful listening, and brainstorming—and the expectation that cases would be written and rewritten many times—had a profound impact on reducing teacher leaders' sense of isolation. For one participant, the ability to share challenges and strategies with peers in this forum proved to be eye opening and rejuvenating:

> I learned that my perspective is skewed. I can really benefit from listening to other people and being around other people—it reminded me to reach out and not be so isolated. I also learned to be grateful for all the opportunities I have had through my job, even though it had been stressful. . . . That was a surprising thing that I came away with. I try to remember that now whenever I get frustrated.

For all seminar participants, the questions that teacher leaders asked one another in their efforts to understand the dilemma turned out to be most helpful in refining the cases. Colleagues' probing queries helped writers determine the amount of contextual information that was necessary for readers to understand the case. Questions from group members also helped some teacher leaders identify the real problem in their case. This part of the process was not always easy—particularly when it meant they needed to start over from scratch—yet

> Questions colleagues asked helped me drill down in and get at what was at the core. Sometimes that can be frustrating. I might be heading one direction and someone would ask me a question that would take me off that path, but that's what made it powerful. My own thinking changed. The power of having a bunch of other people in the room is that they help push your thinking.
>
> **Case Author**

they still appreciated the input. And they also gained insight from others' dilemmas. Seminar participants noted that discussions helped them broaden their understanding of leadership, of the issues that other teacher leaders face, and of reform priorities in other districts.

Although the collaborative writing process was new to most participants, the support they received from their peers produced many converts to the benefits of a collegial writing group. All felt that their writing improved as a result of the group process. As one participant observed,

> What was really hammered home with the writing process at the retreat was that my stuff was better—not because I locked myself in this cave and sweated over this opus, but because I benefited from people who were bright and had a wide range of perspectives. That was very good for me.

Gaining Confidence and Finding New Ways to Exercise Leadership

A wide range of motivations led these 16 teacher leaders to commit to six days of intensive work to write a case about their leadership. For some, the troubling situations they had experienced had shaken them to their cores, and they wanted to analyze what had happened so they could handle similar circumstances more effectively. Others felt a strong need to develop new insights or abilities to help them in their leadership work, and many were compelled to search for new ways to contribute to their profession and have an impact outside their classroom or school.

Even though all of the seminar participants came to the case-writing project as quite accomplished teacher leaders, several began the case-writing seminar plagued by self-doubt about whether they were truly teacher leaders and whether they had the potential to effect change. As the following two quotes demonstrate, the act of absorbing themselves in writing about their work validated and affirmed their leadership contributions.

> I came into this experience really afraid that I wouldn't be able to produce. . . . I was the only one who was still in the classroom, and they had all this administrative experience, and I had no idea what they were talking about. I viewed them as all leaders because they had moved "up" out of the classroom and that was a little intimidating to me. But it's different now having gone through the process, because I realized that what I was doing was definitely playing a leadership role.

I discovered as I was writing cases that there were a lot of ways that I was a leader, yet none of them were what I had perceived leaders to be. You know, the person who is out charging forward and telling other people this is the answer, everybody come along with me. I never saw myself as that kind of leader. But then as we started talking about what constitutes leadership, I started thinking about my own style and the way I do things. And I discovered that in a lot of ways, I was that person in the front.

These testimonials attest to the potential of case writing to help teacher leaders discover new pathways to leadership through their writing. While quite a few teacher leaders were drawn to this project because writing is one of their strengths—one participant joked, "Everybody, especially English teachers, thinks that they are the next Hemingway"—they found that they were able to take their love for writing even farther. As another teacher leader pointed out, the form of writing was new to most of the participants and required them to flex new muscles: "I write for other readers, so that they can understand me, but never in terms of a dilemma that can be analyzed for all its richness and applied to other settings and situations."

Completing the case-writing seminar, and mastering this new form of writing, inspired strong and novice writers alike to hone their writing skills and use them to advance the field. In just two years, one teacher has embarked on a prolific writing side life—"I've had a couple of articles in some journals that I would never have attempted if I hadn't gone through that process . . . a chapter in a math book, and I've done a couple of book reviews"—and others are poised to follow similar paths. Participants who are not comfortable taking on speaking roles at conferences or leading professional development felt that writing about leadership was an effective way to contribute their skills and knowledge to a wider audience. Many of the teacher leaders felt that writing about leadership changed their perspectives on leadership and provided them with tools for being more effective teacher leaders.

> When I first started, I would always say I don't have time to do leadership. I can't. I have a classroom. My students need me. I have a family. I have all these wonderful friends who are doing amazing leadership things running conferences and training other teachers to be leaders in facilitation for National Board or to mentor new teachers. But I just want to teach my class. And yet I want to reach out to other teachers. I love to write. Boy I would love to do something in writing about leadership—it's like the backdoor to leadership.
>
> **Case Author**

FRAMING THE LEADERSHIP DILEMMAS

The 16 cases that you'll read in Chapters 3, 4, and 5 cover a number of fundamental issues teacher leaders encounter in their work. Our analyses of these cases surfaced 10 critical issues that frequently influence the professional lives of teacher leaders. You will find that these issues reinforce the current research on the status and needs of teacher leaders (see Why Invest in Teacher Leaders' Growth? above).

1. *Building support among administrators.* Without assistance from those who control resources and establish priorities, teacher leaders often have to compete for teachers' time and allegiance to reform efforts. Teacher leaders need to cultivate administrators' support to ensure that school and district policies do not conflict with or undermine their work.

2. *Defining roles and responsibilities and straddling roles.* New leadership positions are often experimental and lack job descriptions. Teachers' expectations for teacher leaders' assistance may differ from those of administrators or the teacher leaders. What's more, new positions often lack authority. Establishing agreement on workable arrangements can be a challenge, especially without system support. Too often, teacher leaders find themselves taking on roles and responsibilities beyond what they expected their jobs to be. Role confusion, especially for those spanning established teacher and administrator roles, can create tension for teacher leaders as well as for those they are expected to lead.

3. *Dealing with resistance.* In any new reform, resistance from some faction is inevitable. Learning to work with resistant colleagues (or administrators) is essential for teacher leaders to be effective.

4. *Developing new expertise.* Teachers who become leaders are known for their expertise in some aspect of their work, be it in subject matter knowledge, assessment practices, or relationships with students. However, in their leadership work, new knowledge and skills are needed to be effective in new roles, such as mentoring colleagues, facilitating teacher teams, acquiring resources (grant writing), or working with new constituents (policymakers, parents, or community members). The learning curve for acquiring these additional skills is often steep, with little time or support to become proficient.

5. *Building and sustaining commitment to change.* With the constant swing of the reform pendulum, teacher leaders often struggle to build a critical mass for change. Even when reforms appear to be working, the next reform (first reading, now math) competes for teachers' time and

energy. Leading a reform that challenges the status quo can be daunting. Teachers are often asked to implement new practices before they are proficient in using new knowledge and skills. Teacher leaders may have to push for policy changes to secure the institutional support teachers need to transform current approaches.

6. *Coping with the isolation that comes with changing roles.* Teacher leaders often find that their work is lonely. No longer a classroom teacher but not an administrator either, they struggle to find a professional community for support. For teacher leaders who have built a reputation for competence in one setting, taking on new roles can create a sense of loss of one's identity. Teacher leaders often long for a mentor to guide them in their new role.

7. *Establishing and maintaining credibility.* Teachers can only be leaders if others choose to follow. Credibility has to be earned by demonstrating expertise, establishing trust, and getting results. When competing priorities force hard choices, or when a teacher's years away from the classroom grow, teacher leaders have to work hard to maintain their connection with the demands on classroom teachers. When teachers leave the classroom for new roles, their relationships with former colleagues and school and district administrators change. Establishing credibility and legitimacy as a leader is often difficult in a profession known for its egalitarian norms.

8. *Learning the politics.* Although there are always local politics in schools, the power relationships change outside of the classroom. Taking on new roles requires teacher leaders to understand new power structures, interpersonal dynamics, and political processes that may be foreign, yet critical to their success.

9. *Advocating for others/causes.* Teacher leaders often find themselves in an advocacy role, either fighting for programs or practices they believe in or trying to support others who feel strongly about continuing practices that work. Sometimes, they must push for changing methods that are counterproductive. Given competing priorities of multiple reform efforts, teacher leaders can be perceived as taking sides, which can undermine their influence among certain constituents.

10. *Handling the workload.* Overload is a common problem for teacher leaders, especially those who are still full-time teachers. Devoting time to reform projects while continuing to commit full attention to the students in their classroom is exhausting and often leads to burnout.

Figure 1.2 presents an overview of the leadership issues central to each of the cases in this book. You can use this chart to locate the cases that

Figure 1.2 Teacher Leadership Issues Across Cases—What Is This a Case Of?

Cases	Building Support Among Administrators	Defining & Straddling Roles	Dealing With Resistance	Building & Sustaining Commitment to Change	Coping With Isolation	Establishing & Maintaining Credibility	Learning the Politics	Advocating for Others	Handling the Workload	Developing New Expertise
School Level										
How Hard Do I Push?	X			X	X	X				
Navigating New Waters		X		X		X				
Out of the Closet	X		X	X	X					
Overwhelmed and Underappreciated	X	X							X	
Free Money?			X		X				X	
When Do I Tell?		X				X	X			
District Level										
Filling a Leadership Vacuum		X	X	X			X			
Considering All Voices	X	X	X		X			X		
Crossroads	X				X	X				

Issues

Cases	Building Support Among Administrators	Defining & Straddling Roles	Dealing With Resistance	Building & Sustaining Commitment to Change	Coping With Isolation	Establishing & Maintaining Credibility	Learning the Politics	Advocating for Others	Handling the Workload	Developing New Expertise
Where Do I Stand?		X	X			X				
Preparing for the Future?			X			X		X		X
Is It Just a Crazy Dream?			X		X			X		X
State & National Level										
Truth and Power	X		X				X	X		X
One Step Forward, Two Steps Back				X			X			X
Hanging in the Balance				X	X				X	
Transitions		X					X			X

address the issues that are most pertinent to the groups with whom you work. For example, if you are a curriculum leader who supervises a cadre of literacy coaches and are looking for a new approach to literacy instruction, you might select How Hard Do I Push? Or you might want to use Considering All Voices to engage the literacy leaders in thinking about the challenges in their school improvement efforts. As the figure demonstrates, although each case is situation specific, they share several themes. The issues in these cases will be familiar, as they represent experiences that occur with some frequency in a range of contexts.

In this chapter, we made the case that as the pressure to dramatically improve learning outcomes for all students intensifies, schools are increasingly looking to the expertise of accomplished teachers to lead a wide range of improvement efforts. To support them in their work, the need for engaging approaches to enrich the professional development of teacher leaders is well documented. You will find, as we have, that case analysis and case writing provide a rigorous and provocative way to learn about the challenges of teacher leadership and to broaden leadership skills. We introduced the leadership dilemmas embedded in the 16 authentic cases included in this book. The next chapter will get you started using case analysis to strengthen teachers' leadership capacity in your setting, and it provides a step-by-step guide to help you facilitate case-writing seminars.

Teacher Leader Tip!

If you're part of a group of teacher leaders who meet regularly—a team of mentors or instructional coaches, members of a teacher leader network, or a cohort in your graduate teacher leadership program—consider organizing a book study using this text with your colleagues. Working through the cases together can help your group develop a culture of collegial inquiry and a forum to practice and hone your facilitation and problem-solving skills.

2 Effective Approaches to Case Analysis and Case Writing

In this chapter, we offer an overview of the essentials you'll need to start working with these exciting approaches to professional learning. Before you begin to engage teacher leaders in the writing process, you must first learn to facilitate case analysis; we explain how to do this on pages 25–32. Then, the step-by-step guide to facilitating case writing on pages 33–43 will get you started in planning a collaborative writing process that will support leaders in writing their compelling stories. In both processes, your support of teacher leaders' shared reflection on leadership practice and collaborative discussion provides the all-important scaffolding that turns this potentially risky endeavor into a rich and rewarding learning experience. To support you in your vital role, we offer facilitation suggestions throughout the chapter and in Chapter 6.

FACILITATING CASE ANALYSIS

Case analysis is an integral part of learning to write a case. First, case analysis introduces case writers to the genre and teaches them what makes a good teaching case. Second, teacher leaders very rarely experience the kinds of probing conversations that are pivotal to successful case analysis (Levin, 1999; Miller & Kantrov, 1998; L. Shulman, 1996); these conversations set the stage for the intense questioning that is part of case writing and require participants to publicly take risks by sharing their ideas and observations. Margaret Wheatley (2002) notes that while these risks can be scary, the investment can yield substantial rewards:

> Even among friends, starting a conversation can take courage. But conversation also gives us courage. Thinking together, deciding what actions to take, more of us become bold. And we become wiser about where to use our courage. As we learn from each other's experiences and interpretations, we see the issue in richer detail. We understand more of the dynamics that have created it. With this clarity, we know what actions to take and where we might have the most influence. We also know when not to act, when right timing means doing nothing. (p. 26)

Your skillful facilitation of case analysis will ensure that participants feel free to engage in *courageous conversations* that build their capacity as teacher leaders and change agents. The basic concerns covered in the sections that follow are selecting a facilitator skilled in case analysis, structuring the case analysis session, choosing cases to fit your purpose, and identifying key questions to begin the case analysis process. General facilitation tips and tips on facilitating case analysis with large groups are also included. If you want more in-depth instruction to expand your repertoire of facilitation skills, excellent books on this topic are listed in Resource A.

The Key Role of the Facilitator

Although the purpose of these cases is to teach, the implementation of case-based teaching calls for facilitation, rather than direct instruction. Your role as facilitator is to improve the group process and help participants get the most out the activity. You can accomplish this by stimulating discussion, eliciting observations, and asking key questions.

When facilitating a discussion of a case, you must first prepare your group for its task by setting a clear purpose. Do you want participants to identify the factors contributing to the problem, to analyze the consequences of actions taken, to explore alternative approaches, to draw comparisons with their experiences, or all of the above? The conversation grows by beginning with a description of the events in the case and moving to analysis and reflection. Throughout the discussion, it is important to let participants take the lead. Miller and Kantrov (1998) remind us that the facilitator's role is to create a "case experience," but not to control or shape the discussion. In the course of these collaborative deliberations, cases convey more than a set of facts about a specific situation; they help teach a process of thinking, analyzing, and problem solving (Lundeberg, Levin, & Harrington, 1999; Naumes & Naumes, 1999). Participants in case discussions learn these skills by practicing them while analyzing the leadership problems embedded in a case. With your help and modeling, participants develop the inquiry stance they will need when their experiences call for difficult decisions.

Format for Case Analysis

Our format for case analysis assumes you have approximately two hours to analyze each case. If you have less time, you might want to have your group agree to read the case in advance to maximize the time you have to analyze and discuss the case. We suggest a general agenda schedule that will allow you to thoroughly examine the dilemmas in each case, but we encourage you to be creative and incorporate activities to make the sessions productive.

Session Agenda

1. Introduction—5 minutes

2. Warm-Up Activity—15 minutes

3. Read the Case—10 minutes

4. Whole Group Summary of the Case—15 minutes

5. Discussion Questions Dialogue (small group or whole group)—30 minutes

6. Exploring Implications—20 minutes

7. Wrap-Up—10 minutes

If you are using these cases in a training series, we suggest you reserve a few minutes at the end of each session to discuss assignments for the next session.

Teacher Leader Tip!

If your teacher leader group doesn't have the benefit of a facilitator, you can use this text to support one another in developing the crucial leadership skill of facilitating adult learning among your peers. Take turns assuming the role of session leader. In each meeting, have the facilitator select a case of her or his choosing. The case-by-case facilitation guides in Chapter 6 suggest possible session goals, additional questions, and activities to support your facilitation work. Engaging the group in analyzing carefully selected cases will help your teacher leader community build trust and confidence in facilitating adult learning. You can help one another learn to formulate questions that will challenge colleagues to assess and reevaluate their practice.

Considerations in Choosing a Case

Selecting the cases that will stimulate the most productive learning experience depends on the purpose of the case discussion. It is wise to select cases that contain issues similar to those that participants have confronted. It is less important that the setting or situation is the same. Much can be learned by comparing the similarities and differences in experiences because—like teaching—leadership is fraught with uncertainty (L. Shulman, 1996). Being able to identify the common threads of experiences can help participants deepen their understanding of more generalizable leadership challenges.

All of the cases in this volume can help participants in case analysis learn to approach dilemmas from a more objective perspective, because they have no personal involvement in the particulars of the cases. The lack of personal involvement frees participants to have frank discussions without the added emotions involved when it is their problem. As a third-party observer, it's easier to see the perspectives of other players and to try to understand their motives. Yet because the cases are true, real-life incidents, it is not hard for participants to imagine themselves in a similar situation.

Guiding Questions to Begin the Case Analysis

The following three overarching questions will help you launch a conversation about any of the cases. It's easiest to begin with the concrete information in the case:

1. What is going on in this case?

It's important that everyone agrees on the facts of the case and understands the sequence of events and main characters involved. Encourage participants to make margin notes, highlight key passages, or raise questions about parts that confuse them. An initial discussion of the facts in the case can help clear up any misunderstanding of the details. Then, generate a summary of the case (see the case-by-case facilitation guides in Chapter 6 for a summary you can use to make sure that you've captured the major points). Developing a shared understanding of the case text enables you to explore the dilemmas from multiple perspectives. It will lead to a richer discussion if participants refrain from jumping to solutions right away.

2. What are the leadership issues evident in this case? What is this a case of?

To move beyond the specifics of the case, it is useful to look at more general instances of the issues that surface in the case. For example, there are a number

(Continued)

(Continued)

of challenges inherent in teacher leadership: how to establish and maintain credibility, how to build support from administrators, how to straddle the roles of teacher and leader, and how to deal with resistance. Figure 1.2 (see p. 22) identifies the most salient issues in each case. We suggest you use this chart to select cases that discuss issues that are most relevant to your group. (The case-by-case facilitation guides may also help you with case selection.) Reviewing these common dilemmas will help participants reflect on the parallels to their situations. You can also use Figure 1.2 to draw attention to the multiple dilemmas present in each case; the figure underscores the message that the best cases are complex. You will find that the most interesting cases are those that allow differing assessments of the same situation, which can lead to several equally plausible conclusions, each with different implications for action (Bonoma, 1981).

Finally, thinking systemically, at the school, district, or state level, it's important to ask the third question.

3. What institutional changes are needed to sustain the teacher leadership roles found in this case?

One of the goals of this casebook is to create awareness about the obstacles that teacher leaders encounter that get in the way of achieving real reform. Discussing the barriers and frustrations that other teacher leaders experience may help teacher leaders strategize about how they can advocate for structures and processes that might ameliorate some of the common challenges they confront. Similarly, if you are working with a group of district and school administrators, discussing the challenges faced by teacher leaders can help them rethink how they can support and maximize teacher leaders' contributions.

To go beyond these general steps in analyzing a case, more specific discussion questions appear at the end of each case. Chapter 6 offers additional case-by-case suggestions for facilitating case analysis. However, as you use these cases, you should not feel limited to the questions provided. Indeed, the power of the cases is their complexity and their relationship to leadership dilemmas prevalent in other contexts. Feel free to develop questions to focus your analysis on the most pressing issues in your setting.

Facilitation Tips

Following the advice of experts in facilitation,[1] as well as drawing upon our lessons learned from using the cases, there are a few essential principles that will help make case discussions rich and productive:

---

[1]We have relied on the expertise of many. These principles were derived from the writings of Levin (1999); Merseth (1991); Miller and Kantrov (1998); Miller, Moon, and Elko (2000); J. Shulman (1992); and L. Shulman (1996).

1. *Skillful facilitation requires preparation.* You must be clear about your goals for using a particular case with a group. This requires that you have a thorough understanding of the issues embedded in a case. The more experience you have using a case, the easier it will become to guide the discussion as you become familiar with the variety of responses stimulated by the case. But it is also important to be prepared for unexpected possibilities that might emerge.

Teacher Leader Tip!

The best way to learn to facilitate is to give it a try. The key to successful facilitation is preparation. To assist you, recruit a critical friend to coach you while you practice. Support from a trusted colleague will enhance your experience and help you hone your skills. He or she can help you reflect on your performance and offer suggestions for you to try the next time. In the process, by orchestrating a structured process for analyzing cases and formulating open-ended questions, you will sharpen your inquiry and problem-solving skills.

2. *The facilitator has to create a safe learning community where participants are encouraged to share their ideas and opinions.* As you introduce the case analysis process, provide participants with an overview of how you plan to proceed and your goal for the session. Each participant will read the case silently to decide what is going on in the case. Then, the whole group will review the case together and determine the dilemmas the teacher leader confronts in the case. Reassure participants that there are no right or wrong answers, and stress that the group needs to hear from all voices. By creating a community where the knowledge and wisdom of each participant is respected, yet open to critique, you will be able to use differing views to fuel more in-depth analysis. Warm-up activities to focus the participants' thinking about the issue of teacher leadership will help set the stage. Some ideas for introducing teacher leadership themes might include the following:

- A quick brainstorm about the growth in teacher leadership participants have observed over the course of their careers
- A brief review of key research findings or a short article
- A practice run with a short scenario of an obvious leadership challenge to model the process

3. *The facilitator is an active part of any case discussion.* During the course of the deliberations, your job is to serve as a moderator, devil's advocate,

recorder, and fellow learner. The goal is to structure the participants' work rather than deliver information, give explanations, or provide answers. By carefully listening and observing, you can extend the group's analysis by raising questions that provoke deeper reflection or promote the examination of different perspectives. Sometimes you might need to point out overlooked details or encourage participants to thoroughly analyze all the factors in the case before they suggest solutions. As you listen, write participants' questions and points on chart paper.

4. *The facilitator must bring closure to the group discussion.* As discussion leader, you can help participants collect and synthesize the thinking of the group to make connections and draw generalizations about common dilemmas that teacher leaders face. Review the notes you have recorded on chart paper, and challenge participants to prioritize the most important issues to resolve and to identify missing information they need to know before making recommendations. Or you might wrap up the conversation by exploring the consequences of possible solutions to issues in the case, drawing parallels between the case and dilemmas participants have experienced. This helps participants move from focusing on the details of the particular case to reflecting on how they would handle similar issues in their settings.

Teacher Leader Tip!

As you take turns facilitating case analysis or writing sessions, use the occasions to practice designing and critiquing appropriate agendas and goals for each session. Support one another in making your time together as productive as possible.

Facilitation of Case Analysis With Large Groups

You can use case analysis to gain support for teacher leaders, to model the case analysis process, or to engage a large group of teacher leaders in the process to spur their thinking about leadership roles, skills they want to learn, or resources to learn more about teacher leadership. The Center for Strengthening the Teaching Profession (CSTP) has developed an approach to using case analysis as a springboard to deepen large groups' understanding and appreciation of teacher leadership. We use this approach at national conference events, gatherings at the state level and regional level, and meetings with representatives from institutions of higher education. Although the approach is similar to the case analysis format and process described earlier, it contains some differences that are captured in the summary that follows.

To introduce the purpose of analyzing cases, CSTP facilitators engage large groups in brainstorming how teacher leadership opportunities have changed in the last 30 years. With groups of teacher leaders, the audience usually includes relative newcomers (four to five years of teaching experience), as well as seasoned veterans (20 plus years in teaching). In table groups, participants discuss what opportunities were available for teacher leadership when they first started in education. Often, the responses are limited to "department chair," "host a student teacher," or "become an administrator." Then, the table groups are asked to identify new roles they have seen emerge in recent years, and the list expands tremendously. The difference can be quite eye-opening.

To substantiate the need to invest in teacher leadership development, the facilitators briefly review the research that establishes the need for distributed leadership. For example, they cite, among others, the following:

> Richard Elmore (2000) says the knowledge base one must have to provide guidance on curriculum, instruction, and assessment is vast. His solution is an organization that distributes the responsibility for leadership.

> Michael Fullan (2006) advocates for multiple levels of leadership, all engaged in reshaping the culture of a school.

Facilitator Tip!

One issue that inevitably arises in large group discussions is the diverging points of view among those involved in the case. As a teacher leader writing about a personal experience, it is difficult to understand all the factors that influences others' behavior. A valuable way to gain some insights is to engage in a role-play. In a small group, assign each member to take on the perspective of one of the characters in the case. Have each character voice what he or she was thinking and feeling as the case transpires, and brainstorm what he or she could have done differently to better understand the perspective of the others. What kinds of questions could the character have asked? What opportunities to avoid misunderstandings did the character miss?

Sum up the session by focusing participants on acting on what they have learned by asking them to list three ways to support teacher leaders or to identify a teacher leader role in their district that needs better definition.

LEARNING TO WRITE CASES— A TOOL FOR PROFESSIONAL GROWTH

For some teacher leaders, participating in a case-writing seminar may be the first time they have gone public with their practice or worked in a writing group. Although it may be common in the teachers' lounge to hear colorful anecdotes about students' exploits and reflections on successful lessons—or those that bombed, stories about teachers' leadership work are often kept quiet. Teaching tends to be a profession where drawing attention to one's extra efforts might elicit unwanted notoriety or even resentment. So making one's leadership journey public can be unnerving. For this reason, your role as facilitator is key in reassuring participants that their concerns will be respected.

Step 1: Select a Facilitator

The first important decision in planning for case writing is the choice of a facilitator or facilitator team. To effectively guide teacher leaders through the demands of drafting their cases, the facilitator—whether it's you or someone you choose—must possess several important qualities.

Expertise in writing and the writing process and experience with the genre of teaching cases. If you have writing experience, you know that writing is a slow, iterative process. Even among the most accomplished professionals, it is rare that a writer can produce polished prose in a first draft. Those who write themselves will readily empathize with the teachers' abrupt realization that writing is hard work. As legendary sportswriter Red Smith characterized it, writing is easy: "All you do is sit down and open a vein and bleed it out drop by drop" (Schmuhl, 2010, pp. xix–xx). Although word processors are a welcome timesaver, it's still easy to get discouraged when readers don't understand the message you are trying to convey or when you think you are finished and others are still confused and miss the point you are trying to make. These common frustrations are compounded when learning a new genre of writing. Cases don't just tell a story with a beginning, middle, and end. Writers must reconstruct for the reader a detailed description of a problematic experience without offering a solution. As leaders, these teachers are used to solving problems; yet to be valuable as teaching cases, their portrayals must raise the issues and invite others to engage in analyzing the dilemmas before attempting to resolve them.

Extensive knowledge of teacher leadership. Expertise in teacher leadership will help you keep the writers' focus on leadership issues. In the ill-defined world of teacher leaders, it's easy to confuse relationship challenges, personal problems, or passion for a philosophy or reform agenda with the challenge of trying to lead. It will be important for you to clearly define the parameters of teacher leadership. This requires not only a command of the literature but also real understanding of the practical realities teacher leaders face.

Ability to create a safe and collaborative process that will encourage frank, courageous conversations. Sorting out leadership issues can be a highly emotional experience for some writers. Your ability to empathize with the struggle to find the right words and awareness of the numerous landmines that inhabit the teacher leadership landscape will make it easier to create a safe and supportive place to examine difficult issues. To relieve any anxiety that writers might bring to this challenging work, you must create a secure social process for learning. Working in small writing groups, with ample support, helps teachers quickly develop a comfortable context for sharing their work and receiving feedback.

> It's the opportunity to review a case that you've been intimately involved in and have other people look at it with a different set of lenses. For me, the most beneficial part of it was having the opportunity to write about something that was distinctly troubling to begin with, and then to be able to discuss it in a lot of detail in a confidentially secure setting. That helped me to go to that next deeper level. It's not just surface writing; it is analyzing what I did as a leader and analyzing what truly the dilemma was. I kind of knew what the dilemma was, but it wasn't solidified until I wrote it.
>
> **Case Author**

High expectations. As the facilitator, you must perform a somewhat delicate balancing act. Although care is often required to promote some intense soul searching, you must hold writers to high standards until the case is clear, reads smoothly, and engages the reader in a complicated real-world problem that is unique in the details yet familiar in the issues and emotions.

Step 2: Prepare to Lead Case Writing

One of the best ways for you to develop an understanding of and appreciation for what makes an effective teaching case is to read and analyze a number of teaching cases. Few sources on teacher leadership exist: two casebooks—Miller et al. (2000) and Morse (2009), both about teacher leadership in math and science—and this volume. However, we recommend you read more broadly.

The numerous casebooks developed by Judith Shulman—a leading authority on case writing and the director of WestEd's Institute for Case

Development—and her colleagues at WestEd offer excellent models. In contrast to the Miller et al. text, in which the cases were carefully constructed by the authors to exemplify realistic scenarios that teacher leaders encounter when leading reform in math and science, WestEd's conceptualization of case writing views teachers as the subjects, producers, and consumers of the cases. This approach aligns with our intent to use case-writing seminars to capture teacher leaders' knowledge and experience in a form that can better prepare other teacher leaders for the challenges of leadership work. Figure 1.1 in Chapter 1 suggests additional casebooks to review. Collectively, they offer a variety of perspectives on case methods and cover a range of topics to help you develop a deeper understanding of the genre. Some offer commentary that will give you additional ideas for facilitating case discussions.

Step 3: Create the Context for Productive Case Writing

The most important criteria for recruiting case writers are teacher leadership experience, a desire to examine one's practice, and strong writing skills. CSTP works with an extensive network of National Board Certified Teachers, and this pool provides an obvious source of potential writers. Each year, CSTP advertises through its website the opportunity to participate in a seminar to learn to write a teaching case. CSTP asks applicants to read and respond to a case in 250 words or less. This initial assessment gives us some insight into each teacher's understanding of leadership issues and her or his writing ability. We also ask applicants to identify a few leadership experiences they have had that they might like to write about. Finally, we ask teachers to provide at least one reference able to vouch for their leadership work.

Teachers who are invited to participate must commit to attending both sessions for the full time and must bring a laptop computer. Participants are charged a nominal course fee for the six-day retreat. Lodging and all meals are provided. The retreat is fully equipped with reference materials (casebooks, teacher leadership references, dictionaries, and thesauruses), sticky notes, highlighters, a printer and paper, and plenty of snacks.

Think about possible candidates in your community who could use your support in developing their leadership skills. You may already work with an identified teacher leader network, a group of new teacher mentors, math or literacy coaches, or participants in a writing project who would be ideal candidates for sharing their leadership stories. If you are a district leader or a university faculty member, it may be possible to build case writing into regular meetings or class sessions over many months.

Teacher Leader Tip!

Are you part of an online teacher leader network or listserv? If so, perhaps you can find a partner or partners online who might be interested in writing a leadership case. Is there someone whose blog you admire? Or someone who occupies the same role you hold in another part of the country? Could you create a collaborative writing group in cyberspace?

In our case, we work with teacher leaders across the entire state, so summers are a good time in teachers' schedules to take on case writing. We've found that it's a time when many teacher leaders are looking for a professional development opportunity and one of the few times during the year when teachers can devote concentrated blocks of time to write. Because the writing retreats are intense, it works well to break them into two sessions. A small group of writers[2] commits to five to six days—two three-day sessions with a month hiatus in between—over the course of the summer. This work requires a significant time commitment, so be sure to begin recruiting early (February) before teachers have made other summer plans. It also helps if the retreat allows the writers to gather in beautiful surroundings—a mountain retreat or a wildlife sanctuary—away from the demands of daily lives. Build ample time to write, discuss ideas, walk in the woods, and think deeply about the challenges of teacher leadership into the retreat's schedule.

We've been intrigued by the possibility of having teams of administrators and teacher leaders write cases together, providing two different perspectives on the same teacher leadership challenge. The resulting cases could provide compelling materials for engaging mixed groups of educators in understanding the pressures that constrain each other's work. The case discussions could potentially afford significant policy changes to enable the two groups to work together more effectively to achieve shared goals. Unfortunately, we've been unsuccessful in recruiting administrators to join a writing group, as few administrators have been able to commit the time. Perhaps it's an idea that will work in your setting. (If you find ways to make it work, please share your experiences with us: Jeanne@cstp-wa.org.)

You'll find that it is important to let teacher leaders choose the topics they want to write about. The objective is for writers to use the occasion to delve into experiences they have found troubling, as these incidents hold

---

[2]The average size of the groups is six; we've worked with groups ranging from five to nine teachers.

the most potential for furthering their learning. Yet your job is to ensure that the topics they choose are indeed problems of leadership. Given the complexity of their work, one of the writing challenges teacher leaders face is choosing which of the many difficult situations they have traversed to write about.

Step 4: Design an Introductory Seminar

Designing a case-writing seminar that will fit your needs requires experimentation. Feedback from participants will help you refine your format. A pivotal development in the structure of our seminar was the realization that we needed to start by defining what we meant by teacher leadership. Because we hadn't been clear about the central focus of the work the first year, many writers struggled with identifying a leadership dilemma, as one of the case writers noted, "It's a very slippery thing."

Fortunately, that writer felt the slipperiness made the experience fascinating. She found that "being in a nebulous, foggy area is a great spot to be in because you have to find your way around it, and it seems that it's always a great learning experience." For others, the wandering without direction was more frustrating than invigorating. One writer remembered that after that first seminar was over, she kept wondering, "How is this a case about leadership?" She admitted, "I always felt like I was doing it wrong. I never felt so inept in a writing task."

The feedback revealed a major hole in our training, and we fine-tuned our writing retreats accordingly. Today, each group of teacher leaders spends considerable time collaboratively constructing a working definition of teacher leadership. Participants begin by reading an extensive list of definitions of teacher leadership derived from the literature (see Resource B). Then, working with partners, they look for common themes or qualities that run through most of the definitions. Once participants have reduced the list to the essentials, they discuss different practices by questioning which behaviors actually demonstrate leadership and which are part of the professional responsibilities that all teachers should exemplify. We go beyond listing all of the roles that teacher leaders occupy; we identify the behaviors and responsibilities that constitute leadership. Interestingly, each group of teacher leaders ultimately arrives at a list of qualities (knowledge, skills, and dispositions) that is remarkably similar each year.

CSTP has since published a Teacher Leadership Skills Framework (see Resource C1) that includes a much more concise definition (one that is completely consistent with our working definitions): "Knowledge, skills, and dispositions demonstrated by teachers who positively impact student learning by influencing adults, formally and informally, beyond individual classrooms." We encourage you to have participants generate their own definition instead of adopting this definition; after they have settled on a definition, compare their definition to the CSTP definition. The discussions and exchange of ideas that occur as the group reasons its way to reaching consensus will help all participants develop a deeper understanding of the criteria that define teacher leadership.

The second lesson we learned was to build in plenty of time for reading and discussing cases. It is essential for participants to get the feel of what makes a good case. With this preparation, the writing task will go more smoothly because participants will better understand their targets. The first year was the most challenging because the writers had few models to follow. The cases developed by previous cohorts really helped those in subsequent cohorts grasp the genre and format of case writing more quickly.

It is worth investing time in reading and discussing several cases to learn about the genre, learn what makes a case compelling, and learn what constitutes a leadership dilemma. During the case-writing seminar, participants have time to read a number of cases—the more cases they read, the more the authors will understand the components of a good case. All of this preliminary work will pay off when the writers begin to draft their cases.

To maximize our work time together, before arriving at the retreat, the writers have homework to do. The first step in learning to write cases is experiencing the power and complexity of analyzing a number of cases, so participants are expected to read an assigned teacher leadership case and come ready to discuss it. Sample agendas in Resources D and E explain how we organize our writing retreats. These models are intended to give you a general outline of ideas and activities to help you structure a successful writing seminar.

Writing Retreat—Session 1
Step 5: Get to Know and Trust One Another

The first day of the writing retreat is devoted to getting to know one another as individuals and as leaders and creating a learning community. Participants share who they are and the leadership roles they currently hold. Before launching into the writing work, the group reviews the agenda and establishes norms for accomplishing the work. Teachers need reassurance that the conversations they have will remain confidential. The expectation is that every member of the group will serve as a critical friend by reading drafts, asking questions, and offering feedback.

Writing Tips!

To help the writers develop a feel for case writing, it is worthwhile to complete a second read of each case you discuss. The second time through, focus on the techniques the author uses to give the case its vitality. Notice how the opening grabs the reader's interest right away by creating an element of drama or suspense. With a page limit of six double-spaced pages or 1,600 to 1,800 words, like a good short story, the author has to be discriminating and make every word count. Study how the author brings the reader into the scene to experience the tension created when one encounters troubling dilemmas. Dialogue helps recreate the action and introduce characters, while internal talk reveals thoughts, feelings, questions, and concerns the writers experience as they try to navigate difficult situations. Pay attention to how the author weaves sufficient background details into the scenario to help the reader understand the context, but in the end, the author leaves the reader wondering. The dilemmas are intentionally left unresolved to serve as a springboard for collaborative learning and problem solving.

Step 6: Start Writing

Writers begin their work by brainstorming leadership dilemmas the participants have faced. Each person shares one or two ideas he or she is considering to get the words flowing. Then a 10-minute quick-write helps to get the ideas on paper. A brief read-around can help generate additional ideas from the group to further develop the story line before the writers get to work fleshing out their cases or developing a "case seed" (Shulman, Whittaker, & Lew, 2002). Some writers will choose to take their laptops outside, while others might retreat to the quiet of their room. We encourage writers to attend to their needs to stay productive—including taking breaks or going for a walk to clear their heads when the words won't come.

Teacher Leader Tip!

Engage in a writing activity to generate possible topics for a case. Have each teacher leader describe one recent experience when she or he was responsible for facilitating a meeting or discussion of an issue. Include in the descriptions the goals for the session, the issues that came up, and an assessment of what worked and what didn't. As you discuss each incident, explore the possibilities for developing a case about leading the work.

When the writers are satisfied that they have captured the gist of their dilemmas, encourage them to share initial drafts with others for feedback and suggestions. As facilitator, you become the head writing tutor. Be sure you confer frequently with each participant and encourage each author to seek input from several colleagues. Regular feedback, as one author explains, helps the writers stay productive throughout the retreat.

> It was all the clarifying questions that people would ask—"What do you mean here?" Those clarifying questions made me reexamine what I had written and look at it in a different light. And then reading other people's work, and having conversations with them about their case made my case improve, just by thinking more about what I had written.

The writing process is never easy. Constant questioning of the core dilemmas at the heart of the cases, discussion, feedback from peers, and writing and rewriting multiple drafts are integral aspects of a productive experience. Feeling "inept in a writing task," at first, is common. Letting go of the need to be experts and open themselves to learning from peers can be especially challenging for teacher leaders who are very strong writers.

> I've had a lot of experience with writing, and I was thinking this shouldn't be too tough, but it was really challenging on two levels. One was analyzing the experience that I was writing about, and then trying to make sure that I understood all the levels and perspectives. And then there was writing for a particular kind of audience. Eventually, knowing that I was writing for the benefit of others helped me to not have as much ownership about what I was writing, so that it could be taken apart and it could be examined.

As the case develops further and sensitive incidents are fleshed out, some authors may become concerned about possible ramifications if someone in their school or district reads their case. For this reason, it is essential that case writers have the option to publish their cases under a pseudonym. The ability to remain anonymous seems to give authors permission to be honest about problematic interactions or circumstances that contribute significantly to the dilemmas in their cases.

Writing Retreat: Wrapping Up Session 1
Step 7: Whole Group Feedback

Before leaving the first half of the seminar, borrowing the "author's chair" idea from the National Writing Project (Lieberman & Wood, 2003), each author has a chance to read his or her draft aloud to get feedback from the whole group. Collectively, the group examines each case and asks, what is this a case of? to be sure that the dilemmas represent a larger category of difficulties common to the work of teacher leaders. Often, colleagues will identify dilemmas that the author hadn't thought about. More than once during these discussions, writers have realized that the issue they thought was a leadership dilemma was actually a personal challenge and that they needed to change their direction or start over on a new case. This process gives each writer much to think about, and the feedback helps the authors make revisions and refine their cases.

In between the two sessions, participants agree to continue working, submitting drafts, and getting feedback from the facilitator via e-mail. Each writer is expected to arrive at the second half of the seminar with a completed rough draft.

Teacher Leader Tip!

If members of your teacher leader group want to take on the challenge of writing their cases, the guidelines in this chapter will provide support. However, we don't expect teachers to be able to write their cases by reading this book without the support of colleagues who are also engaged in the process. The fact that you are actively seeking to improve your leadership skills by writing a case gives you a head start. If your group has literacy coaches or teacher leaders who have participated in the National Writing Project or another writing network, these leaders' understanding of the writing process makes them excellent candidates for facilitating case writing. Recruit them to lead your group through the work—it will be a learning experience for all of you!

Writing Retreat—Session 2
Step 8: Revise, Revise, Revise

Writers spend the second three-day session refining their cases through multiple rounds of reading and revision (see Resource E for a sample agenda). The goal is to have each writer leave the second half of the retreat with an almost finished product, needing only polishing and fine-grained editing. As the facilitator, you will need to pay close attention to each writer's progress and decide the next steps to take during the time together. If someone is in need of more one-on-one help, schedule time to confer with that author. As you read drafts, note the areas where several writers need additional help. This will signal when a minilesson is called for to review some aspect of case writing. For example, if several in the group need help strengthening their openings, it's wise to take a break from writing and print out a page or two of everyone's first paragraph with no names attached. This will allow the group to focus on the effectiveness of the first few sentences without the surrounding text. As a group, read and discuss each one. Ask participants, How does it make you feel? Does it create emotion or intrigue? What do you want to know next? Does it make you want to read on? How could it be more compelling? This is one way an individual author can benefit from others' recommendations to help him or her craft a more captivating start to a case.

Frequently, writers struggle to decide whether there is sufficient detail for the reader to understand the context and to identify extraneous information they can cut. Sometimes capturing the right tone presents a challenge. For example, some retreat members may interpret an author's attempts at humor as arrogant or even contemptuous sarcasm. Learning from feedback is not always easy, but in the end, it can impart valuable lessons, as one of the case writers concedes:

> I had to make myself teachable, but thanks to the perseverance of everyone on the team, my writing went through many, many changes. Finding my focus was the most difficult thing. I had so much generalized frustration about so many things that it was very difficult to pare it down into the main part of my case.

Writing Tip!

Titles can be another tricky topic. After each author reads his or her case aloud, invite the group to compose a title that captures the essence of each case. This will generate a number of ideas the author can choose from or combine to form a more fitting title for the case.

Before departing from the writing retreat, conduct one more round of author's chair read-alouds. Once again, have the group reflect on the critical question, what is this a case of? Does the case elicit multiple responses to this query? If so, it indicates that the case is rich enough to be a case of many things. It will also reveal whether other readers will relate to the leader's experience.

To wrap up the case-writing seminar, the group must agree on a target date for completing the cases. Writers make a commitment to continue working via e-mail with the facilitator until their cases are completed. By the end of the six days, the writers have often completed seven or eight drafts. However, it is not uncommon for a teacher leader to go through a dozen rewrites before the writer and the facilitator agree the case is "finished." It is then sent to an editor.

CSTP contracts with a professional editor who reads the penultimate drafts with fresh eyes. In addition to copy editing the manuscript, the editor provides all authors with queries and suggestions to help them further strengthen their cases. During the editing process, the editor is careful to maintain each author's unique voice while offering ideas to improve the flow of ideas, to engage the reader, or to enhance clarity. When the authors review the edited manuscripts, they have the opportunity to ask the editor follow-up questions. Then, the authors make the final decisions about all changes. CSTP has published the finished cases in small pamphlets and on its website, without the background and facilitation support included in this volume.

This chapter describes the central role that facilitators play in making case analysis and case writing a productive learning experience. The guidelines presented here will get you started in using case methods to expand and strengthen teacher leadership. They are intended to help you become skilled at facilitating case analysis and to motivate you to embrace case writing as a powerful professional development experience that will help teachers grow as leaders. We encourage you to use your experience and expertise to adapt our ideas, or create your own, as you think about possible ways to use the cases in this book.

The next three chapters revolve around the teachers' cases. They are organized by the arena in which the teachers' leadership work takes place—at the school level, district level, or state and national level. The characters and events in these cases are authentic, but the names, genders, and titles may have been changed to protect identities. These stories invite professional communities to engage in conversations to scrutinize the issues present in a particular case, to reflect on their experiences and to learn from one another about possible solutions to dilemmas they find in their settings. As you orchestrate discussions of these cases to strengthen teacher leadership in your area, use the facilitation guides for support, and incorporate ideas from your staff development tool-kit.

3 School-Level Leadership Dilemmas

T he school-based teacher leaders in this chapter are full-time teachers who, in addition to their work in the classroom, strive to make a larger contribution. These teacher leaders' dilemmas are not necessarily unique to individual schools; however, without official leadership positions, questions of authority and role definition create additional challenges. Obtaining support from principals to sustain reform efforts is essential, as schools often juggle multiple mandated district initiatives that compete for teachers' limited time. Moreover, because these teachers are still in the classroom, few professional development opportunities are available to help them develop the facility they need to lead. As a result, these leaders often have to depend on their interpersonal skills and their ability to model exemplary practice to persuade colleagues to invest in their cause.

The most common issues that school-based teacher leaders face are trying to resolve the ambiguity that surfaces as they straddle the roles of teacher and leader, needing to build support among administrators to facilitate their work with other teachers, establishing and maintaining credibility among their peers, and managing the workload of extra leadership responsibilities while still teaching full time. To help you select cases that address your priorities, the following brief preview highlights the primary focus of each case in this chapter.

How Hard Do I Push? follows a teacher leader as she introduces and develops an in-depth professional development program, lesson study, to engage a grade-level team in improving mathematics instruction. The success of the project leads to rapid expansion throughout the school and to other schools in the district. But district restructuring, new initiatives, and a new principal make it hard to sustain a productive program.

Navigating New Waters raises the issue of how to transfer one's credibility as a teacher leader from one school to another. Eager to share her experience and expertise with her new colleagues, the "new teacher" is not sure how to gain acceptance in a new setting: lead by example, offer ideas, or wait to be asked?

Out of the Closet . . . and Out the Door? shows how taking leadership on behalf of marginalized students can be risky, but rewarding. Having established a safe haven in one school, this teacher leader wonders if it is wise, safe, or possible to extend his work to other schools.

Overwhelmed and Underappreciated addresses the perennial problem that classroom teachers face when they take on leadership work over and above teaching full time. In this case, one teacher leader appears to reach a breaking point, in part because of overload and in part because she feels unappreciated.

Free Money? demonstrates how leadership carries with it responsibilities for both intended outcomes and unexpected events. In a small school, the loss of one or two partners can mean the work falls disproportionately on one person, leading to overload and exhaustion.

When Do I Tell? explores ethical issues about a teacher leader's responsibility to support a struggling colleague when the welfare of children is at stake. In this case, the teacher leader reasons about walking the fine line between support and evaluation and the potential consequences of either choice.

Case 1

How Hard Do I Push?

by Debra Rose Howell

What a relief! Another strong finish to the school year! Again, our kids' test scores climbed. Yes, lesson study work *is* continuing to make a positive difference in student achievement. The administration once again will be pleased. We have cross-grade-level professional discussions happening. People are getting along better than ever.

Oh my, is that Angie asking Valerie for feedback on a geometry lesson? I never thought that would happen! Don and Terry are looking over each other's student work from the recent lesson they worked on together. What a great conversation they are having. Staff members really seem to feel valued and respected by one another and by the principal. Nothing could be better!

Wait! What is that I just heard over the clunking of the copy machine? No, that can't happen! Did I just hear Harriet say that she has accepted a science special-ist position in another district for next year? I don't care if it is her dream job! She has been our strong, quiet, and experienced leader of the fourth grade, who has really advocated for lesson study.

Mike looks up from reading over last night's school board minutes. "Hey Deb, Amy has been granted a leave of absence through December for maternity leave next year. Isn't that great news?" You have got to be kidding me! She has been my resource for working on the district curriculum realignment of the math strands. I thought she would be back at least part time in the fall. I walk gloomily back down to my classroom.

I see Jody with a huge grin on her face running toward me. "Debra, I just got a call from the district office. I got the third-grade position over at the other ele-mentary for next year! I'll finally get a continuing contract," she explains with elation. I am finding it difficult to look even slightly thrilled. I didn't even know she had applied! She was the one who really helped bring the entire second-grade staff on board last year during our school's reconfiguration.

Over the intercom, the secretary reminds us, "The new principal will be meet-ing with us in a few minutes to introduce herself to everyone so we can *feel more comfortable and less uncertain about next year.*" Oh, let's just throw a new prin-cipal into the mix? Help! Now what will happen to lesson study Monte Cristo Elementary style? Can it survive with all these changes?

We just finished our fourth year of lesson study in our newly reconfigured K–6 elementary school. Five years ago, I secured two years of funding through a lead-ership grant. Our group's initial focus was to establish collaboration between our nine fifth-grade and multiage program (fourth-, fifth-, and sixth-grade) teachers. We wanted to create an environment for critical reflection and focus on increas-ing our state test results specifically in math. I began by presenting to the fifth-grade and multiage staff just what lesson study is. Lesson study brings teachers together with specialists and other educators to design lessons, make revisions, observe student learning, and engage in professional discussions about improving student learning. When a lesson is fully developed by the group, one member teaches it to a class while the others observe and note the interaction between the lesson and the students. The entire group then meets to analyze and reflect on the lesson. This is further refined until it is ready to be tried out in another classroom. This cycle continues until the group is satisfied that the students fully understand the lesson.

I purposely chose this group to start with, as fifth-grade state math scores in rounding and estimation had been nose-diving over the past few years. Their classrooms were spread all over the building with no common planning time, so there was no teaming except in the multiage program. Most were experienced teachers with firm differences in philosophy on how to teach mathematics. The newer teachers were still "star struck," trying to find their way to eventually elbow in and share newer educational approaches. Many "behind the back" discussions were taking place regarding what and how we taught when the classroom door was closed. Further, teachers were suspicious of the multiage program, which many saw as the program that got all the special favors from the principal. Many staff felt that only high-achieving students (i.e., no problem kids or special needs kids) were placed in these multiage classrooms. I wondered if lesson study could help us get past all of these misconceptions.

To my amazement, every fifth-grade teacher not only attended the informational meeting but they *all* volunteered to participate the following fall. In addition, some of our specialists, an instructional aide, and the building principal asked to join us. By purposefully deciding to focus on just one math strand, it seemed to help everyone feel more comfortable and eager to join. Things were going smoother than I could have ever hoped.

After three rounds of lesson study, staff members continued their lesson study discussions during lunch and in the hallways. In addition, they realized through classroom observations that we all have needy students, including multiage classes. The bonus was that all of our state test scores in math went up significantly!

I knew we had found a good thing when Andrea, our music specialist, wrote to me,

> Personally, the most beneficial part of lesson study was the camaraderie it built within our staff. We began with a group of teachers who were in no way a cohesive team. We now have people teaming up to plan education and extracurricular activities. I consistently say hi to people that I never used to. This might seem inconsequential, but it is actually hugely significant. When teachers are comfortable with each other and respect each other's abilities, more cross-curricular planning occurs. Student learning benefits as a result.

In the second year, I actively recruited and invited more grade levels to join, and our lesson study group doubled its size to 26. I deliberately asked Harriet and Amy to speak to the staff to help expand leadership in lesson study. I asked them to help me share with the staff their observations and reflections on the time spent on lesson study. Harriet has taught for many years and commands respect.

Although Amy is less experienced, her devotion to aligning the math curriculum hooked the newer staff. They figured if she felt it was worth spending the time and energy on, then perhaps it was the right move for them as well. Nearly every teacher on staff became involved in the second year of lesson study; it was now "our project" instead of "my project." With more staff members participating, the professional development continued to thrive!

I have to make sure I have the right mix of staff personalities and teaching experiences working together in these small groups. This isn't always easy. Keeping a balance within each group of experienced to new staff, from outspoken to introverted, from organized to disorganized, I didn't always anticipate the problems that occurred. Sometimes I found it best to mix across the grade-level groups; while other times, it was best to keep a grade-level team together to work on their lesson development. Moving a quiet leader such as Harriet to be the small group leader of her team brought forth her organizational skills, and it also gave Sarah and Lynn a chance to see how children in their differing grade levels worked on this math strand.

As we moved into our third year of lesson study, new challenges arose. Without the leadership grant, I had to secure funding for substitute teachers and meeting time spent outside the school day. My principal, Wayne, quickly offered to use some of his building budget to fund this successful professional development. Since he had become an active participant in the group meetings, he saw the positive interactions and powerful lessons being developed. He also saw that using the staff to learn from each other, rather than paying for staff to attend expensive trainings out of the district, was cost effective.

During the third year, our focus moved to reading. With little time during the day to read this kind of research material, I chose to add professional journal reading to our tasks during our half-day release time. This additional task helped nurture and inspire professional discussions across the building, as all groups were reading the same piece of research. Even staff members who were not in the lesson study groups started picking up and reading the research so that they, too, could be part of the discussions in the staff room and hallways. Our superintendent, another elementary building principal, and a school board member came to the large group debriefings. We continued to give presentations to our staff, sharing the ways we found to better refine and present lessons. We were even asked to share our form of lesson study with the high school and middle school math departments, and they, too, started a joint math lesson study team. We continued to grow and change with the needs of our students and staff. Securing further funding, lesson study seemed to be becoming a permanent part of the professional development in our district.

That is, until we hit year four. Our two elementary buildings were restructured from one K–3 and one 3–6 elementary building into a K–5 building. My elementary building changed to become a K–6 school. Half the staff from each building made a move to the other building to round out the complete configuration of grade levels. My building seemed to comprise newer staff. Unfortunately, most of my devoted lesson study participants moved to the other building. Add to that a new reading curriculum for kindergarten and first-grade classrooms that needed intensive training outside the classroom day, and you have a recipe for too much change too fast. How was I going to convince the new staff that we had something that really worked? How was I going to lead this inexperienced and overwhelmed staff into another year of lesson study?

Kindergarten and first-grade teachers simply couldn't take on another big commitment and decided to bow out. Our third-grade staff members wanted to do their own staff development because most of them were new teachers. This left the reluctant second-grade teachers, fourth- and fifth-grade teachers who had little teaching experience, an experienced multiage staff, and our music specialist Andrea who were willing to participate. I started this year grouping by grade levels, hoping that would reduce stress. I had to do some coaxing to convince Marie, a new fifth-grade teacher, that lesson study was worth trying during her very demanding first year of teaching. I shared with her all the positive aspects of lesson study whenever I saw her. She dove in with every ounce of energy she could give it.

Unfortunately, early on, her group bombed, with several members choosing to leave meetings early, not participating fully, gossiping, not staying on task, and purposely trying to sabotage the group's work. Marie came to me ready to throw in the towel and swearing to me that she would *never* put herself in that position again. Terrific. Did she feel conned by me for convincing her to do this? Was it my responsibility to report back to the principal on this problem in her group so that he could deal with it? Should I intervene and talk to the other group members? How far did my leadership role stretch?

As I approach the start of another school year and potentially a fifth year of lesson study, I am again meeting new and complex challenges. After losing many of my strongest advocates to the other elementary school last year, and with a handful of the lesson study leaders of the current staff—such as Harriet, Amy, and Jody— leaving as well as Wayne, my supportive principal, I am left pondering many questions. The new principal is a rookie who will have her concerns and demands of starting a new career in a new district. As the teacher leader, do I make the move myself and try to reorganize in September, or do I present it to this new principal simply with the hope that she will continue to make it happen? And now, with the expansion and implementation of the new reading curriculum to second and third grades, have I now lost too many supporters to make it work? Am I pushing too hard because I believe so strongly in lesson study? What are the boundaries of my teacher leader role? Should I let it go or try to keep it alive? How hard do I push?

Questions for Discussion

1. What are the boundaries for teacher leaders in a school? Where does/should a teacher leader's role stop?

2. What do you think of the author's strategy to start working with the least collaborative grade level first? What are the risks and benefits of this approach?

3. How can the dynamics of dysfunctional teams be addressed to ensure that their issues don't undermine progress in the rest of the teams?

Case 2

Navigating New Waters
The Voyage of a Teacher Leader on the Sea of Change

by Claudia McBride

As a fourth-grade teacher moving to a new school, I am navigating new waters. In doing so, I am relearning a life lesson that cannot be found buried inside a text—starting over is *scary*. As a teacher leader, it is good to relearn how unsettling a change in course can be.

Since 2000, I have experienced the richest part of my professional journey so far. When I began teaching at my preK–8 district, I could not imagine the successes it would achieve. I have worked in "the little school district that could"—could empower teacher leaders, could teach minority students, could provide high-quality professional development, could support site-based management, and could support professional learning communities (PLCs). Its "could" attitude was evident in the rising state assessment scores, community pride, and parent support.

I became a National Board Certified Teacher (NBCT), and I trained to be a state Teacher Advancement Program (TAP) mentor teacher and an NBCT candidate facilitator. I guided colleagues through the National Board process. I mentored new teachers and provided district writing training to elementary staff. I served on the school improvement committee, principal's advisory committee, and student assistance committee. I thrived on contributing to the positive growth. Now, as my PLC colleagues are completing their first National Board candidate year, I am accepting a new teaching position. To an outsider, it might appear that I am simply moving to another fourth-grade teaching position in a different school. Yet there are other professional considerations. I am enticed by my new school's decision to form PLCs to improve student outcomes. Currently, it has no National Board Certified teachers, and I will have the opportunity to help the district develop the promising practices and strategies that transformed my old district.

There are five new staff members, and Don, the principal who hired me, is also new. Don was selected to lead this building because he demonstrates a passion for growing people and creating opportunities for positive growth. He is dedicated to establishing PLCs. My new colleagues are veteran teachers, but they have little or no PLC experience. They might well be apprehensive. One of my strengths is that I have learned from both good and bad PLC experiences. I can be a reassuring voice backing up the captain when we sail through rough seas. But will my colleagues see me in that light? Will they see me as the first mate or the new guy's lackey? Don has already told me, "I am counting on you to help me establish PLCs. You will bring a wealth of experience to our process." How will I determine the right amount of assistance to offer? I want to make the crossing safe for all of us but be savvy enough to gently dissuade would-be mutineers. Can I build the positive relationships necessary?

I am joining a staff that is not as cohesive as my old team. Yet when I think about my old team's early days, it, too, was divided between the energetic solution seekers and the defenders of the status quo. My old school did not transform overnight, but I was there during six years of dynamic growth and change. We all grew in new directions while cultivating individual strengths that allowed us to collaborate effectively. Our PLCs were stronger because we understood and honored our diversity. Everyone had a place in our learning community. Learning to listen to the "old grumps" and recognizing them as "school historians" allowed us to develop relationships that became part of our shared foundation.

Once again, I will need to build a shared foundation with colleagues. Yet this time, I am an unknown quantity. I will no longer be a valued and respected teacher leader in a dynamic learning community. I will not be a key part of a math, reading, and writing team. I am leaving behind my two fourth-grade teaching team members and my four NBCT candidates for a larger school district with nine schools instead of one. My new school houses only Grade 4–6 classes, with support specialists and classified support staff. I will be one teacher on a much larger team—one of nine fourth-grade teachers.

How significant will my role be as a new fourth-grade teacher? How will I fit? Will my new team be a regular nonagon or a concave, irregular nonagon? I consider what Sheri, a fourth-grade teacher from the interview team, said: "You will be such a welcome addition to our staff. I was so impressed during your interview that you talked about 'shared success, our team, together we,' and so on. We need strong team members at the fourth grade." What will my new team expect of me? What do I expect of them?

I know that I will need colleagues to orient me to the learning culture, curricula, and "nuts and bolts," and I will need to hook up with positive staff willing to mentor me. My friends from my old team reassured me that when I was hired, my listening and questioning immediately put them at ease. The more we teamed, the more they grew to respect me and value my input. Now, I have to do it again. I wonder how long it will take my colleagues *this time* to see that I come early, stay late, and take on tasks and projects because I have a deep passion for teaching students to be successful learners.

Will I find colleagues who share this passion? Already, I am anxious to get into my new building and begin unpacking. If I go in before school starts, will I meet other teachers who feel the need to be planned, prepared, and ready to begin preassessments as soon as the second bell stops? As I was unloading classroom materials from my old classroom into my new room, Bonnie, the math coach, asked me, "Are you sure you have the time to start looking over the math curriculum while you are moving? You must be really dedicated or absolutely crazy! Either way, I am glad you are excited about teaching math." I hope that I will find others who are "really dedicated or absolutely crazy" about teaching. I will be the lone NBCT, but I will certainly seek out teachers who embrace or embody the following five core propositions, as I did in my old school when I recruited a group to undertake the NBCT process:

- Commitment to students and their learning
- Knowledge of the subjects they teach and how to teach them to their students
- Responsibility for managing and monitoring student learning
- Thinking systematically about their practice and learning from experience
- Membership in PLCs

Even as I look for like-minded colleagues, I will have to be aware of the multiple personalities involved in my larger team. Will I remember to listen and not judge others when teacher talk is not positive? Will I politely and respectfully redirect comments based on observations I am making of staff? As an experienced teacher leader, how can I successfully join the culture, foster the collaboration that I value, and contribute my skills and knowledge?

Upon reflection, in my old school, my emergence as a leader came from my classroom work. I threw my energy and skills into helping my students become competent writers. After two years of solid performance (90% mastery) from my students on the state assessments, my colleagues started asking me how I was helping my students perform more successfully. I joined a PLC team that adopted a consistent writing strategy and developed rubrics for all elementary teachers to use. Then, I became one of the core teacher trainers, as we retrained the whole elementary staff to teach writing more effectively.

My new colleagues will discover my abilities through the success that my students demonstrate, and patience will be my best ally. Yet, while it is unquestionably a virtue, I have a limited supply of patience when I am pushing for students' success. I've learned that improving student success has to be a schoolwide goal, and I know that many of my new school's students do not meet the performance standards on our state assessment. Will I be able to still my inner voice that cries out, "This is a way that worked!" and wait for my team to find a way that works for all of us? Will I allow others time to grow, even when I have a vision of what the future landscape could look like? How can I challenge the status quo of marginal growth in core subject areas and find ways to share my expertise without seeming overly pushy?

Now, in the waning days of my summer break, I feel adrift on this sea of change. But I remember a wonderful old maxim: "Ships are safe in the harbor, but that's not what ships are for." The saying reminds me that while it is indeed scary to start over, I must make the journey. And I will. I long for my new colleagues to value the journey to becoming a true PLC as much as I do, but I know that I cannot force their processes or their journeys.

Instead, as I scan my new horizons, I will watch for learning opportunities that will connect me with my colleagues. There will be trainings, curriculum issues, and student challenges for us to tackle that will help build new foundations and trusting relationships. As we work together, I must remember that my new colleagues care little about what we did at my old school. My job—our job—is to focus on moving forward here, today. We must sail through inevitable storms as a crew, but we will be stronger if we all survive the voyage.

Yet questions still haunt me. Will I be content to sail patiently beside them, or will I itch to steer the ship? If I don't try to steer, will the others see that I have skills that can help us navigate? Will they recognize me as a leader who can help us stay the course? In the end, as I take a deep breath and prepare to enter uncharted territory, my biggest question is not, How will I navigate this sea of change? but, Will I navigate this sea of change successfully—for my new students, new colleagues, and myself?

Questions for Discussion

1. Some say that keeping the focus on what's best for students helps prevent adult egos from blocking progress. How can you address the lack of learning in some teachers' classrooms without challenging a colleague's competence?

2. How does a teacher leader act as a leader while still establishing trust and credibility as a team player?

3. When an experienced and accomplished teacher joins a new staff, do you expect him or her to be a leader? What do you want to learn about that teacher before you look to him/her for leadership?

Case 3

Out of the Closet . . . and Out the Door?

by Christopher Drajem

The sun is shining outside my window, and I try to harness the attention of my 9th- and 10th-grade humanities students, as the screams and shouts of students leaving on field trips make their way into my room. Amid this cacophony, Jeffrey shares his year-end letter to next year's students with the class. "One thing I'll tell you," Jeffrey reads, "don't ever use the phrase 'that's so gay' because you will just be *destroyed*."

This does not exactly communicate the message I prefer; yet, the essence is there. As a gay male teacher, I am pleased to know that students understand the need to use respectful language in my classroom. Our small high school, set in the shadow of the Space Needle in the midst of an amusement park, consistently proves itself unique. It flaunts its difference in size, in location, and in the school culture—which is accepting, affirming, and, for the most part, devoid of bigotry and hate.

As a teen, I struggled to accept my sexual orientation in a very different atmosphere. High school was challenging and painful. I felt confused and cut off from my family, my friends, and myself. Attending a private, Catholic, all-male school in the early 1980s did not ease my tension, and the religious education encouraged me to hide deeper in my shell.

In part, I became a teacher because of this experience. I did not want other teenagers to suffer as I had. I knew that schools could be supportive places for young people who question their sexual orientation. I also knew that if I became a teacher, I would need to take a leadership role in making some major changes. Curricula would need to address issues of fairness and discrimination. Teachers would need to confront bullying, harassment, and language as they relate to sexual orientation. Finally, to lead the change, I had to be visible—out of the closet, and I had to drag writers, historical figures, and artists out with me. But what would this look like in reality? How could I make any of this happen while teaching my content? Did I really have the guts to come out to 180 14- and 15-year-olds?

The staff at the school was supportive, and I came out to a small group of students halfway through the year. Word spread quickly, and I was pleasantly surprised that there was very little negative response. Sarah, a sophomore, told another student that she would kick his ass if he had a problem with the fact that I was gay. Again, this was not necessarily the way I wanted it handled, but it was nice to know that students supported me.

I approached my principal and asked if I could start a gay-straight alliance (GSA) at the school. Nationwide, GSAs give students who are gay, lesbian, bisexual, or transgender (GLBT) a forum to gain support from their straight allies. Her response was a bit tepid.

"Why do we need a group just for GLBT students?" she asked. "It's a small school; why not start a multicultural club?" So we started a club where all minority students could meet to . . . do what? I'm not sure. Perhaps that's why it was a dismal failure.

In year two, to continue to create a climate of acceptance, I mentioned my partner and the home we share on the first day of class. Despite a few raised eyebrows from freshman boys, the news was not a big deal. Early in the year, I also enlisted the help of Lisa, a district health education specialist. To orient Lisa to the school's culture, I described the support I received from staff and students, and I shared some of my concerns. Were students out to each other? How much support did GLBT students feel? How willing were the principal and staff to support GLBT issues? How ready was the school to deal with issues of language and harassment?

Lisa absorbed the information and went to speak with the principal. She shared the importance of GSAs, and she showed the principal a letter written by the superintendent that supported GSAs' existence in every school. I was very pleased to have Lisa in my corner. We were going places—albeit cautiously. We announced a series of lunchtime GSA meetings, but students had to see me to find out the location and meeting time. At the first meeting, we created a secret knock so the five students who showed up could use it to attend future meetings.

All went smoothly until a junior verbally assaulted a sophomore who he assumed to be a lesbian. Students were shocked and sought me out to process the incident. They wanted to know why the principal did not discipline the perpetrator. I was also upset. The slap on the wrist the student received was bad enough. Worse still, the principal did not come to me to strategize how to increase student awareness and sensitivity. Perhaps she thought it would be more damaging to draw attention to the incident? I had a different perspective, and I decided to take action.

Lisa and I brought in students and educators from other schools to help our fledgling GSA develop an antiharassment training for students and staff around GLBT issues. The training received great reviews, and the school newspaper published a supportive editorial. Emboldened, the GSA shed its secretive mantle and literally came out of the closet. (OK, it was actually a small office.) We met openly in my classroom and our numbers swelled, but there was more work to be done—particularly in engaging staff in our efforts.

A few teachers attended GSA meetings, but we needed more staff to proactively address GLBT issues. In addition, two gay teachers seemed less visibly out to their students, and I felt their openness would benefit our community. I engaged them in ongoing discussions about the struggles and successes of being out, and Lisa recommended we create a "safe staff" list of those willing to discuss GLBT issues. When I e-mailed colleagues about the list, I was shocked by their lack of response. Was my e-mail lost in the crush of school business? Was this evidence that teachers did not want to deal with these issues? Slowly, I determined that staff needed information and strategies to help them discuss GLBT issues. We found resources, developed a training, and our safe staff list became obsolete when all staff members signed on.

By year three, the GSA had one of the highest attendance rates of any club, and my classroom was overflowing. The change in just a year's time was amazing.

Sarah, the student who vociferously supported me, was a senior now and a GSA leader. She kept pushing: "Mr. Drajem, what are we going to do about trannies? I met some this summer, and we have done *nothing* to address their issues." The gauntlet was thrown. The students felt there was still work to be done. How could I continue to empower them to be agents of change? How about a schoolwide community meeting to highlight some of the issues faced by GLBT students? The GSA embraced the idea, and the meeting was hugely successful. Students and staff thanked us for taking on this work, and the GSA was encouraged by its accomplishment.

Besides working with the GSA, I wanted to address GLBT issues in my classroom. I researched lesson plans for inclusion, with depressing results. Most of the lessons merely defined terms: "What is a homosexual?" "What is a heterosexual?" Some had lists of historical figures who were gay (Michelangelo [1475–1564], Italian sculptor, painter, architect, and homosexual). Simplistic and cursory, these lessons did not engage students in discussing the struggles and controversies concerning GLBT civil rights, discrimination, harassment, and violence.

I urged my 9th- and 10th-grade humanities teaching team to include a GLBT civil rights unit in our yearlong study of the Americas. We agreed that an exploration of U.S. history must address the long, varied struggles for civil rights by minority groups, so why not include the fight for GLBT rights? My team members embraced the challenge. I raced to collect relevant materials, secured copies of a play about the reactions of Laramie, Wyoming, residents to the murder of gay college student Matthew Shepard, and arranged for friends and community members to serve as interviewees for a culminating oral history project.

Students dove into rich conversations about challenging topics. Our team marveled at the way they reflected on the varied responses of Laramie residents following Matthew's brutal death. We were transfixed by their oral history projects. Several students in each class turned their interviews with individuals fighting for GLBT civil rights into powerful dramatic pieces.

With the success of the unit, I realized that I'd met all of the goals I had set for myself when I ventured forth on my path as a teacher leader. As an out teacher, I am a valuable role model for students and for staff. I've helped create a safe, welcoming environment for GLBT students, and I've advanced curriculum reform. And . . . what's next? At year's end, when a student's main piece of advice to incoming students is "don't ever use the phrase 'that's so gay'!" it tells me that this is an amazing place to teach and that it might be the right time to leave. Something is pulling me away from my safe environment, goading me to build on the work I have done to make high school a safer place than when I was in school.

Outside my safe bubble, social barriers and taboos flourish. As a nation, we are very far from a culture of acceptance based on our common *humanity*. I am appalled by students' stories about the prejudices and lack of safety that prevail at other schools. Colleagues elsewhere in the state tell me that their schools do not discuss GLBT issues *at all* because teachers, parents, and administrators feel they should not be raised. Lisa talks about the negative phone calls she receives from parents, community members, and other district staff each year when she hosts a GLBT family dinner.

In light of all this, how can I stay in my sheltered environment? How can I do more to affect the system as a whole? Could I work with building and/or district staff in Seattle or beyond to establish GSAs in all schools? Are there state or national organizations that could benefit from my experience with incorporating issues, leaders, and writers into curricula? Do I have the drive to become an administrator and be a visible role model/advocate at a larger level?

I have an urge to move beyond this safe zone I helped create, but the thought of leaving is tough. Will the changes I helped to make as a leader in my school survive after I move on? Will Lisa lead our GSA? Will my humanities colleagues teach our unit on GLBT civil rights? Will my gay and lesbian colleagues continue to be out and proud role models? Will the staff and administration continue to deal with GLBT issues in a positive, proactive manner?

I am at a crossroads. Where can I do the most good for the struggling teenagers that need my support? Is there more work to be done right here—more curricula to change; more outreach to be accomplished by the GSA; more discussions, movie nights, consciousness raising, stories to share, and victories to celebrate? Or, now that I'm out of the closet and the GSA is out of its closet, is it time to head out the door?

Questions for Discussion

1. How critical are mentors in the development of teacher leadership? How does one find a mentor when exerting leadership can be politically risky?

2. How does a teacher leader know when it is time to move on to the next challenge and hand off the leadership role to others?

3. What steps can teacher leaders take to secure the longevity of their work after they leave?

Case 4

Overwhelmed and Underappreciated

by Louise Tolson

As a teacher leader, my efforts to make our quality school even better can be very satisfying. It is rewarding to work with talented, committed professionals who want what is best for students, especially when they are fun and interesting. However, we are seeing an awful lot of each other lately, and some of us are a little frayed around the edges.

The stale smell of cafeteria food wafts into the tiny office where I am setting up a table. There is no room to negotiate, but with a little effort, we can squeeze seven people around it. I am not thrilled that this is our working space for our half-day instructional leadership team (ILT) meeting, but in our regular spot, the only other place in the building to work, our parent organization is lovingly preparing a staff-appreciation lunch. Suddenly, Karen enters. Her anger is palpable. "What are you doing? We are not meeting in here!" As Karen disappears to find our principal, her over-the-top reaction perplexes me. Is she having a bad day, or is something more going on here?

I am a middle-grade English teacher and ILT member at Northside, a very small K–8 public school with 200 students. Our principal is a part-time principal and a part-time district administrator, and we have 18 staff members, 11 of whom are teachers.

You would think that running such a small school would be simple.

Ten years ago, when Northside was in its planning stages, our advisory committee optimistically thought that shared staff leadership would eliminate the need for a school principal. While the committee ultimately decided that Northside needed a part-time principal, the school still has an expectation that staff will help plan and lead. From the beginning, teachers made many decisions about the character and focus of the school program and worked together to determine curricular direction. However, the realities of full-time teaching and the numerous demands on our half-day principal quickly demonstrated the wisdom of not having the school run solely by its staff.

Northside changed principals four times in five years, and the direction of the school's shared leadership shifted constantly. Each principal had his or her own style of working with staff. Often, the principal just did his or her job, and we did ours. During our brief staff meetings, we did not have enough time to engage in desired whole school collaborative planning.

When our current principal joined us three years ago, he offered us an array of decision-making tasks. At first, we thought he was a bit lazy and wanted us to do his job, too. Instead, he began a process—featuring the ILT—that helped institutionalize our school's collaborative leadership process.

The ILT's mission is to shepherd the work of student learning. Unlike most other committees that are responsible for short-term tasks, the ILT has a yearlong commitment and multiple responsibilities. The team meets as often as necessary, often weekly, and looks at schoolwide learning goals, grant-funded responsibilities, assessment results, projects, and initiatives. Although the principal is an ILT member, he is often absent from meetings due to the many demands on his time, and he is content to allow us to make many decisions without him.

Ideally, the entire teaching staff would serve on the ILT. In fact, we have made efforts to encourage each staff member to rotate in for a time. However, this voluntary participation system has not brought in any new staff members. Some excellent teachers are content to use their time and energy for their classrooms, and several of the newer Northside staff members have not bought into the school's shared leadership philosophy and expectations. They are willing to serve briefly on committees, but they feel that long-term commitment to a group with regular meetings such as the ILT is "too much."

Our ILT members are, therefore, "willing over-timers" who usually agree to participate in trainings, preside at evening school events, or provide summer school and other out-of-school learning experiences. This small core group is interested in moving the school forward, even if it means taking on more responsibility and spending more time in meetings. Strongly committed to the small school philosophy, and anxious to see Northside's unique character continue, we are fearful that other staff members do not have the same commitment to our school's vision and potential. However, we also are keenly aware of the personal costs of the leadership responsibilities that we assume.

Knowing how busy I am already, I usually take on just a few ILT responsibilities. I worry about becoming overwhelmed, so I prefer to provide secretarial support to the ILT, and I occasionally offer to help lead meetings, represent the school at parent or district meetings, or help arrange staff development activities. Karen, our second-grade teacher, does the lion's share of our work. She has been with our school since its founding, and she has a strong commitment to its vision of shared leadership.

Despite our shared leadership values, Karen is disproportionately burdened. Her understanding of our charter's mission leads her to commit time and energy to many challenging tasks related to our school reform efforts. She is anxious to pull the staff together and build a cohesive focus on improving student achievement. She feels strongly that our very existence is tied to student performance, and she worries that the district could pull the plug on us at any time.

Today, our special ILT meeting with our grant-funded school reform coach is about the sustainability of our improvement efforts. It is unfortunate that it also is the day our Hispanic parents are creating a fiesta in our workroom, but Karen's loud, angry reaction is oddly intense. After she returns from unsuccessfully searching for the principal, she is still upset. "There is no way we are going to use this small, smelly office for our meeting! The parents will have to move!" What is going on? We have been flexible before.

Not wanting to offend our parents, I invite the team to meet at my home. On the drive over, Karen confesses that she feels that our ILT group is not valued. Being relegated to the small, smelly office indicates to her that we do not matter. She also suggests that the principal's lack of regular attendance shows that we are a low priority. Ironically, the staff appreciation lunch is just one more example of others' needs superseding the work we do. Karen feels that the hours and hours of work she has personally committed to helping Northside move forward to achieve its goals are irrelevant to the principal and others at the school.

Is Karen reacting this way partly because she has chosen to be responsible for so much of what the ILT does? Perhaps she is uncomfortable delegating to others. It is clear that she might be on the verge of burning out. Yet, if she were to quit entirely, it is very unlikely that someone else would be willing to shoulder her ILT workload.

Currently, teachers volunteer to take on shared leadership responsibilities. But should *all* staff members be required to participate in the ILT? I am afraid that if individuals are forced to take on leadership roles for which they have no interest, it will adversely affect the quality of work and decision making. However, more involvement would lighten the load for everyone and provide broader investment in the school.

As the anchor member of our ILT, Karen is overextended. However, the principal's lack of expressed appreciation and commitment to attending meetings also is a major part of her frustration. The principal rarely thanks—verbally or otherwise—people for their work, and his numerous roles at our school and with the district keep him very busy. Is it necessary for the principal to leave his other responsibilities if he trusts the group to proceed without him?

In thinking about Karen's concerns, I find myself wondering, "What is a principal's role in shared leadership?" How can a school community define that role, and how should the principal and staff negotiate responsibilities? Our principal has helped establish a unique environment that allows the staff great autonomy in developing programs and setting a direction for the school. Would we really welcome more administrative involvement and control?

I am proud of the ILT's accomplishments, and I am strongly committed to shared leadership. I can see that the staff's collective knowledge of our students gives us the unique perspective to address their changing needs and goals. The investment of time by our school leaders makes our school a great place to learn. But does shared leadership require equity in responsibility? I consciously choose to limit my responsibilities to avoid overload, but am I being fair to Karen and to the group? I hesitate to do more. As my middle school students put it, I am "whelmed," not overwhelmed yet, but getting closer. I really do not want to cross that line. I feel a responsibility to provide leadership within my school. However, I do not want to take any more time away from my family or students.

After talking to Karen, I find myself grappling with some serious questions. Karen's leadership strengthens our school, yet she feels unappreciated. What is the best way to reward leadership contributions before leaders burn out or begin to resent others and the job? Extra pay or other tangible and extrinsic rewards? Personal thanks? Chocolate? Whose job is it to provide this appreciation? How might I help the principal understand that it is important to Karen and other teacher leaders that he more actively and publicly recognize that our work is relevant and important? He does not like to be told how to do his job, and I am afraid of putting him on the defensive.

Nurturing and thanking teacher leaders for the work they are doing is important for sustaining school reform efforts. I would like to help Karen and others feel valued, because I truly believe that Karen's efforts are the heart of what makes our school effective. Despite all that she does, *would* Karen be so overwhelmed if she felt more supported and appreciated?

Questions for Discussion

1. How might the idea of shared leadership look from the principal's perspective? Karen's perspective? The perspective of new staff members?

2. The author suggests that nurturing leadership contributions could be helpful in sustaining teachers who choose leadership roles. What do you think nurtures and sustains leadership?

3. What solutions are posed for sustaining leadership? Which do you believe would be effective or not? Why?

Case 5

Free Money?

by Irene Smith

The e-mail note describes a terrific opportunity: "The National Council for the Social Studies (NCSS) invites you to apply for a CiviConnections grant." As a middle school language arts/social studies teacher, I am always looking for ways to enrich my students' learning; this grant to promote service learning connected to historical issues sounds exciting. To apply, I need to form a cross-disciplinary team with two other teachers in my school. If we get the grant, the three of us will collaborate in planning lessons and engage students in a variety of interdisciplinary service-learning activities.

I gather Lisa and Sue, my Discovery Lab School middle school colleagues, and have a quick meeting. Lisa, a science teacher, and Sue, the sixth-grade teacher, agree that this grant is a perfect fit for our small K–8 school; project-based learning and community involvement are important Discovery Lab values. They ask me to lead the group, do the actual grant writing, and communicate the project to our funder and the community. Together, we determine how to integrate our subject areas to develop a service focus, and I help Lisa and Sue write their sections of the proposal.

I send the grant to the Yakima School District office so they can approve it before it goes out. We are nervous about making the deadline, but the district financial officer and grant specialist must sign off on anything binding. They also need to track and report on how Yakima schools use grant money. Grants are legal contracts, and no district wants to incur surprise responsibilities. Fortunately, the district approves the grant application, and we submit it in the nick of time.

Lisa, Sue, and I are so happy when we are accepted! We will use the $10,000 in "free money" to pay for our projects, summer training, and a winter trip to Washington, DC, for the NCSS conference. Even as we celebrate, fate changes our plans. Lisa is rushed to the hospital after she suffers a brain aneurysm during our eighth-grade graduation ceremony. Although her health improves over the summer, she needs to take a medical leave, and the district hires a substitute for the year. Simultaneously, Sue announces a happy surprise; she is pregnant! She, too, will need a substitute when she goes on maternity leave in the spring.

So we regroup. I invite Cathy and Shari—our third- and fourth-grade teachers—to participate in our grant training and planning. Now, we are a team of four. I plan to work with the seventh and eighth grades and assist Richard, Lisa's substitute, with his participation. Sue has the sixth graders, at least for a little while. And to make this opportunity more seamless schoolwide, I resolve to include the fifth-grade team once school begins.

The summer training is terrific and gives us time to develop our CiviConnections project. We decide to focus on the Yakima River; we will engage students in finding out how people have used the river historically and identifying the problems it faces today. Unfortunately, I hit a roadblock when I try to include Richard in our planning. He is overwhelmed with the demands of his classes. To help him, I offer to weave science activities into my CiviConnections activities, shifting some instruction from my language arts curriculum to infuse more of the science components. What choice do I have? Who else will step in?

Another challenge comes during our first weekly planning meetings. Quickly, we realize that we must narrow our focus and split grant responsibilities. Each class has to determine how it will fulfill the grant requirement of 25 service hours per student. The younger students will do trash pickup and create antipollution kits. The older students will do historical research, create informative maps and exhibits, record oral histories, and make documentaries. Cathy and Shari ask me to wait to invite the fifth-grade teachers to our planning sessions until we have our budget and plan fully complete. "It's not about sharing the money," they tell me. "It's just that it is difficult enough planning for four classrooms." I understand their point, but shouldn't I include everyone in the planning stages?

It also would be great to have more help during this phase. The grant will support a big group field trip to visit the river, a wastewater treatment plant, and the Yakama Nation Cultural Heritage Center. It's a great opportunity, but the logistics are mind-boggling; it's hard to line up the buses, get chaperones, and arrange everything for the big day. It is even more challenging to coordinate our community partnerships with organizations that hold a stake in our issue—the Bureau of Reclamation and Yakama Nation Fisheries—a key grant requirement. When I connect with our community partners, they offer me more ideas and opportunities than I can manage. They are eager to be involved, which is great, and they also have a lot of their own initiatives in which they'd like us to participate. Can we go to their trainings? Can we acquire more money for buses to take our kids to see the salmon migration? Would we like to do habitat restoration or mapping? Suddenly, there are many more decisions to make and demands on my time. Do I need to write another grant? Should I be spending this much unpaid time in meetings, on the phone, and writing e-mails?

Now we are in a countdown to meet service-learning grant requirements. During our next team meeting, I ask again about involving the fifth grade, and Cathy and Shari respond, "Wait a little longer. We still haven't fully decided how to implement all of our plans." Wait? But time is almost up! Now I'm afraid that our inability to include the other teachers is undermining our Discovery Lab cohesiveness and leaving the fifth graders out of a great learning opportunity. I'm not sure how to reply this time. Do I have veto power here? Should I ignore my partners' concerns and involve the fifth grade? I'm really worried, but also we have major concerns about the budget to sort through.

Our team finds out that $10,000 is not much when we deduct our training costs and the first bus field trip. Gas is expensive, so we modify our budget to pay for substitute teachers so we can take a few students via parent vehicles to the river for activities. The NCSS conference airfare and hotel bites another big chunk out of the budget. Sue can't go because of her pregnancy, and Cathy and Shari altruistically decide that they won't go to preserve funds for our projects and activities. So I am the only one to represent our school at the conference. While in DC, I am thrilled to show how well we have integrated our different subjects and grade levels. I am proud of the learning our students exhibit, as I share our display board, student essays, and maps.

Back home, the Bureau of Reclamation arranges habitat restoration activities for our sixth, seventh, and eighth graders. The students love the experience: "Wow! This is cool!" they say. "Take a picture of me with the tree I planted!" "Look at the way we've created a fish nursery by weaving these twigs!" Unfortunately, time is passing too rapidly. We still have to schedule many more student service hours, and I can tell that we will struggle to complete our grant requirements by the April deadline.

Finally, I meet alone with the fifth-grade teachers and ask them how they would like to participate. We decide they will do a special art activity related to salmon. I begin grant writing to see if we can make that happen—all of the CiviConnections grant funds are fully allocated—but we quickly learn that we are too late. We have missed the deadline. I feel terrible that we have left out 30 students who would have benefited from participating. As I wonder what I should have done to prevent this, an even more pressing concern arises—my students' learning.

I notice that my students' writing scores have fallen because I haven't given as much attention to focused writing instruction. Even as I try to concentrate on my students, my attention is pulled in different directions—from budget snafus to staff issues. The district finance office is upset because NCSS hasn't sent the promised check. This serious problem could threaten my future grant writing opportunities! I drop everything and start investigating. It turns out that the check was mailed but never cashed by the district. After a flurry of e-mails and faxes, the issue is resolved except for my vague unease that both the district and NCSS are now annoyed with our project.

When Sue has a beautiful baby boy and goes on maternity leave, her substitute is so overwhelmed by her new responsibilities that she can't participate in CiviConnections. Again, I pick up the slack. My time on the grant adds up to many more hours than I originally anticipated, and my family wonders if I live at the school, but how else can we get everything done?

It turns out that not all of my partners are as worried about this as I am. I notice that Cathy and Shari have not used their budgeted substitute hours for taking small groups for service activities. Cathy explains, "We'd love to do that, but we're just too busy!" Shari adds, "Instead, we'd like to use our substitutes to give us time to plan together instead of working with students, okay?" But the point of the grant was to give students opportunities! Besides, if we don't do what we said we would do, I feel that we're not fulfilling the contract. Am I wrong?

There's no time to argue now. I tell Cathy and Shari that we'll need to ask for the district's approval, and I tackle the other paperwork that needs to be finished. I spend hours tracking down receipts and forms and completing reports and federal surveys. In the midst of this, Cathy and Shari unhappily tell me, "The district won't allow us to use the substitute hours!" Because it's so close to the end of the year, the district is ending all further spending and that part of the grant will return to the funder. Cathy and Shari are frustrated that they've worked extra hard all year and will not be able to use the additional money they saved by not going to Washington, DC Was it my job to find out when the district was cutting us off and remind them of the deadlines? On the other hand, shouldn't Cathy and Shari have used the substitutes as we originally planned?

Despite all of the glitches along the way, our spring celebration of our CiviConnections work is a wonderful evening. We meet at the local arboretum and share displays, music videos, and PowerPoint documentaries. Parents and project partners come to see the students' projects and to hear them talk about community service and helping the Yakima River. The history museum thanks us for our donation of oral histories and other records. Local scientists and ecologists join us. We are so proud. Overall, we feel that we have accomplished something really special. Several parents, impressed by our efforts and the students' fine work, come over to chat. "What grant will you be pursuing for next year?" they ask. "We hope that you will do something like this every year."

I would love to pursue another grant for next year, but what can I do to make things run more smoothly? This year showed me the high cost—for my students, my family, and my relationships with colleagues—of free money.

Questions for Discussion

1. How might the author have built support among her colleagues to share the workload instead of simply doing it herself? What other sources of support could one call upon?

2. How can a teacher leader ensure that instances of extraordinary effort don't become an expectation in future ventures?

3. What kind of resources do teacher leaders need to sustain themselves as they take on additional leadership work?

Case 6

When Do I Tell?

by Christy Glick Diefendorf

The phone rings, "Mrs. G., I need your help *now*. I tried the science lesson, and the kids just destroyed it!" I try to listen to Ryan as he explains to me everything the students have done wrong. I can hear his students in the background. Loud laughing and yelling make it difficult to hear. He is having this conversation in front of his students in the middle of class. What has gone wrong? Has all of my work been a waste of time?

When he pauses for breath, I glance around my classroom and see that my student intern has the first graders actively engaged. I sigh in exasperation as I ask, "Ryan, how can I help you?" As his words pour out, I think to myself, and, can I really help you?

While most new teachers have a mentor only during their first year, Ryan, a second-year teacher, is a special mentoring case. Five months ago, human resources enlisted me to mentor Ryan because he was clearly struggling. He couldn't seem to adjust to teaching a new grade in a different building in the district. After talking with Ryan about his situation, I felt that he was committed to improving his teaching skills and, most important, was eager for help.

At first, I was optimistic. I have been a successful mentor for 15 years, and I know that the skills I've developed can help new teachers become accomplished professionals. I also know that effective mentoring depends on whether a district invests in the work—ours does. The district is providing release time for me to work with Ryan—two days to use in any way we see fit. We have been meeting weekly, and I am in his class at least twice a week helping him teach lessons and providing modeling and feedback.

During the past three weeks, Ryan and I have been focusing on classroom management. He is trying out the new strategies to get his class under control that I've shared with him, while mastering the use of the science kit. I taught the first six lessons to model how to plan, prep, and deliver the lessons in an organized, systematic way. Now, Ryan is beginning to take over the responsibility of the lessons a little at a time, with me coteaching. I am using a gradual release of responsibility approach with Ryan so he can concentrate on his classroom management skills. Recently, he has begun to teach some lessons on his own, as I watch in the background, taking notes for him. Things have been progressing slowly, but I am fearful that Ryan's progress is not enough to convince me that he will become a successful independent teacher. Today, he is panicking because he knows that he is on a plan of improvement; he has to show professional growth to keep his job, and he has once again lost control of his class.

I am discouraged as he begs, "Can you come down and help me get the class organized again?"

As I head to Ryan's room, I am determined not to bail him out this time. I march down the stairs, questioning if I am the right mentor for him. Surely I have provided enough modeling and practice for him to develop the skills he needs to be successful. Am I meeting his needs?

Entering Ryan's room, I see some students working at their desks and others up wandering around. Several students are at the sink, playing in water, using some of the science equipment to squirt each other. The noise level is off the charts, and Ryan has fallen back into the pattern of yelling out directions in a fast clipped voice, "Tommy, sit down! Derek, get away from the sink. Elli, I already explained where to put the composting bag."

Why is he shouting again? I thought he had that under control. What is happening? Have I done too much modeling and not enough supported practice with him leading the class?

He looks at me and pleads, "Can you get them to sit down and listen?" My first impulse is to take over the class and teach them myself. But I know that is not my role, nor will it be helpful to Ryan.

"How would you suggest that this be done?" I quietly ask. "What is it you want the students to do?" I need to support Ryan and, at the same time, help him establish his authority while managing this class. How do I help Ryan gain the independence that he needs and not make him dependent on me?

Ryan explains, "All of the students are supposed to be in their seats writing in their science journals about what they have observed. If they finish early, they need to get out books to read silently while others complete the assignment." I feel that I cannot step in and take over at this point. I quietly say, "Ryan, get the students' attention and have a class meeting. Work with the class on what is expected of each of them."

Why don't I see any progress? At what point do I let the principal know my concerns about what is happening here? When do I tell?

When the students are finally all sitting down on the carpet, I hear, "I had to call Mrs. G. because you are not behaving and following directions! Derek, I specifically asked you to go to your seat, but instead, you went over to the sink and were playing around with the water and eye droppers. You've got to stop screwing up! You kids need to behave because I am going to get fired if you don't."

Internally I cringe. Wow, he is not getting it. Did he really just say that? We need to sit down and talk specifically about word choice and negativity, yet again. This will be hard because we have already had this conversation, and I know that I will have to be more direct this time. Ryan participated with the majority of staff in a book study of *Choice Words*. He heard how everybody felt that word choice was a critical issue for teachers. How do I help him understand that ethically there is a line of professionalism that you do not cross? I feel that Ryan falls back into his bad habits whenever I am not in the room. As I continue to observe, he sends students back to their seats. I notice some students look defeated and others look as if they don't care. Ryan looks up with relief when the bell rings and the students run to recess.

I feel like I have spent the last five months working with someone who is clearly not making strides in becoming a proficient teacher. Have I wasted my time? Perhaps mentoring is something I should give up!

"Do you have time to talk?" I ask. "What do you think worked in the lesson?"

"Nothing worked. Why is it that when you come into my room the students start to behave better?"

How do I show Ryan that *he* is the reason his class is falling apart? I am out of ideas.

I need to show him the things he says are unethical and inappropriate. "Ryan, one area that I am concerned about may make you uncomfortable, but you need to be aware of this. You are negative with the kids and punitive when you talk with them. Professionally, you need to be careful with your word choices. Telling a student that he 'screwed up' is not acceptable. Telling a child this in front of the whole class is damaging to the child, and he may take the blame very personally and deeply. When you have a behavior issue to address with a child, you need to do it in a positive and private way."

Do I really have to say this to a second-year teacher once more?

Ryan appears to be listening carefully to what I am saying. I wonder if he is really getting it, though. "Ryan, do you understand what I am talking about?"

I wait while Ryan thinks about this. I am surprised at how long he thinks. He finally says, "Well, I guess using 'screwed up' is not okay. But Derek was messing around, and he is the problem a lot of the time."

Is Ryan really not getting that *he* is the cause of some of this behavior?

I keep trying to get through to Ryan, asking "But Ryan, when you tell a group of students that your job is on the line, what do you think this does to your credibility?"

Ryan doesn't give a clear answer, "Well, I guess I lose it, maybe?"

Ryan has grown in some areas. He is able to write up lesson plans that are connected to the standards. He is getting work graded and back in a more timely fashion. He has an attitude of "I really want to make this work." However, his growth in the classroom is sporadic, at best.

Ryan is at a critical juncture that new teachers face when they are consistently unsuccessful. At this point in his career, he should be showing huge gains in management and instruction. Instead, his students are academically behind the other second grade classes. And there is clearly a discrepancy between his responsibility to ensure that his students make appropriate gains and his performance. Should the district allow him to continue to teach? How much time and effort from mentors is enough? When do you stop and recommend another profession for a teacher in crisis?

As I wrestle with these questions, I reach a crisis of conscience. I cannot put myself in an evaluator role—doing so would go against everything I learned in my training and 15 years of experience. I must focus my efforts on providing support and help for Ryan. I must also maintain confidentiality and be careful not to provide his evaluators with information that would impact his performance evaluation. At the same time, I cannot let his students suffer. Ethically and professionally, I need to find a way to be honest and fair to all. In my heart, I am torn as to what I should do.

The time is nearing when Human Resources will ask me if I want to continue supporting Ryan. I have to ask myself, Am I the right person for this mentoring relationship, and do I want to do it again? Is now the time for me to tell?

Questions for Discussion

1. It's normal for new teachers to be in "survival mode" during their first few months of teaching. What is the mentor's responsibility if that survival phase stretches well into a second year?

2. Is it ever appropriate for a mentor to breach confidentiality? If so, when and how can a teacher leader divulge concerns about a teacher's competence?

3. What strategies help mentors promote self-sufficiency in new teachers? What mentoring behaviors may have contributed to Ryan's continued dependency?

4 District-Level Leadership

When teacher leaders work at the district level, even though most of their work is with teachers, a consistent challenge they face is building support among administrators at both the school and district levels. District-level priorities sometimes call for different approaches than teacher leaders feel are best for the teachers they support. As a result, they often find themselves caught in the middle between the central office and the schools, trying to negotiate the implementation of new policies and practices.

From this intermediary position, teacher leaders deal with resistance to change on many levels. They must learn to navigate fluctuating political dynamics across schools and departments. As each school has its own unique culture and goals—that may not align with district priorities—these teacher leaders need to develop new skills of diplomacy to work successfully with a broad range of schools.

In addition to dealing with competing allegiances and resistance, these teacher leaders often feel isolated and miss the camaraderie of being part of a school staff. They find themselves with few colleagues who do what they do. No matter how committed one is to a reform agenda, sometimes leadership can be a lonely enterprise. One of the case authors aptly characterized the challenge: "As a teacher, you have goals and you develop lesson plans to get there, but with teacher leadership, you have goals, but how you get there is so tricky because there are so many unknowns. It's really complex."

All of these dilemmas come to life in the cases in this chapter. The following brief summary of each case will help you select cases that match issues you want to address in your setting.

Filling a Leadership Vacuum raises questions about a teacher leader's ability to lead a district reform without support from the building principal. This is particularly challenging in this case, because the reform provided professional development for only one department, leaving the rest of the staff anxious about making their practice public and open to feedback without the benefits of training and previous experience working with an instructional coach.

Considering All Voices describes a teacher leader caught in the middle between district leaders and the group of teacher leaders she has nurtured for several years. The trade-off between subject matter expertise and the need for broad-based teacher involvement in the process complicates the group's participation in the reform.

Crossroads reveals the challenge of trying to move from an isolated specialist position to provide leadership at the district level. Does a teacher leader have to remain "one of them" to be able to credibly advocate for the group, or can one provide leadership from the outside?

Where Do I Stand? Leadership in a Culture of Us and Them highlights the division that often exists between schools and central office personnel. When a teacher leader moves into the nebulous area between the two, loyalties are often questioned, and teacher leaders have to weigh the pros and cons and find ways to bridge the divide.

Preparing for the Future? Reliving the Past? takes up the pressure a young emerging teacher leader feels when he's asked to fill the shoes of a legendary veteran leader. His task is to get his team to overcome the historical disjunction between the middle school and high school to vertically align curriculum that will raise standards and prepare all students to succeed in the most rigorous courses.

Is It Just a Crazy Dream? explores the struggles of one teacher leader as she works to transform the role of school counselors from reactive behavior managers into proactive teachers of positive interpersonal skills and responsible behavior. She wrestles with how to make inroads and convince her colleagues to give change a chance.

Case 7

Filling a Leadership Vacuum

by Joanna Michelson

One by one, the 25 high school teachers wander in and start posting their "What Learning Looks and Sounds Like in My Classroom" charts. My pulse rate doubles. Is this meeting I am about to lead going to be a waste of time? Have I misread this situation? The teachers' charts suggest they are more on the same page about teaching and learning than I thought. According to their posters, this seems like an ideal school for the literacy reform. Do these teachers really need to change? Have I underestimated their school culture?

As a district literacy coach, I work with several of the school's English teachers, supporting them through one on one, classroom-based coaching sessions, often with many other teachers, consultants, and administrators present. This residency model of embedded professional development is designed to build several strong laboratory classrooms in the district, in which other educators can easily observe teacher practice and learning alongside student learning. The residency teachers at this site have been enthusiastically involved in the work for two years; their practices have become increasingly student centered, with more students achieving at high levels.

This spring, however, I have begun to notice a change. The residency teachers ignore the e-mails I send to schedule coaching dates. When I manage to contact them, I have a very hard time coordinating visits to their classrooms because they say they're too busy. During my few successful visits, I sense that teachers no longer want my feedback. And more and more students in these previously high-functioning classes are visibly opting out of learning, without consequence. It seems the teachers are less committed, sharing a feeling that one teacher voices: "Haven't we done enough to change our practices? What about the rest of the school? I can't work any harder."

In desperation, I seek Principal John Henderson's support. Uninvolved in the reform work this year, John is becoming increasingly difficult to locate. When I finally catch up with him in the hall, he seems like he's in a rush. "Do you have a minute?" I call out eagerly. "Just a minute," he replies, checking his watch. "Will you support a visit to another school in the district?" I ask nervously. "The residency teachers really seem like they're burning out, and I want to show them that there's room for more growth for them and their students!" While John quickly agrees to the visit, he declines to come along or facilitate any follow-up. "Can you ask the district for substitute money?" he calls over his shoulder as he heads to his office.

The trip is a great success. The residency teachers are inspired by the other school. They are most struck by the schoolwide emphasis on student voice and the clear, shared school vision led by the principal. They also are convinced that the rest of the school must support the values they are cultivating in their residency. Eager to engage staff in a process to unite them in sharing a vision of effective instruction, they want me to facilitate the discussion. Of course, I will do anything to move the literacy reform forward and honor these teachers who feel so isolated.

So here I am, a literacy coach, running a staff meeting. As requested, teachers have made posters of various sizes and shapes that express the values of the student-centered literacy reform. All charts mention ideas such as "students are talking," "students are working independently," "students know how to work collaboratively," and "students are advocating for their own needs." Perhaps the other teachers really do share the residency teachers' hopes and expectations for students. But if this is true, why has the reform stagnated?

As teachers start settling into their chairs, the door swings open and John walks in. He smiles at me and takes his seat with the staff, producing his best principal poker face. Several teachers start whispering. This is the first meeting John has attended in a while. I wonder if the teachers are sharing my thoughts: What does he want for the students at this school? And where has he been all year? My doubts about facilitating this meeting intensify.

Ted and Susie, two of the residency teachers, introduce me to the staff and, after sharing the highlights of their visit, they note that the other school's classrooms felt truly consistent and student centered. Susie adds, "We can't move forward as a school unless we have this discussion about our visions for our students in *all* our classrooms."

"Thank you for agreeing to initiate a difficult conversation today," I begin, pausing to point at the posters. "Judging by these wall charts you have prepared, you are already thinking about ideal conditions for student learning, and you want these conditions to be a reality for all of your students. Our conversation today will shift between the theoretical and the concrete—the larger guiding principles you value and the nitty-gritty of what those principles look like in practice. In my experience, we cannot have one without the other. And we can't hold each other accountable without both the general and the specific."

Mark raises his hand. "I take issue with the word 'accountable.' That feels entirely negative to me. Is this about punishing each other for messing up?"

There is a rumble in the group. I glance at Ted and he shrugs. I respond, "Okay. The idea is that we can't work in isolation. Accountability, in my mind, means we are aware of what each other believes and is trying out. . . ." Silently critiquing my words as I speak, I cringe. Why am I using the term *we* when I am not a teacher in this school? Why am I running this conversation? Why doesn't John speak up? He's the principal, and he should be leading this.

Mark seems to accept my response, at least superficially. But he has cracked the veneer of the meeting. Whispers continue between tablemates, and I become more anxious. This conversation will be awkward, and its implications will be uncomfortable. I glance at John. He shuffles the handouts on the table in front of him. It is clear I am on my own in leading this conversation. It's no surprise that students at this school are reluctant to work collaboratively or take risks. John models isolation and does not seem to support risk taking. Why should students expect to be held accountable or to have high expectations for each other? They see their teachers resist public accountability, too.

I return to my opening, explain the agenda for the day, and provide a rationale for each part—professional reading, discussion of individual core values, gallery walk, discussion of shared core values, and intervisitation schedule.

Sandy, a special education teacher, cuts in: "Personally, I am not comfortable with anyone visiting my classroom. You have to acknowledge," she looks up at me, "that not all of us have had the coaching that the residency teachers have had. And keep in mind, any time anyone visits, it is just one moment in time, one moment in the curriculum, one moment that might not represent all the other moments. Plus, I've been pulled out of my room for other duties all year."

I am floored. We have not even started the agenda, and the very last part of it is already generating the most anxiety. I expected some balking around figuring out shared values. Yet it seems the most terrifying component is the fear of being exposed in the classroom. This staff throws parties together and goes rock climbing on the weekends, yet they clearly do not trust each other as professionals.

I gather my teacher voice. "Okay. I hear the concerns about the intervisitations. We will have time to address those issues later." The residency teachers are quiet. I can see in their faces that, on some level, they anticipated this; the staffwide resistance has been their reality all year.

Hmm. So this is one reason the residency teachers have grown subtly resistant. Over time, they have gotten burned out by the pressure to move their practices further than those of the rest of the staff, and they are tired of the public nature of their learning. What happens to a group of teachers who receive substantially more professional development support than the rest of the staff? What if that professional development conflicts with the school's existing "closed door" norms? In this case, without a principal's voice to focus the school's vision, the strong residency teachers have gotten reabsorbed into the school's culture of distrust. Suddenly, I have even more respect for their desire to initiate this meeting. They want to address it, but as I sit there quietly, I feel the burden sitting even more precariously on my shoulders.

Against all odds, however, the meeting slowly begins to gain momentum. To my amazement, when I engage the group in a discussion of shared practices and personal core beliefs about teaching and learning, everyone actively participates. No one argues about the process, and Sandy and Mark volunteer to synthesize the patterns they notice and read them out to the group while I write them on an overhead. When I look up from the projector, however, my heart sinks. John has left. Was he threatened by this conversation? Does he honestly not care?

Puzzled, I pull out the chart I have designed to organize and schedule intervisitations. As I tape the chart to the board and start to introduce the schedule with a possible protocol for observation, Mark interrupts, "Again, I am not comfortable with this idea of accountability and visits."

This spark ignites other voices. "I don't feel we have enough time to plan this right now." "Whether or not we admit it, there are power dynamics at play in this room." "Will we ask first? How much notice do we give?" "I don't know what we are looking for . . . and how will the debrief work?" "What if we only offer positive feedback first?" "What about first-year teachers? Can we be excused?"

I don't know how to respond to this snarled web of worries and fears. This meeting reminds me why I am not—and do not want to be—an administrator. Still, it would be helpful to be able to *mandate* something. Without John present, this process has no teeth.

We have to stop at noon. "Why don't you work out your schedules over lunch?" I suggest, wondering if I should quickly track down John and try to enlist his help. The group halfheartedly invites me to the potluck luncheon. I decline and, as I head away to my office, I'm haunted by where this all went wrong. I thought this conversation was essential to the coaching, and the residency teachers certainly wanted me to help, but what will happen to the coaching now? How could a group so seemingly on the same page have this level of distrust? Did I just make the situation worse for the residency teachers? Maybe I should stop my work at this school. But if I stop trying to improve the school culture—and students' learning—who will take over? Who's in charge here? Can teachers reform a school without the principal's support?

Questions for Discussion

1. How can the professional learning experiences of a small group (e.g., language arts teachers) help change the culture of a whole school? Can this approach to reform be effective without strong principal leadership?

2. Where did this coach's process fall apart and why? How might this coach have avoided this situation?

3. How can an instructional coach help make it less threatening for teachers to make their practice public?

Case 8

Considering All Voices

by Diane Kane

While sitting around a table in the math cubicle with my teammates and the district curriculum director, I find myself concerned, defensive, and puzzled. The district curriculum director is unhappy and directing his comments at me: "You don't want this to move forward. You don't trust the process. The voices of all teachers must be represented, not just those of the 'expert' teacher leaders."

We are at the meeting to plan the initial sessions for refining the K–6 mathematics curriculum for our district. Using our state's grade-level expectations for reaching standards in mathematics, the K–6 curriculum committee will identify the concepts and skills each student must have before moving to the next grade level. These concepts and skills are called *power standards,* a term coined by Douglas Reeves, an authority on academic standards. After considerable research, the district curriculum director has outlined a process for the committee to identify power standards.

A few minutes ago, I was shocked when I scanned the list of teachers being invited to participate in the committee. Some are novices, and others have resisted changing their approach to teaching mathematics and fully implementing our current mathematics program. Many of our mathematics teacher leaders are not on the list at all.

Each building in our district has a teacher leader for mathematics. Over the last five years, many of them have dedicated their Saturdays and afterschool hours to attending seminars and meetings to examine student work to better understand how children learn mathematics. So when I studied the list, I wondered why only a few of the teacher leaders are being asked to serve on the committee.

Taking a deep breath, I share my concerns with the group: "Why aren't we using the expertise of all of our teacher leaders? How will we know if we are identifying the standards most important for students learning mathematics? How will we address the negative feelings some teachers will bring to this work?"

In asking these questions, I am following the norms our math team has developed during our two years together. We approach our work in a thoughtful, critical manner, and we all raise questions to examine as many aspects of an issue as we can anticipate. Unfortunately, my questions and comments have frustrated the curriculum director.

After the curriculum director's outburst, the room is tense. I feel defensive, and I begin to fear that my mathematical content knowledge will not be tapped as we work to identify the power standards.

As the district specialist for elementary mathematics, I was hired for my knowledge and my experience with how children learn mathematics. Will I be allowed to contribute in a useful and meaningful way to this work? I harbor a deep and abiding appreciation for mathematics, and I am passionate about the need to make it accessible for all learners. The power standards represent a significant and necessary effort to increase students' opportunities to learn, and it is important to me to participate.

The meeting ends abruptly, leaving me with an uneasy feeling. How can I help the curriculum director understand that my questions are framed by a genuine desire to understand how our current work to identify power standards meshes with my knowledge of the teaching and learning of mathematics? The following morning, as we prepare to begin our first session with the committee, I try to explain my approach to our curriculum director, but my attempts to assure him that I am open to his ideas fall on deaf ears. He remarks, "You have strong ideas about how things should be working." I am shaken. How can I contribute to this important district work if the ideas and knowledge of the teacher leaders, as well as my own, are not valued?

Teaching mathematics effectively today requires a considerable commitment to acquiring content knowledge and an understanding of how children acquire mathematical concepts. To fully implement our program, teachers must make a significant shift in pedagogy, moving from an emphasis on teaching procedure and arithmetic to building on students' existing knowledge and experience with mathematical ideas. The mathematics teacher leaders are committed to understanding how to make the shift and to improving their teaching practice from year to year. I am eager to serve as a resource and to learn right along with them. We have a great deal of faith in our math program, particularly as districts using it show an increase in students demonstrating they have reached standards on the state assessment test. This makes sense, because our state standards are based on those set by the National Council of Teachers of Mathematics (NCTM), and our program is a standards-based program. In my teaching experience, I am encouraged by my students' growing knowledge of concepts and enthusiasm for mathematics. Each year, I am impressed by their academic progress.

In many public forums, our superintendent emphasizes the need for a coherent district mathematics curriculum, consistent from school to school and grade to grade. He also stresses inviting and listening to the voices of all teachers in the district. Without adequate teacher buy-in, our curriculum cannot be taught effectively, or even used, in classrooms. The superintendent understands the importance of teachers believing in the curriculum, and I respect and admire his ideas regarding teachers and curriculum.

In my current staff development position, I often deal with the fallout from teachers receiving little support to develop the knowledge of mathematics necessary to successfully implement our program. Much of my work involves chipping away at the wall of resistance of some teachers. My experience with teacher leaders indicates that when the staff increases its content knowledge and has a clear understanding of the flow of ideas moving from one grade level to the next, much of the resistance melts away. The power standards seem like a good way to identify this flow for district teachers and a powerful vehicle to ensure that a consistent curriculum will be taught across the district.

As I reflect on the comments of our curriculum director, I realize that his focus is the buy-in of all teachers. I believe in the vision that he and the superintendent share, but I see some possible problems that I do not know how to address. Some of the teachers who will serve on the committee view the power standards work as an opportunity to get rid of our current program and return to one that requires less teacher preparation. Is the K–6 curriculum committee the proper place for them to air their grievances? I also know that these teachers do not necessarily understand the NCTM standards and the need for us to change our instructional strategies. I realize that it is important to hear all teachers' voices during this process, but I wonder about the decision to ignore the voices of some of the teacher leaders. What role are they to play?

The teacher leaders are committed to planning and carrying out professional development in mathematics in their buildings, modeling how to teach our program, and introducing instructional strategies to their peers. I have been working with many of the teacher leaders for several years, and I know that some of them will interpret their exclusion from the K–6 curriculum committee as a lack of appreciation for all they have learned and for all of the time they have dedicated.

Fast forward: Over the course of five months, the committee identifies the power standards in a series of daylong sessions. Teachers work in grade-level groups to identify standards and then compare standards across the grade levels. There is a logical flow to analyzing requirements by grade, and the expectations for teachers and students seem realistic. Opportunities arise to introduce the NCTM standards and for teachers to learn about mathematics content. The resistance of some of the teachers on the committee softens considerably as they acquire more knowledge about teaching and learning mathematics.

I am able to participate on the committee as a member of a grade-level team. I frequently refrain from actively participating in discussions, because I do not feel that the curriculum director will value my views and input. My work with the teacher leaders for mathematics continues in our monthly meetings. Teacher leaders often ask me questions about the progress of the committee and the rationale for excluding some of the teacher leaders. One remarks,

> I have to tell you; I am feeling angry and insulted. Why weren't the teacher leaders asked to create the power standards? I feel as though all of my hard work and leadership efforts are completely discounted and unvalued. I will not be a teacher leader next year.

In late August, the power standards will be presented to teachers when they return to school, with the explicit understanding that the standards are a "working document." Early in August, the mathematics teacher leaders will meet to design a professional development experience to help district teachers understand the process used for determining the power standards and how the power standards will be addressed during instruction.

I am wondering how willing excluded teacher leaders will be to carry this work forward. It will be important for them to collect data in their buildings relating to the successes and issues associated with the power standards. They will also be relied on to help their colleagues adjust to some changes in instruction. As the person responsible for coordinating the mathematics teacher leaders, how can I validate the work they have done and motivate them to continue in their leadership roles? When the buildings' staff raise questions and issues, will the excluded teacher leaders feel empowered enough or armed with enough information to address the issues?

Questions for Discussion

1. How can a teacher leader nurture and sustain the enthusiasm of other teacher leaders over time?

2. How can teacher leaders work with administrators to build strong collaboration and support for teacher leaders?

3. Is it critical for all teachers to agree to support a new program or effort? If so, how do you achieve agreement among all teachers?

4. How can teacher leaders use their expertise to inform and influence district leadership practices?

Case 9

Crossroads

by Jean Henderson

As a veteran resource room teacher, I wanted to make changes in my district to strengthen special education and support my colleagues. Instead, I hit a major dead end in my work, and I burned out. There seemed to be no alternative except to leave the field that I loved.

Three years ago, I sat at my desk, took another sip of coffee, and gazed at my endless to-do list. After seven years of working in isolation in special education, I could sense that I was starting to wear out. In my role as a resource room teacher for a small, rural school, I juggled countless responsibilities. I needed to know all of the regular curriculum for Grades K–5, keep current on special education laws and procedures, and help families in crisis. While continuing to attend multidisciplinary team meetings, individualized education program (IEP) meetings, and care team meetings, I also participated in building meetings. All of these duties were on top of responding to the everyday needs of my students as well as supervising and creating lesson plans for five educational assistants.

Suddenly, the phone rang. It was Sue, a new resource room teacher in my district, and her voice sounded panicky, "Jean? I'm not sure what to do. I'm having a problem with this parent, and I don't feel like there's anyone else who can help me. Do you have a few minutes?" The minutes turned into an hour that I didn't have to spare, but I had to help Sue. I knew exactly what she was feeling.

Sometimes, it seemed like special educators, like Sue and me, were at the bottom of the district's pecking order when it came to trainings, materials, and status. While the regular education teachers in my district had some collaborative opportunities available to them, the resource room teachers did not. Unsurprisingly, the district's turnover rate among special educators was higher than that of any other segment of the specialist population. Many of my colleagues moved to regular education because of the isolation, tremendous workload, and lack of professional development support.

I was committed to informally mentoring my colleagues. Teachers like Sue often called me with questions about the law, protocol, or simply how to survive in the isolated state of special education teaching. Even as a seasoned teacher, I shared the need to connect with my peers. I yearned to keep growing, and I was also eager to take on leadership roles in my district. It seemed like I was off the administration's radar, though. In seven years, the special education director came to my classroom just once—and then she was looking for someone else. Overlooked and overloaded, I knew that I needed to make a change.

When the opportunity to take on the challenge of National Board Certification came along, I quickly applied. I thought that certification might be the solution to my problems. In some ways, it was. As a National Board Certified Teacher (NBCT), I gained access to professional development opportunities outside of my school district. For the first time, I was encouraged to become a leader, and the Center for Strengthening the Teaching Profession (CSTP) gave me newfound faith in my leadership abilities.

Becoming an NBCT was a pivotal point in my career. I was positive that district administrators would be pounding on my door to utilize my experience to work on special education teachers' needs. Unfortunately, no one ever called to request my help and, postcertification, I felt like I hit another dead end.

With great trepidation and soul-searching, I decided that I needed to leave my resource room and move into a regular classroom. To be tapped for leadership roles in my district, I felt like I had to understand the full scope of how special education impacts regular education and gain a broader sense of the relationship between the two. The change was not easy for me to make, and it created a lasting inner turmoil. Looking back, I wonder if I could have stayed in my resource teacher role and realized my potential as a teacher leader. Did my leadership journey really need to take me out of my resource room?

Even as I left my resource room behind me, the work never left my heart. When I heard about some CSTP-sponsored minigrant opportunities, I began to envision a networking idea for elementary resource room teachers. This grant would allow me to bring these teachers together and help them avoid the burnout that I had experienced. I e-mailed all of the resource room teachers in my district, asked if they would be interested, and received a resounding and enthusiastic yes! The special education director's response—"Go ahead and apply for it, as long as it doesn't take time or resources away from the district"—was more restrained, but I was thrilled to have a green light for my project.

With the CSTP grant, I could support others in a way that I had not been, and I could help retain quality special education teachers. I was excited, yet nervous, about the group's first meeting. Would my move away from my resource room affect the special education teachers' participation? Would they feel like I had jumped ship? Did I still have enough credibility with them to serve as a mentor?

I was relieved to find that the group understood why I left special education, and they truly appreciated our time together. The newest special education teacher told me, "I look forward to our monthly meetings. Finally, I have a chance to talk to someone who understands what I am going through!"

Throughout the year, we met almost monthly. Teachers exchanged curriculum materials, brainstormed students' care plans, and discussed the roles they played within the context of their building environments. Group members enjoyed sharing their challenges and success stories, and they created a strong support network for each other.

During the last meeting, the group expressed its appreciation for the support and resources they had received. One teacher who planned to pursue her administrative credentials in the coming year said, "I wish we could have incorporated this grant into our district's special education committee. These folks really need to hear what is happening down here in the trenches before they make decisions. They need another piece of the puzzle presented to them by teachers, not principals."

I agreed with her. I had accomplished my initial goal—to produce results that would benefit the participants and the district's special education mission. Now, how could I continue the momentum and gain the district's buy-in and support? I still felt uncertain about my district's recognition of me as a leader. Would anyone listen to me? What was the best way to help move the project forward?

As I worked to complete the CSTP grant, the special education director contacted me. I was excited to tell him about how successful the grant had been, but he cut me off with a quick question, "Why is there money left over in the budget? I would have liked to use it for other purposes." At first, I felt hurt. I saw my dream of special education leadership minimized. After my initial shock, I realized that the director faced a perpetual budget crunch from all sides. He was looking at the unspent dollars left in the grant and not the professional development potential of the collaboration. When I took a step back from my first reaction, I understood the director's perspective. Still, his question and apparent lack of interest in the project felt like a sharp slap on the wrist to me. What did it mean for the project? How could I reapproach him to talk about building on the work of the grant? I felt like I'd driven myself into another dead end.

Today, I firmly believe in the idea of networking special educators for collegial support, and I continue to contribute my experience by mentoring a new special education teacher via the teacher assistance program. I also attend the district's special education meetings to stay abreast of changes in the law and procedures, even though I am a regular education teacher. Yet I feel like I must continue to venture outside my district—as I moved beyond my resource room—to find avenues to serve as a teacher leader.

At the local university, my leadership skills are valued and respected. I now teach a professional certification class for new teachers at the university, and two university administrators rely on me to teach and support beginning teachers through their initial 15-credit professional certification programs. As a National Board facilitator, I have successfully guided other teachers through the rigorous process, and I serve on the executive board of my local union.

However, with each new class that I teach at the university level, I am concerned that I am moving farther away from my dream of special education leadership. No longer at a dead end, I find myself at a crossroads. Do I need to move back into special education to effectively make changes, or can I do it from a distance? Why have I not been able to create a leadership position and a credible voice within my own school district? Should I try to rethink my expectations and approach the new special education director with plans to lead a special education teacher mentoring group? Without question, I have "earned my wings" as a teacher leader. But is it the kind of leadership that best fits my skills and experience?

Questions for Discussion

1. What does it take for a teacher leader to gain credibility among peers?

2. Is it possible to overcome the isolation of a specialist and advance as a teacher leader?

3. What does it mean to be a leader in a small district? How can a teacher create opportunities to lead?

Case 10

Where Do I Stand? Leadership in a Culture of Us and Them

by Molly Daley

Was I being watched? I stood talking with Linda, the coordinator of our elementary peer-coaching program, in a district meeting. My suspicions were confirmed when Linda walked away, and Janet, one of my fellow coaches, rushed over to save me.

"They're not trying to suck you into a curriculum specialist position, are they?" she asked, scooting me quickly back to our table.

"No, I don't think so," I lied. The director of curriculum and instruction had just announced that the district was adding several literacy, math, and science specialist positions, and Linda was encouraging me to apply. I was not only listening to *them,* I was considering becoming one of *them.*

Why was Janet so suspicious? She and I had worked in our buildings as peer coaches for several years, but this was the first year our district funded literacy and math coaches in every elementary school. Throughout this pilot year, coaches repeatedly requested more training and direction from the district. Now, the district was responding by adding content specialists to work with coaches, teachers, principals, and leadership teams. Wasn't this what we wanted?

Linda served 20 schools—she scrambled to train and support two or three coaches per school. The district funded our part-time release from the classroom, but there was little evidence that it valued our work. In fact, we weren't sure that the coaching program would continue. Didn't hiring curriculum specialists specifically to work in buildings *with coaches* mean the district was finally behind us? As I slid back into my seat, I asked Janet why she wasn't excited.

"This big change will be followed by another big change and so on. In the end, we'll be right back where we started—with no real commitment to peer coaching in our district." Janet felt like she was alone in her battle to maintain coaching and quality staff development in her building. Years of struggling to secure funding and gain recognition for her school's improvements in teaching and learning had taken their toll. She felt abandoned by the district, and now *they* had lost her support.

From my staff lounge chats, I knew that many teachers would respond as Janet had. So I decided not to tell anyone that I was considering applying. The "duck and cover" and "wait out the storm" mentality was common. Several teachers were probably watching the seconds tick by until coaching fizzled out. Veteran teachers often recognized my enthusiasm for peer coaching as something they once felt. "Don't get too attached," they warned. "This, too, shall pass."

Yet I could tell that some of the coaches also were excited by the new specialist positions, and on the drive back to my building, I weighed the pros and cons. In our model, we coached part time and taught part time. This meant that I could practice and experiment with the same things I asked teachers to do. I was in the trenches with them. If I stopped teaching, would my colleagues still trust and listen to me? I loved teaching, but I was invigorated by the challenge of supporting teachers. Would I have to sacrifice one passion to pursue another?

Also, Janet had a point. The district had a pattern of implementing but not sustaining changes. After six years, I could see the waves of new ideas wiping out reforms that came before. But our new superintendent and the director of curriculum and instruction listened to us, and they shared my belief that teacher development is the key to improving student learning. They also viewed job-embedded peer coaching as one of the most effective ways to develop teachers. If anyone could bring focus and continuity to our district, these folks could. I did not want to hop on this wave and end up washed out to sea. Still, I believed that the district was moving in the right direction, and I thought I could contribute. If we don't find some sort of wave we are willing to ride, aren't we just left washed up on the shore?

I decided to trust my optimism, and Linda, who said she was "never more hopeful" about the direction of our district, and I applied. Before my interview, I told my principal. I knew *they* might contact him for a reference, and behind closed doors, he was supportive. He said that while it was always disappointing to see the best teachers leave the classroom, he knew I would be great for the job. His words reminded me of what Janet said about being "sucked in" by the district, as if moving out of the classroom was some terrible fate he'd watched good teachers succumb to over the years. Why did he make this sound so final? Couldn't I return?

The next day, it became clear that my principal didn't understand I had told him about the interview in confidence. When I returned to school after a field trip, one of the few colleagues who knew about my decision to apply quickly grabbed me.

"Steve told the whole staff you applied to the district office."

"What?" Why would he do that, especially when I wasn't at the meeting?

"He also joked we should shun you like the Amish do when a member of the community chooses to leave."

Here it was again—us and them. I knew he was joking, but I felt even more worried that I would be viewed as an outsider if I moved into a district position. I didn't even know if I had the job yet, but I already felt like I violated the trust of the community.

Of course, everyone asked me why I applied. I shared my reasons: "I think there are some really good changes happening in our district, and I am excited by the possibility of being involved in the process." Their responses were always the same: "What changes? Why haven't we heard about this?" Apparently, our administrators hadn't communicated with teachers about the restructuring. More important, they hadn't shared with teachers that they were making changes to better support schools and building staff.

Still, I was excited when Linda told me I got the job. She would supervise me in her new role as curriculum manager. As she shared the names of the other new specialists, I was certain I had chosen wisely. I would work with several colleagues that I hugely admired. This was a great opportunity for me to learn and grow as an instructional leader. I was feeling so positive I barely hesitated before answering the standard questions for all new administrative hires:

"Do you understand you will no longer be represented as a member of the union?"

"Uh, sure." I could always join again when I returned to the classroom.

"Do you agree to support all decisions made by the school board and the superintendent and to represent our district in a positive way?"

"Yes, of course." This would be easy since the needs of schools were at the center of recent district decisions. Restructuring the curriculum department to better support schools with curriculum and staff development was evidence of this new era of district leadership.

When I hung up the phone and skipped over to the classroom next door to share my good news, I found several other teachers huddled around my colleague's computer.

"Looks like you won't be our building coach anymore," he said. How could he possibly know?

"What are you talking about?" I asked, slipping in among the group of teachers to see what they were looking at. It was a job posting.

"They're eliminating the part-time coaching position. The new position is full time." That seemed okay. The district obviously wanted to increase the time and resources devoted to peer coaching in each school. He continued, "Look, it says the new position requires willingness to pursue administration." Huh? Why are administrative credentials needed for a coaching position?

I scrolled through the job description, and there it was: *evaluate certificated staff*. How could this be? We worked so hard to establish ourselves as peers, learning alongside the teachers we supported. It takes time for teachers to trust a coach and take the risk of learning in the presence of a peer. With a coach as evaluator, would anyone be willing to take that risk?

Over the next few days, the building buzzed with gossip: "Who will apply? That salary is huge! Has anyone checked with our union rep? Did you hear how much the district is spending on this?" I was skeptical about the decision, but I couldn't join in spreading negativity and fueling mistrust of the district. I usually just left the room. It seemed I was now on the outside.

At our first curriculum department meeting, I learned that the administration added evaluation to the coaching role because principals requested support with their overwhelming workload. This was a trial solution—based on good intentions—that we would evaluate in the upcoming year. But were good intentions enough for me to support a decision I felt was wrong?

Good intentions weren't enough for Linda, and she resigned. Janet was not interested in administration, and she left her role as a coach. In fact, most of the existing coaches did not reapply. Now, I need to support a whole new group of people using a very different coaching model from the one with which I found success. I did not expect this, but can I really be certain this model won't work?

I need to keep an open mind and try to contribute to its success. My principal continues to say that I joined the "dark side." He did so in front of families at our fifth-grade graduation and with staff on the last day of school. He's joking, but how widely is this view shared? Is Janet right not to trust the district? While I know it is not as sinister as the dark side, I am stepping into a gray area. How can I sustain my energy in a system where so much is beyond my control? How can I support the district while remaining true to my beliefs? Is there some way to bridge the middle, or must we all take sides and ally ourselves in the ongoing struggles that exist in any educational organization? If so, which side am I on?

Questions for Discussion

1. What role can teacher leaders play in bridging/mending a history of distrust between teachers and administration?

2. How can teacher leaders work within the bureaucracy to ensure that teachers' voices help shape policy?

3. What conditions would be necessary to incorporate evaluation into a peer coaching role?

Case 11

Preparing for the Future? Reliving the Past?

by Matthew Colley

"What is her problem? Some people are too insecure," grumbles one of the high school Advanced Placement (AP) Program teachers. A middle school Highly Capable (HiCap) Program teacher cries silently. Her colleagues console her, but they, too, are angry and hurt that the high school AP teachers are ignoring their concerns. The AP teachers are frustrated by our vertical team's lack of progress. Our task is to create an aligned, usable curriculum for our middle school language arts classes, but our team is in turmoil. As the team chair, I need to get us back on track.

Four years ago, we formed our team to engage HiCap and AP teachers in joint planning. We wanted to make students' experiences more uniform (e.g., consistently high expectations, common text experiences, shared terminology) as they journeyed through the system. We also sought to move toward AP open enrollment. Students who were underrepresented in AP classes because of grades, economics, and test scores deserved a chance to participate in the classes.

It wouldn't be easy to achieve this goal. To succeed, we needed to change the way we saw our students and ourselves. The middle school teachers were balking: "That's fine with your kids, but mine can't do that. I won't set them up for failure." The team was charged with raising teachers' expectations, and, in the beginning, it made great strides.

The AP teachers learned that the HiCap teachers were not sticker-pasting rubes, blithely sending kids forward, unprepared for what lay ahead. The HiCap teachers found that the AP teachers weren't the elitist, disrespectful barbarians they had believed them to be. Together, they quickly recognized that the most pressing need for the team to address was the middle schools' lack of a language arts curriculum. The absence of a set curriculum meant that there was little consistency between classrooms in a particular building—let alone across the three middle schools—complicating open AP enrollment.

The team tackled the issue head on. The AP teachers identified skills students would need when they became freshmen, and the HiCap teachers set some concrete, reachable goals. Their discussions began to build relationships, plans, and commitments.

That was four years ago. I joined the team a year after those first productive meetings. As the energy of those meetings waned, and we realized the Herculean nature of the task, the chairman stepped down. Mr. Brown, the driving force behind the open enrollment movement, was nearing retirement. He knew we needed to cultivate new leaders. I was honored that the team chose me to be the new chairman, but it was daunting to follow in Mr. Brown's footsteps. As alpha an English teacher as has ever wielded a red pen, he was able to affect great changes through the force of his personality and obsessive dedication. (His school day began at 3:00 a.m.)

Changes in leadership often slow momentum, and the contrast between Mr. Brown and me was quite stark. A mere second-year teacher, I was unsure of myself. How could I, a neophyte with little credibility and political capital, lead a group of experienced teachers in achieving lofty goals? How could I build on a trust that had existed for only a short time and was already beginning to show cracks? The group had an influx of young teachers. None of these new members, myself included, had participated in the meetings that successfully built camaraderie and dispelled preconceived notions.

While my first meetings went well, several HiCap teachers refused to participate, citing the uselessness of the meetings or problems with Mr. Brown. Initially, the associate superintendent made participation in the team mandatory for *all* HiCap and AP teachers. After the first year, however, it became clear that there would be no consequences for dropping out.

"What harm can come from participating?" I asked one HiCap teacher during a private meeting. "Why not be sure your voice is heard? Isn't it clear that we have to develop a more unified approach to teaching in the middle schools?"

She was implacable. "No, I don't think it's obvious. You can't just tell us what we need to do. I don't think you high school people realize that we have to meet the standards of the state test. The AP things are all fine and good, but we're under the gun to raise scores now."

I couldn't convince the HiCap teachers that challenging students with higher standards can improve test scores. Instead, they complained that the team focused too much on AP standards. I knew they were under tremendous pressure to address our state's specific standards. Yet how could they ignore opportunities to improve? Why couldn't they see that our state standards were not rigorous enough for kids to excel on AP tests and in university coursework? How could they purposefully put our students at a disadvantage?

Blinded by my biases and fear of failure as chairman, I could not think critically about how to solve the problems. I could not even see the real problems. Our district was changing rapidly. School improvement facilitators were using scare tactics and guilt to force the middle schools to make changes, and now the high school was hectoring them. It was a stressful time, and the team needed a leader who would strive to remedy all members' concerns. Instead, I lost sight of the HiCap teachers' needs and our shared goal of quality education, and I began to channel my energy into trying to get all of the HiCap teachers to participate.

I spent a lot of time asking myself, "How can I compel these people to be active members?" I tried holding team meetings at different schools, but attendance continued to drop. Few people responded to my request to e-mail me about the priorities they thought we should target. Nothing helped, and I felt ineffectual.

Many team members and administrators complimented me on the team's progress, but I disagreed. True, the math and science vertical teams flamed out and disbanded, but did we deserve praise just for existing? Sure, I could accept the status quo, meet with those who showed up, and continue to accomplish little. But where would that leave the students who should be able to go as far as their abilities and ambition could carry them, regardless of their cultural heritage or socioeconomic status? How could I rally the team to better serve our students' needs?

In my efforts to round up the stray teachers, I ignored the core group of teach-ers who were present at every meeting, willing and able to improve the quality of instruction at all levels. As a result, they were frustrated. We constantly discussed "fixing what was wrong" with the middle school. As I stuck with strategies that worked in the early days, such as backward planning from the AP tests, our exchanges became less and less collegial.

"I don't understand why we even bother looking at this," said one HiCap teacher. "There's just no way my kids can do any of the things we're talking about."

"Don't you *want* them to be successful?" an AP teacher asked patronizingly.

Another HiCap teacher chimed in, "Perhaps you've heard of this test we have to give in the seventh grade? The WASL (the Washington Assessment of Student Learning—the state's standardized educational assessment system)? I don't see how any of this connects with our state standards."

An AP teacher retorted, "Yeah, we have that, too, in case you didn't know."

"And 95% of my kids pass it," I snapped, staring down the two teachers. Needless to say, this sort of point-counterpoint debate did not help.

Inevitably, the team imploded. The HiCap teachers wanted us to slow down. Instead, and on top of the demands of their school improvement facilitators, we asked them to teach history as part of the interdisciplinary HiCap program. We ignored their concerns, and our insensitivity drove one overwhelmed teacher to tears. She was in a dual assignment—language arts and math—and felt over-whelmed by both. I, unfortunately, kept saying, "Don't worry about that now. When the time comes, we'll help you."

I don't think the blowup was my fault alone, but I was in the best position to address it. I reexamined my vision for the group. I wanted us to adopt a workable curriculum so that all our students would have a fighting chance at passing the AP tests, and I wanted our students to attend and graduate from four-year univer-sities. Our team included committed veteran and energetic new HiCap teachers, and I decided to start focusing on who showed up—not the malcontents—even if only one person from a building came.

Before our next meeting, I met with some AP teachers to tell them that our meetings would focus on the HiCap teachers' needs. More important, I told them that we would change how we acted in the meetings. "Whether we admit it or not," I began, "we don't think the HiCap teachers are doing their jobs. Nothing about our behavior says we have confidence in them."

"Yeah, but . . ." began one of my colleagues, rolling his eyes.

I continued, "We are fools if we think we can improve the system without working with them. This issue is bigger than us, bigger than our egos or our per-ceptions. So please, just keep your mouths shut unless you have something pro-ductive to say."

During the next meeting, a HiCap teacher mentioned a program by the AP test developers. The HiCap teachers saw the program as a possible solution to our alignment problems. Earlier in the team's work, the AP teachers had vetoed this program—we didn't think it was rigorous enough. Upon reflection, however, I realized that alignment, not rigor, was our number one goal. Couldn't we use this program in Grades 6 through 8, bringing the three middle schools together?

The high school's curriculum and standards were already more closely aligned and calibrated. Why look for a revolution when a movement was needed?

Yet I struggled. How could I, in good conscience, say that this was a good curriculum for the middle school but too easy for our high school classes? Wouldn't this attitude widen the rift between the HiCap and AP teachers? Still, the HiCap teachers, through research and experience, had identified a program that would work for them and would unify and raise the middle school standards. If we truly valued their opinions, we had to listen to them and trust their judgment. So we listened, and we did not roll our eyes.

That meeting was a turning point for our team, and we rose from the ashes of our implosion. Now, we have good camaraderie and a shared vision, but have we truly progressed? Our team had strong relationships in its first year. To achieve real reform, don't we need to get *all* teachers to change their attitudes? If we start to focus on getting folks to buy in, will we lose track of our vision again? Have we accomplished anything? Have I? Was F. Scott Fitzgerald right? Do we ever move ahead, or are we "borne back ceaselessly into the past"?

Questions for Discussion

1. How important are age and experience as criteria for leadership? If they are not important, what is? What are the qualities required for teacher leadership?

2. How does a teacher leader balance a commitment to his or her beliefs with the give-and-take negotiation required to achieve share goals? Does collaboration always require compromise?

3. What were the key turning points in this case? What caused the work to stall? What moves got the committee back on track?

Case 12

Is It Just a Crazy Dream?

by Jane Oczkewicz

"You've got to be crazy! I can't do all that!"

I close my eyes and shake my head, saying, "That's not what I wanted to hear."

Thinking back to when I was a classroom teacher, I remember when my school counselor asked me the "counselor question": "Do you have any students who would benefit from a friendship group?" Without hesitation I said, "Sure!" thinking of my one little girl with flashing eyes and a temper to match. "Suzie will be a great candidate." So once a week, at 10:15, Suzie left my classroom to join the other "Suzies" for 30 minutes in Room 7, the counselor's office. When Suzie returned, I asked, "What did you learn today?" With a smile on her face she replied, "Oh, I don't know. . . . It was really fun. We played a game and talked." I sensed that she was *loving* getting out of class.

"Something's wrong with this picture," I said to myself, thinking about Suzie and also making the connection with my principal's concern about too many discipline referrals. "It's easy for us to think that the problem is with the kids, but I think the problem is with the system. If I were a counselor, I would teach friendship and anger-management skills and, most of all, conflict-resolution skills to *all* the kids. I would teach the lessons in classrooms, involve teachers, and create opportunities for everyone to learn to use tools to solve their small problems. I think tattling and discipline referrals would drop drastically and playground and bus safety would increase and that our school culture would change dramatically."

I could tell that our principal, Mrs. Renard, also was frustrated. She was a seasoned professional who prided herself on running a "well-organized school," and preferred to be an instructional leader, not a police officer. "I'm tired of taking care of too many kids' problems," she told me. "I can't do my job!" Thinking that I had a solution, I confided my fantasy to her. "Our kids would grow up with words to say and things to do when things don't go their way. Kids would be able to learn, and teachers would be able to do their job: teach."

To my surprise, Mrs. Renard was not only interested in my vision, but she also hoped to incorporate it with a plan of her own. I was part of that plan. Encouraged, I pursued my dream. I achieved the required master's degree and certification in school counseling.

Now here I am, Mrs. Renard's full-time elementary school counselor—making headway in my school and finding myself butting heads with change-resistant counselor colleagues—like Betsy and Sam.

I am discarding the old rules of "how to be a good school counselor" in my school. Instead of working quietly in my office, I am becoming the school hub—linking staff, administration, students, and parents; I am as visible as possible with adults and children alike. I meet buses in the morning, hang out on the playground, open a "Kids' Café" to promote restaurant manners, run a peer-mediation program, coordinate tour guides to welcome new students, train the playground attendants in conflict-resolution skills, and, yes, teach lessons in classrooms. We see results. The kids make better choices, our school climate improves, and discipline referrals to Mrs. Renard have dwindled from six to seven a day to one or two a week. Since I am teaching lessons to everyone, there is less need for friendship and anger-management groups. My job also is getting easier. Classroom teachers reinforce my lessons and expect their students to apply what they learn from me.

The district counselor meetings, however, are a challenge. My counselor colleagues are spending considerable time commiserating about their jobs: problem kids, problem parents, problem teachers, and the problem of how to solve the problems. I want to yell, "Hey, you guys, let's focus on some solutions!" Betsy and the other elementary counselors, however, have legitimate complaints and fears. They use a reactive school counseling model in which kids are diagnosed with a problem and sent to the counselor to be "fixed."

With naive enthusiasm, I share my success with the counselor group. "What do you mean, initiate a schoolwide counseling program?" laughs Betsy. "I barely have time to squeeze in all of my divorce groups, grief groups, and anger-management groups. And I was just asked to add a fourth-grade test-prep group. How can I teach classroom lessons, too? Remember, I've got too many needy kids at my school. There just isn't time. Also, there's no way my principal will go for the idea."

"You're right!" chimes in Sam. "Time is definitely an issue. I already know what the teachers in my building will say. I can hear their polite excuses: 'I'd love to have you come into my classroom, Sam, but there are just not enough minutes in the day.'" I smile and respectfully listen as the other counselors eagerly share their litany of daily responsibilities and excuses. Betsy, Sam, and the others are very hard working and dedicated to their students. I just wish they would redirect all that hard work to produce more effective outcomes.

To me, the resistance is like a thick cloud of black smoke, choking out exciting possibilities. Out of the corner of my eye, I see Betsy and Sam, rolling their eyes and shaking their heads. I think to myself, "They're probably whispering, 'She's crazy! She just doesn't understand!'"

Somehow, I find the courage to continue speaking. "A proactive counseling program meets the needs of all the students," I explain. "In my school, I teach skills for success to everyone instead of patching up schoolwide wounds with Band-Aids. It's making my job easier." This good news falls on deaf ears and is greeted with a chorus of "Yeah . . . buts." I empathize with the frustrations of my colleagues and wonder, "How do I go about initiating change without coming across as an autocratic bully?"

Part of the problem is that none of the other elementary counselors have been teachers. They have never acquired the skills needed to settle down 25 wiggly first graders or 32 giggly fifth graders, nor have they learned how to teach quality lessons that are informative, motivational, and developmentally appropriate. None have been taught the importance of data, test scores, or schoolwide collaboration to improve school climate, instruction, and students' lives.

On a quest, I charge ahead to find more ways to expand my school program. I attend state committee meetings and report that schoolwide counseling is the "in thing." Counselors are becoming catalysts for educational change and assuming leadership roles in reform, working to shift from a mental health program to a guidance program that uses a proactive, systemic approach.

I learn that the American School Counselor Association (ASCA) suggests radical changes in the counselor job description. The biggest obstacle is leaving the safety of working with small, controllable groups of students in an isolated counselor office. Counselors are asked to teach lessons to whole classrooms of students and assume responsibilities such as collecting data, assessing results, participating in schoolwide academic reform, and perhaps even going to PTA meetings.

I suggest we form a book club to study the ASCA National Model handbook. To my surprise, nearly everyone signs up to attend—even Betsy and Sam. "School counseling programs are designed to ensure that every student receives the program benefits," I read from the manual. "A comprehensive school counseling program will focus on what all students, from prekindergarten through twelfth grade, should know, understand, and be able to do in these three domain areas: academic, career and personal/social. . . . The emphasis is on academic success for every student."

I am excited as I prepare for our first meeting. I know that the challenge of designing a counseling program delivery system that includes pushing our elementary counselors beyond their comfort zone will be tremendous. I hope our book club sessions will be the golden opportunity to start an overdue conversation. I look forward to analyzing our counseling programs by looking at where we are now, how we got here, and where we want to be. Yet when the first meeting rolls around, my hopes are dashed; as high school and junior high school counselors fill the room, all of the elementary school colleagues are noticeably absent. How could they pass up this learning opportunity?

Instead of being a leader with an enthusiastic following, I feel like an ineffective rebel. I am a person who needs appreciation, and this is not a comfortable position. Ready to retreat into my shell, I focus instead on the questions that are spinning in my head. Do these particular counselors even want a leader? Do they perceive me as a threat to the status quo? I thought I was offering a more attractive alternative. Don't they get it?

Disappointed, but not defeated, I rethink my strategy. How can I take new ideas, make them attractive and user friendly, and be a catalyst for change? What skills do I need to learn to work effectively with resistance? How does a group change its program philosophy? How can I help the counselors use their skills more effectively? Reeling from self-doubt, I become a candidate for National Board Certification, thinking that the process will be an opportunity to redirect my energies. I need a boost, a new challenge, an opportunity to reflect and to grow, and maybe an excuse to separate myself for a time from the counselors' scrutiny. To my surprise, my vision of schoolwide counseling is once again validated: The National Board requirements for school counseling certification are based on the ASCA model. "Ahhh!" I muse. Now, perhaps, Betsy and her group will see the light! But do I have the energy to try again?

I'm feeling lonely in this crusade. I recall an incident, years ago, when I found Mrs. Renard at a staff function, sitting all alone. "It's lonely at the top!" I commented to her.

"Sometimes it is," she said. "It's lonely having the courage to carry out a dream." I wonder, will I be able to persevere and keep on smiling when people say, "She's crazy!"

Questions for Discussion

1. What can a teacher leader do when data and results are not enough to convince others to change? What more can one do to inspire others to follow a new path?

2. Rather than proceed alone, how can a teacher leader build a coalition? Who might be potential allies for this cause?

3. What is causing this teacher leader's colleagues to resist? What can a teacher leader do to address the reasons behind the resistance?

5 State- and National-Level Leadership

The teacher leaders spotlighted in this section are breaking new ground by taking on leadership roles that span an entire state, regional, or national context. Many of these teacher leaders' roles are one of a kind; there are often no training programs to prepare them for the responsibilities and skills their roles demand. Further, as pioneers, it is not easy to find mentors who have the wisdom of experience to guide them.

Although these teacher leaders are not immune to some of the same dilemmas found in the cases in previous chapters, they also face some unique challenges. Politics seem to be more prominent and problematic. Policymakers operate in a different culture, often quite distinct from the work world of teachers. Learning to work with constituents outside of education, such as the legislature and the media, is critical, as these groups can be influential in policy decisions that will ultimately impact teachers' and students' lives. So these teacher leaders must find effective ways to advocate for others who are rarely mobilized to act on their own behalf. Too often, this work is done solo, without the support of a professional community.

As a group, these cases invite the reader to contemplate the following:

- What is distinctive about the cases in this section?
- What are the unique skills teacher leaders need to work in these larger contexts?
- How can these teacher leaders acquire the new skills they need to be effective at this level?

The cases in this chapter focus on the following challenging situations:

Truth and Power describes a clash of cultures within an organization whose purpose is to advance teacher development. As the organization grows, its leaders hire business people with no background in education to play key roles as trainers and managers. The teacher leaders who have been essential in the development of the organization appear to be losing clout as the organization evolves.

One Step Forward, Two Steps Back recounts a campaign by a school librarian to restructure the role of school librarians to enable them to actively participate in the state's reform agenda. The need to upgrade school librarians' skills and knowledge to prepare them to serve as instructional leaders is essential if their positions are going to survive budget cuts, but some of the author's colleagues are the major obstacle to implementing the new standards she fought so hard to achieve.

Hanging in the Balance follows the journey of an isolated specialist who tries to create a professional network for herself outside her school and district. The more involved she becomes in the state organization, the more she gives of herself, until she begins to question the return on her investment. As her sense of exploitation grows, she reflects on how to find balance in her professional work—how to give enough to feel fulfilled, but not so much that she burns out.

Transitions discloses the uneasy emotions that a teacher leader experiences when she leaves the classroom for a new position at the state level. The transition leaves her in between two communities, gradually losing membership in her former group while struggling to adapt to an unknown arena.

Case 13

Truth and Power

by Kate Ryan

"So what do you think, Kate?"

I never imagined that this seemingly simple question could be so complex. However, a quick rewind of the last few years has all of the red flags in my head standing at attention. Should I say what I really think; do the potential ramifications outweigh the benefits?

The red flags signal uncharted territory for me. As a teacher leader in my school district, I was always confident that administrators valued my input. With that experience as my training ground, I have moved into leadership roles on the district and then the state level. In almost every case, I've felt that my colleagues appreciated my thoughts, and I never dreamed that speaking up might have unintended consequences.

So when Cindy, a colleague who I've known for several years, invites me to work on a planning committee with other teacher leaders, I go in assuming that the national organization where she works operates in a similar fashion. The organization's focus on teacher development naturally leads to using teachers' expertise, and I know many teachers who, like Cindy, have worked there over the years as consultants or employees.

The work is so exciting! I am in awe of these amazing teachers, and have to pinch myself to make sure I am really sitting at the table with them. Nina is legendary; the organization has tapped her expertise in many capacities over the years, and she definitely holds the mission and vision of the work in her head and heart. Cheryl is equally knowledgeable and has served as a trusted consultant in numerous paid and volunteer positions. These teachers are among the most highly regarded in our teacher leader community. With 10 other teacher leaders from around the country, we pool our collective experiences and complete a draft of a new training series. We are also asked to become the first group of trainers to offer this professional development nationally. I am proud of what we've accomplished and eager to stay involved. As we head to lunch that day, Cindy tells us that the organization has hired a new manager named Jon, who will join us for lunch. He wants to get to know us and hear about our work.

At lunch, Jon tells us about his prior experience and asks each of us about ours. He outlines his vision for the organization, and says he wants to work on better outreach. He wonders aloud how the organization might harness the energy and enthusiasm of teacher leaders around the country. And then, he asks the question: "What do you think?"

The room goes surprisingly quiet, with just a few short comments about how it sounds like he has good ideas. In hindsight, I probably should have taken this as a sign. After all, many of these teachers have been involved with the organization for a number of years, so I should have wondered why they were staying quiet.

But instead, I say what I'm thinking: "If you are serious about expanding out-reach to teacher leaders, you are really going to need to put some resources into it. Everyone in this organization has the equivalent of two full-time jobs already, and adding this work to their duties would make it impossible to move forward. It is critically important work, and I think there should be dedicated resources so that it becomes a priority, not an add-on."

"I guess we'll have to work smarter—not harder," Jon replies, but I'm focusing on his body language, rather than his words. He turns away stiffly, and I have the distinct feeling that he does not appreciate my comments. The conversation moves on, but the nagging feeling that I said too much lingers. Oh well, it is done. Or is it? Every time I run into Jon over the next few months, his reaction is always the same—no eye contact, closed body language, and as little conversation as possible. I ask a colleague what his interactions with Jon are like, and he says Jon is always really friendly. Hmm.

But that is not the only bad sign. Although I remain a member of the training team, over the next year, the requests for me to run trainings slow considerably. I wonder casually to myself if this has anything to do with my interaction with Jon. I've heard stories about how he feels about "troublemakers," and I can't help but wonder whether I am in that category. But I have plenty of work to do with my regular job, so I don't think too much about it. I figure I am probably reading too much into the situation.

Then Cindy abruptly leaves the organization. Her boss, Kevin, takes over her duties in the short run. Kevin and I have worked together on a different project, and we have a good rapport. I know that his background is in business, so it makes sense when he tells the training group that he plans to hire another teacher to take over Cindy's work permanently. In the meantime, he is going to put some teachers on contract temporarily. I hear that he is offering the job of managing the training to Nina, which is perfect. I feel confident that she'll be great at leading the project.

Months pass. One teacher is hired for a specific project and then suddenly disappears. No one knows why. Finally, Kevin tells us that he is hiring someone named Rochelle to lead the trainings. Rochelle is not a teacher, but Kevin believes that her business experience will be beneficial for the training. With Nina's help as the "content expert," Rochelle will revamp all other aspects of the training. This seems like a strange strategy to me, but since Nina will be involved, I know that everything will be fine.

Then I meet Rochelle. She's only been on the job a few weeks but tells me that she has already hired another nonteacher. As an expert in adult learning theory, the new hire's job is going to be to "fix" the training.

"Teachers are fine in the classroom," Rochelle explains condescendingly, "but they don't necessarily have the expertise to handle training for adults."

Taken aback, I say, "But you hired Nina to work as the content expert, right?"

Rochelle stares back at me blankly.

"Didn't I get an e-mail from you about Nina's role?" I ask.

"Oh, that's right," Rochelle nods slowly. "Nina is going to help us *some*. But only for Phase 1."

I don't ask about Phase 2, but reading between the not-so-subtle lines, it is pretty clear that it does not include Nina or the other teachers.

I don't know quite what to do with this information, but fortunately Kevin schedules a meeting of the group of trainers for the next week, and I go in eager to better understand what is going on. The second I enter the room, I can feel that the air is thick with uncertainty and suspicion. It is clear that I'm not the only one who has questions and doubts about the changes. Kevin begins by thanking us for our work and assuring us that he values what we have done. He talks about how Rochelle and her assistant are gathering information about how we can enhance the training and how Nina will help.

After a few minutes, Cheryl speaks up, "What *exactly* do you plan to change about the training, and why? The evaluations have been strong, and I've heard participants say again and again how valuable the training is. So what is this really about?"

"Any training can be improved," Kevin responds, and he moves on without explanation.

When the meeting adjourns, I leave knowing that I have not misunderstood Rochelle. This is about a noneducator mindset that teachers do not have the expertise to plan and implement an initiative. First, I feel sad and disappointed. Over the next couple of hours, I work my way to furious. How can *this* organization, that supposedly values teacher leaders, go down such a path? How does that saying go? If these are our friends. . . .

I spend a restless night trying to decide what to do. This is so wrong for so many reasons. First of all, teachers are the experts in this content and the only ones who can authentically plan and deliver it. Period. Second, incredible leaders like Nina and Cheryl deserve this organization's utmost respect, and seeing their expertise dismissed makes my blood boil. Finally, all of us deserve to be told what is really going on rather than having to decode the difference between what is being said and what is being done. So what should I do about it?

I think about conversations with a former boss, someone for whom I have great respect. In situations like this, she always repeats the same mantra: "Speak truth to power." That saying is incredibly bothersome to me. Every time I think of it, I'm forced to examine my motivations and actions as a leader. On the one hand, who could argue? Of course, everyone should speak the truth. On the other hand, many situations are not quite so tidy. The fact is that sometimes "power" doesn't care about my "truth," so while speaking it might gratify me, it is naïve to think that it is always the best way to get something accomplished.

I then think back to the situation with Jon. It is clear that the organization's new management does not appreciate advice. Should I speak up now and let Kevin know that I am upset about the training and the way the organization is treating teacher leaders? It is possible that doing so will mean that I am officially blocked out of any continued work with this group. I'm not sure if I really care about that, as I don't want to put my energy in a place where it is not valued. But I do care what happens to this work. And I really care that the expertise of teacher leaders continues to be used as it has over the long history of the organization. Would it be better for me to be quietly diplomatic so that I can work to change this attitude from the inside of the organization? And there are the other teachers to consider. If I speak up this time as part of this group, will the consequences extend to the others? Will they be painted with the same troublemaker brush, by association?

This dilemma swirls in my head as I make my way down the hallway the next day. As luck would have it, I run straight into Kevin.

"What did you think of the meeting?" he asks.

"It was fine," I answer vaguely. "What did you think?"

"I thought it was sort of . . . odd," he responds.

"In what way?" I reply, dodging, trying to decide where to go next.

"Well, for one thing, I'm not sure about Cheryl's comments. It seems like she is pretty upset about something." Here we go again. Cheryl speaks out and is now under suspicion. Kevin continues, "I got the same feeling from other people, although many of them remained quiet."

Then *the* question came. "What do you think about all of this, Kate?"

I pause for a moment. But then I think, "Who am I kidding? I can't keep quiet— this is too important." Speak truth to power, right? So I tell Kevin about my concerns with Rochelle's comments and that it seems that the teachers are being removed from the equation here. I explain my disappointment and my worry that the organization is taking a wrong new direction by not capitalizing on the expertise of teacher leaders. I tell him how highly regarded teacher leaders like Nina and Cheryl are and how much I am bothered by what seems like disrespectful treatment of them. In the end, Kevin thanks me for my honesty, and we part.

Later that same day, I run into Kevin again. He doesn't acknowledge me. No eye contact, no hello. Sigh. I've been here before.

Now weeks have passed with no communication. Did speaking my mind make any difference at all? What do I need to do to get this organization to see how wrong these decisions are?

And in the larger picture, does "speaking truth to power" ever really work?

Questions for Discussion

1. How does positional power (or the lack of it) in an organization affect one's ability to exert influence?

2. What strategies might be effective in convincing the "powers that be" that the wisdom of accomplished teacher leaders is vital to achieving their mission?

3. What options does this teacher leader have if she wants to work from within the organization on behalf of teacher leaders?

Case 14

One Step Forward, Two Steps Back

by Sarah Applegate

"Sarah . . . my principal said he was going to cut my library position in half and I am going to have to teach fourth grade part time. . . ."

"Sarah . . . our library program is going to be all planning time next year; how can I work with students to develop their research skills in only 20 minutes?"

"Sarah . . . have you talked to the union about how it is unfair that the art and music specialists get to be full time and the library program is being cut down to part time?"

"Sarah. . . ."

"Sarah. . . ."

"Sarah . . . help!"

This is getting exhausting and depressing. Messages from around the state are consistent. To save money, schools and districts are cutting school library programs. As a board member of the Washington Library Media Association (WLMA), our school librarian professional organization of over 1,400 voluntary members, my job is to save them, right? And if we do make inroads politically, in the midst of standards-based reforms circling specifically around math and science, what does another RCW (Revised Code of Washington, the laws that govern our state) or WAC (Washington Administrative Code, the guidelines for implementing the laws) involving school libraries really mean for the daily workings of schools and districts trying to make adequate yearly progress (AYP)?

After hearing that the State Board of Education was going to edit the Common School Manual and remove any mention of "school librarians" or "school libraries," our organization sprang into action.

Our legislative liaison Jennifer began making phone calls, building relationships and sending fruit baskets to key folks in the decision-making loop.

"Larry says we can present to the state board at the end of the month. And he is going to coordinate a WAC revision meeting in Olympia next week. Can you go to represent WLMA?" Jennifer asked.

"Of course," I responded quickly. But then I stopped to think. "What exactly should I say? I have never spoken at a hearing—what can I expect? How does it work?" I began to panic.

"Well, you need to figure out what to say . . . that is what *you* are good at. Here is what you can expect from the hearing. . . ." Jennifer described the setting I could expect in front of the state board. I breathed a sigh of relief that she was among our ranks. Her passion for the political side of our work will surely come in handy, since there are few school librarians who are eager to be a part of the political process!

I began e-mailing and corresponding with other WLMA leaders, including professors from university training programs, to figure out what we wanted in reframing our job. As a state organization, we had been struggling with job cuts around the state, and had determined that a radical shift in our job description was in order. No longer could we allow "book babysitting" to be the order of the day in school libraries. Taking a cue from Mike Eisenberg at the University of Washington's iSchool and the K–12 Library Initiative, a federal grant in which over 500 school librarians were trained in a common curriculum while redefining their roles, we were ready to move toward an exciting and challenging shift in approach. Instead of just being "happy librarians"—cataloging and selecting books, shushing students, and straightening the shelves—we needed to become instructional leaders in our buildings, fulfilling the mission of the American Association of School Librarians (AASL) to ensure that students and staff are effective users of ideas and information.

"I think we need to emphasize the research skills we bring to the table," said one professor. "Let's clearly establish the steps that school librarians should be teaching in the research process."

"We have to emphasize the need for a certificated school librarian in every building," responded a school librarian who had faced cuts in her district. "We are being replaced by paraprofessionals who are not running programs but just checking books in and out. We have to emphasize the importance of the professional."

"What can we do for education reform?" questioned another school librarian leader. "What are the holes in state-mandated initiatives that we can take leadership in? If we can take something on that the state says has to happen, we will become indispensable."

At the first WAC revision meeting, I was excited by the range of people wanting to have a say in what the new WAC might say and what my job might look like. From building principals to classroom teachers to university professors, these were people who cared about school library programs and wanted to help save them from the chopping block. The challenge was definitely going to be building consensus about how to get there.

"School librarians can take on a wide range of instructional and leadership roles in a building," I shared. "For example, a school librarian can do a lot of the staff training and development around curriculum initiatives." For the library people in the group, this made sense and fit in with their schema. For the nonlibrary people, their quizzical faces told their story. "Uh-oh," I thought silently, "they haven't seen an active, involved librarian in action, have they?" I knew this was a crucial moment.

Drawing upon my experience facilitating the K–12 Library Initiative, I began to share what a school librarian should be doing every day. "School librarians have three specific jobs: information literacy teachers, reading advocates, and information managers. They also can fill many other roles in a building, and actually, they are a very cheap date for all the skills they bring." Again, the library people nodded, and the nonlibrary people look puzzled. But they looked willing to hear more. "If we recommend high standards for librarians in the WAC, then administrators can have clear expectations and can evaluate them effectively." The wheels began to turn in the group, and heads began to nod. We were making headway. The other school librarians described what they do in their daily work, and they shared their value to the school community to an increasingly warm audience.

"This sounds great, but I haven't seen it before," said one administrator. "Our librarian won't let more than one class in the library at a time and restricts what students can check out. The staff doesn't look to her for inspiration or instructional help. I would love to have the person you are talking about, but where do I find him or her, and how do I shape who we have right now?"

The door opened.

"WLMA has an annual conference at which we work to build capacity based on the three roles I described. We have regional groups that meet and mentor each other. We have highly skilled board members across the state. We have over 35 National Board Certified Teachers (NBCTs) from all parts of Washington who are willing and able to help improve practice. We can help your librarian become better." And as I said this, I knew I had stuck my foot into a vat of quicksand. How were we going to make every librarian around the state better? I just knew that it would fall on the shoulders of our organization.

We created a draft proposal to present to the state board describing what a "teacher-librarian" should be doing to improve teaching and learning. The proposal was long and prescriptive, and I loved it. However, the executive director of the state board explained that WACs cannot be prescriptive. We whittled and edited the language down. While we lost some of the meat, we essentially retained the core values of information literacy teacher, reading advocate, and information manager that we knew were crucial to our schools, as well as demonstrated that we were willing to fill in holes that the state needed leadership in, such as Culminating Projects, High School and Beyond Plans, and classroom-based assessments.

The following week, I nervously presented our proposal to the state board. I don't think I looked up for the three minutes I spoke, but when I was finished, I saw they were still listening and even smiling at me. They made a motion to approve and everyone agreed. We were in the WACs! Success!

Or so we thought.

A few months later, the governor created a study group to evaluate preK–20 education in the state. Part of her directive was to dilute the authority of the state board.

"Sarah, we have some bad news," Jennifer called to tell me. "I just got off the phone with Larry from the state board, and they will not be supervising the library WAC anymore. . . . In fact, they won't be overseeing very much." She sounded as deflated as I suddenly felt. "Our only hope is to propose something to the legislature and push for an RCW."

"Jennifer, that sounds impossible."

"It will be hard but not impossible. We can do it. We have 1,400 members around the state . . . and c'mon, everyone loves a library! We already have a great brand!"

I always admired Jennifer's tenacity and optimism.

"Just tell me what to do, and I will do it."

Jennifer began crafting our next plan to get our WAC rolled into an RCW. This would be huge. While WACs merely govern procedure, RCWs are laws that everyone in the state must follow. Getting an RCW would be our holy grail. We would finally be legitimized as teacher-librarians. Students around the state would be assured quality information skills programs that would prepare them for their future. And I would stop getting those depressing e-mails.

We restarted our campaign. We educated our members about how to contact their legislators. We gave them talking points that captured the vital role that teacher-librarians can play in schools, and we worked to create a sense of urgency. Jennifer arranged meetings with key legislators on the education committees so that we could share with them the research of how a quality teacher-librarian would impact students. And we rallied other supportive educators to help speak for us.

Meanwhile, positions were being cut in my district. The e-mails and calls kept coming, even from teacher-librarians just miles from my school, telling me that at staff meetings, classroom teachers were being asked to choose what they wanted to cut out of the specialist rotation in their building: music, art, or library. One teacher-librarian watched as her staff essentially voted her out, saying they could cover the information skills curriculum, that the trained teacher-librarian wasn't essential to their daily work. "I was voted off the island, just like that," she said in tears. "I have developed a student-run television program here at school, I collaborate with many of the teachers, and I have students in the library working all day long. What am I doing wrong?"

When I spoke in front of the legislative education committee, urging them to support the RCW language, I held this woman and her students in my heart. She is an amazing teacher and an amazing teacher-librarian, but the pressure of present-day education reform ended up pushing her staff to make difficult choices about how to organize their school. The realization that we, as teacher-librarians, have to make more public and more visible what we do to improve student learning became more evident. I hoped that the RCW would not allow schools to make these devastating choices and allow teacher-librarians around the state to grow to their full potential.

In August, Jennifer called me to tell me the RCW had passed. We were now official, signed into statute. We are teacher-librarians. We are expected to collaborate with teachers to help students meet standards on the WASL (the Washington Assessment of Student Learning—the state's standardized educational assessment system), on the classroom-based assessments, on the Culminating Projects, and on the High School and Beyond Plans. And if a school does not have a certificated teacher-librarian running its library and information skills program, the school is second tier and merely has a library.

We were ecstatic. We sent out press releases to principal organizations and teacher groups. We shouted from the rooftops that finally we were legitimate in the eyes of the law, and, moreover, we had established high standards and expectations that schools, districts, administrators, parents, teachers, and students could expect from their teacher-librarian. Now we were ready to move forward with systemic change within our ranks. We could get our people trained, build capacity, raise the bar, demolish the old-fashioned view of the library, and create a new vision of library and information skills programs.

However, the e-mails don't stop.

Districts large and small continue to cut back their teacher-librarian positions and even eliminate their library and information skills programs in favor of less expensive models. Paraprofessionals are checking out books, but no professional is providing instruction to students or participating in the curriculum collaboration with teachers we envisioned four years before. We have shared the new RCW with principals and administrators, both through our members and through specific letters to individual district leaders. We have tried to educate members of the education community about what the new guidelines for library and information programs say, but little has changed. We are still endangered, and while we have stunning programs, we still have members of WLMA who are not rising to the standard that we, as statewide school library leaders and vocal advocates, have set. This message has not filtered down to the district level, and despite the RCW, the challenges still remain.

I wonder if this struggle was worth it. I put myself out there, speaking for teacher-librarians around the state, and still, I hear stories of ineffective teacher-librarians, teacher-librarians who are cut back to part time (or even cut entirely) and "the staff doesn't miss them," and paraprofessionals teaching "library classes." What do we do with those who don't carry the leadership vision of the RCW we worked so hard to get passed? Whose fault is it? Should the state be enforcing the standards of the RCW, should the Office of Superintendent of Public Instruction, or should WLMA? Who has the power, truly, to ensure that quality teacher-librarians are in every building? And what do we do with those who don't have the capacity to rise to the occasion? Because in reality, whether they are in the classroom or the library, they bring us all down.

Questions for Discussion

1. What is a teacher leader's responsibility for improving the professional practice of colleagues who don't meet standards? How can teacher leaders mentor peers who don't see a need to change?

2. What political knowledge and skills do teacher leaders need to shepherd needed reforms at the district level? At the state level?

3. What perspectives can teacher leaders contribute to policy discussions?

Case 15

Hanging in the Balance

by Krista Swenson

"Krista, can you present three sessions at the conference this year instead of just one?" "So I know I said I'd partner with you on this, but I don't have time." "Look, I can't come to meetings and help you plan. Let me know if there's anything I can do on the day of the event." As a world language teacher leader, giving back—to advance my field, to support my colleagues, to improve my school—is really important to me. But when does giving back become getting taken advantage of? This is the question I'm wrestling with lately.

"Aren't There Any Sessions for World Language Teachers?"

"I got it!" I am thrilled when I get my first job teaching six levels of Spanish to students ages 6 to 18. I can give my students the priceless gift of another language. Oh, what lives they will lead—earning higher salaries due to their bilingualism, traveling the world. I imagine the excitement I'll share with other world language teachers as we collaborate, make the world a multilingual wonderland, and . . . wait a second. As the lone Spanish teacher, I don't have anyone to collaborate *with*.

Desperate for ideas and inspiration, I can't wait to participate in my first district professional development day. I show up eager to meet and learn from other, more experienced colleagues. But wait a minute. Are there no sessions for world language teachers? Unsure of what to do, I choose a technology session. I happen to sit next to a woman with "French" on her nametag. "Aren't there any sessions for us?" I whisper. She laughs sarcastically and says, "No. There never have been, and I'm pretty sure there never will be." As our session starts, her words sink in. I know there must be other world language teachers in the district. Why are our needs being overlooked?

Frustrated, I decide to join the Washington Association of Foreign Language Teachers (WAFLT). Unlike my sessions during my district's professional development day, *all* of the WAFLT conference sessions relate to my job. I am blown away by the presenters' skills, expertise, and enthusiasm. I take so many notes my hand hurts, and I leave full of ideas. I also am impressed by the awards luncheon. As teachers stand up to accept awards, they say things like, "I wouldn't be up here without my peers, who took the time to help and support me," and "After years of benefiting from this conference, I knew I had to give back to my profession." These teacher leaders are very selfless and inspiring. I, too, want to give back to my profession. Little do I suspect that I will soon have the chance.

"Me? A Vice President? Me? A Presenter?"

A few years later, at another WAFLT conference, I'm surprised when a well-known and respected teacher asks if I have a minute. "We need a regional vice president for the American Association of Teachers of Spanish and Portuguese," he says, "and everyone I talk to says you will be an outstanding candidate. I agree." I am floored, honored, and so privileged. It doesn't take me long to say yes and join the eight-person board.

Soon, I'm racking up miles on my car to attend the bimonthly board meetings held around the state. Intimidated but thrilled, I participate in planning the conference, raising funds, and strategizing how to prevent programs from getting cut by working with legislators. I really enjoy the camaraderie of being with other teachers who not only understand the issues world language teachers face but do something about it. And more opportunities arise each day. "Krista, would you be willing to share your class website at next year's conference?" asks my fellow board member, Pat. It's great that others appreciate the website and find it valuable. But presenting? I'm not too sure about that. Then I think about what a lifesaver the conference has been; it is the only place I can learn the skills I need. Maybe someone urgently needs *my* guidance. I remember the comments about "giving back," and I nervously agree to present. Happily, my first session is a success and many teachers come up to thank me afterward. One older participant, who has flown in from Canada just to come to my session, says that because of me she is no longer afraid of computers. Hooked by the positive responses and gratitude, I present my site numerous times and eventually branch out to present and copresent other topics.

"Can I Say No?"

Teaching gets easier every year, and I begin to take on more and more leadership roles. After achieving National Board Certification, I become my school's technology coach and union representative, and I form a Spanish club. At the district level, I research the world language teachers and create an e-mail distribution list, which I use to forward information about resources and upcoming events. At the state level, I continue my work on the board, including hosting "idea shares" around the state, driving to various cities to meet with other Spanish teachers on a regular basis.

During one board meeting, I hear that some conference participants are upset that there have been no sessions on National Board Certification, a session I've done previously. Others are requesting that I do my songs and digital portfolio sessions again. "Krista," Pat asks, "can you present three sessions at the conference this year instead of just one?" I'm not sure what to say. I think, "The conference is the highlight of my year. There are only five hours of sessions; if I present for three, I'll only be able to attend two. Our board's policy is that presenters pay the same as everyone else: Is that fair? Still, it's flattering that my sessions are in high demand, and I'm not as desperate for ideas as I used to be." I waver, but when the "giving back" voice pipes up in my head, I reluctantly agree, still worrying about the consequences of my decision. Am I on a slippery slope? Will they ask me to present four or five sessions next year? What if I am asked to do more in my other leadership roles? Will I be able to say no? I haven't been able to so far.

"Let Me Know If I Can Help on the Day of the Event."

Although my board position is losing some of its appeal and demanding more of my time and pocketbook than I would like, I decide to run for reelection. It pays off when I find out about a grant-funded program called Western Initiative for Language Leadership (WILL). WILL provides world language teachers working in isolated areas with collaboration and professional development opportunities. I think I've died and gone to heaven when I am accepted to the program and go to Oregon to take part in a week of training. All participants work as sole world language teachers in schools and districts that overlook their need for support. And all of our schools and districts are slashing our classes because of increased emphasis on standardized testing of the "core" subject areas and underestimation of the value of world languages. We discuss our shared challenges and brainstorm. Energized, I return to my district to develop my WILL leadership project.

One night, it hits me. World language teachers need to get together, and our programs are in jeopardy. So I decide to write a grant that will engage all K–12 Spanish teachers from across the state in planning and offering an amazing competition for our students. I attended a similar competition in Oregon, and I am confident that we can pull one off. We can even invite the media to highlight the importance of world languages and hopefully save some programs! The more I think about it, the more excited I get. I submit the grant at the end of the school year and soon find out I have won! My dream has finally come true. I am going to collaborate with other teachers who share my passion for advocating for world-language learning. We are going to create a competition that will blow people away and be a blast for students. Fourteen teachers promise to help me plan the event. I am exploding with ideas and can't wait to get started!

When school begins, I plan our first meeting for 9 a.m. to noon on a Saturday. I write an agenda outlining the areas we need to focus on and all of the roles we need to fill. I collect information about the Oregon competition and make binders for my partners. The morning of the meeting, I go to Starbucks to get goodies and coffee and arrange everything carefully. Then, I wait. A little after nine, the first participant shows up. Two more show up at 9:30. I start the meeting but keep looking at the door, waiting for the other partners to walk through. Instead, some of them send e-mails saying they are sick or too busy, but that they will definitely be at the next get-together. Yet at the next meeting, there are only two other teachers and myself. I wait for the calls or e-mails about why there are so many absences, but none come. After I send multiple "Where were you?" e-mail queries, two teachers tell me they can no longer commit to helping me plan because of illness. A couple more cite lack of time. Some never even bother to reply, and some write, "I can't make the meetings, but let me know what I can do to help you on the day of the event." I am incredulous. I don't need help on the day of the competition, I need it now!

To the credit of the two partners that stick with me, we get a lot accomplished. We meet often and lay the groundwork for when the competition happens at some point in the future. Yet I am devastated that my vision for a competition that will inspire students to continue in a subject area that is rapidly disappearing never comes to fruition. I can't understand how teachers who seem to share my enthusiasm and who made verbal and written commitments can so easily walk away, especially when one objective of this competition is to help make their jobs more secure. This completely unexpected turn of events pulls the rug out from under me and forces me to weigh the costs and benefits of my leadership roles for the first time.

"Am I Giving Back Too Much?"

All of my leadership roles take time—time away from my friends, family, and interests outside of school. Also, it seems that no matter how much I do, everyone wants more. When I try to get others to help share the burden, they often don't follow through. And what about the fact that my salary is the same as teachers who don't have to worry about these extra demands? Maybe I should try doing the bare minimum, too. But if everyone had that attitude, where would that get us?

When is it time to stop giving back? I think of the selfless teacher leaders at the awards ceremony, and I wonder if they ever have this debate with themselves. Maybe they started out like me, saying yes to too much too often, but eventually found a way to balance their roles and stay energized and happy. For me, my decision to remain a teacher leader is hanging in the balance, and I'm not sure which side will win.

Questions for Discussion

1. How can a teacher leader inspire collaboration?

2. Does teacher leadership always require self-sacrifice? What makes the sacrifices worthwhile?

3. How does a passionate teacher leader learn to balance professional responsibilities, voluntary leadership work, and personal needs?

Case 16

Transitions

by Terese Emry

I never considered myself a teacher leader. In my mind, teacher leaders were those really smart people who stood up at staff meetings and always seemed to have the right answers. I was a worker bee, someone who would much rather do the work of the committee than lead the committee. And I did a *lot* of work. I did so much work outside of my classroom that, when I heard about National Board Certification, I saw it as the clear path to refocusing my attention where it belonged, on my classroom and my kids. How could I know that achieving this certification would catapult me into the unfamiliar and confusing world of teacher leaders?

My achievement of National Board Certification in 2000 coincided with the launch of a statewide, grant-funded initiative aimed at increasing the number of National Board Certified Teachers (NBCTs). The initiative also sought to create and maintain an NBCT leadership network. The initiative's coordinator was amazing in her ability to find or create numerous leadership opportunities, and with only 71 NBCTs in the whole state, there was plenty for everyone to do.

Excited for a new challenge, I decided early on that I would do as much as I was able as long as it didn't have anything to do with politics or the media. I facilitated a group of National Board candidates, went to leadership trainings, presented at meetings and trainings, received a grant to begin a new teacher support program in my district, and traveled across the state and the country doing work related to National Board Certification.

Then, with just one year of the grant left, the coordinator of the initiative called me. She was starting a new project and wanted to know if I would take over for her. Take over for her? There had to be some mistake. Had she already asked the teacher leaders we both knew to do it? Had she run this past the initiative's funders? Had she asked her boss? Did they know I was *just a fourth-grade teacher?* I was completely flabbergasted, but intrigued. After much hand-wringing and weeks of sleepless nights, I decided to go for it. I asked for and received a one-year leave of absence from my school district. The coordinator position would phase out over the course of the year, so I wouldn't be on my own, and anyway, it was just for one year. What could happen?

Things started smoothly. The coordinator oriented me to the office and gave me a list of the numerous project components. We reviewed our calendars and divided duties. We attended events together to make the transition public. The first month was great, and then suddenly things changed. I e-mailed her my questions, and she did not respond. What did this mean? Was I supposed to know how to run the project now, because I certainly did not. I knew she was really busy, but why was she avoiding me? This obviously was not going to work out.

I realized that I had made a horrible mistake, and I thought frantically about whether I could get my real job back. I had to talk to her. "Did you get my message about the upcoming meeting?" I asked. "No," she replied. "Well, I sent several messages to your new e-mail account," I responded indignantly. She said,

"I just had this same conversation with our secretary. What e-mail address are you using?" I rattled off the combination of letters and dots, and she stopped me. It was the wrong address. None of my e-mails were making it through. A sense of relief washed over me. I was not alone after all. I could still ask questions and receive guidance, and she would be there to help me through the year. With her as a resource and mentor, I knew I could make it. From that time forward, I never took the support I received for granted. I haven't forgotten my feelings of complete isolation and utter terror when I thought I'd been tossed into this new world of leadership by myself. A mentor made all the difference.

The year progressed, and I began to get my feet under me. I gained confidence in my ability to make sound decisions. I also learned that, when I made a mistake, I could figure out how to fix it and the world would keep turning. But there were many things I couldn't figure out. One puzzle was the dynamics of what was happening around me and how I fit in.

At first, the people who I encountered in my new job saw me as a strange creature. During meetings, people pointed out that I was a teacher and others would turn to look. I felt like a visitor from another country, and, like a tourist in a strange land, I was often confused by the customs and culture. I went to meetings where the topic was innocuous, but the tension was so thick you could cut it with a knife. It seemed that there was always something else going on besides the subject at hand, but what? What were the hidden agendas and cloaked grudges that filled the room? Who could be trusted? What were the unwritten rules? I heard rumors—"those two had a falling out, so now they are on opposing sides of everything"—but even that information was spotty at best. I was now the worker bee in the wasp nest, trying not to get stung too hard.

As spring approached, I learned that the project would be funded for one more year. I could stay on, but now I would be on my own—no mentor. Ironically, my job would now require working with the media and the legislature, the exact two areas into which I vowed never to venture. I knew that I didn't have the experience or skills to pull it off. I remembered back to a time when I had been interviewed for a newspaper story, and it was so traumatic that I felt sick for weeks afterward. Fortunately, I heard about a speakers training, and I jumped at the opportunity. During the training, I learned techniques to effectively communicate with reporters and the legislature. That fall, I talked to several reporters around the time of the National Board score release. I even appeared on a local TV talk show, something that I would never have done before. I testified at the legislature, and I organized an event for legislators and NBCTs to meet and talk. I shudder to think about what might have happened had I been thrown into these new situations without the training. Luckily, I had access to this resource when I needed it, and I learned the skills I needed to be successful.

Even with the mentoring and training, this ongoing transition has difficulties. There are nagging questions. First, to what community do I belong? When I was teaching, that answer was obvious—*my fellow teachers are my community*. In my mind and heart, teachers are still my community, but something has changed. Teachers who I meet now know me only as the state coordinator, so they see me as something other than a teacher. Understandable I guess, but so strange. I was shocked recently when a teacher at an event commented that he liked that I spoke to the group "like a teacher." He was surprised and looked skeptical when I told him that *I am* a teacher. His eyes seemed to say, "You are one of *them* (administrators) who still happens to have some qualities of one of *us* (teachers)." Is that true? When do I stop being a teacher? Is it something that gradually wears off, or was it stripped from me as soon as I walked out of my classroom? What if I don't want to let it go?

While that kind of experience is uncomfortable for me, the question of community turns hurtful when I find that even my connection with teachers I've known for years is different. When I first went on leave, I was able to maintain my relationships fairly easily. I attended many of their social events, and I was up on all of the latest news of our school community. Over time, that connection has waned. Now, when I hear about staff events, I am seldom able to attend. When I can make it, I find that I am more and more an outsider—a visitor in my own country now. No one tries to make it so, but the passage of time just changes things. I'm not there to share in all of the little things, and I'm not there to help with all of the big things.

More and more, I get the feeling that people think I've sold out. I didn't know that some had that opinion until I signed on to remain in this job for a third year. I could not get another year of leave, so I had to resign from my district. The week of my resignation, I had dinner with a teacher for whom I have great admiration. She and I were hired about the same time and worked together for many years. I could tell that she didn't think I had made the right decision. Since I was not even sure it *was* the right decision, I pressed her to tell me what she thought. She said that she couldn't believe that I would leave the classroom. How could I accept a job that took me away from kids—especially now, with all of the really hard work to be done? The message was pretty clear to me; I am a traitor, making a conscious decision to abandon the trenches, leaving my friends and colleagues to do the hard work without me.

I struggle with this. On the one hand, I know that my current job is important. I know that what I do makes a difference for teachers and for kids. But on the other hand, I can't help seeing the faces of the kids I've had in class. I know they needed me then, and I know that there are just as many who need me now. Have I done the right thing? Is working on the systems that indirectly affect a large number of kids as good as being there to directly impact a few? These questions haunt me.

Questions for Discussion

1. What kind of professional development and/or support do teacher leaders need to develop leadership skills?

2. Can a teacher leader maintain a "teacher identity" after leaving the classroom? If so, for how long?

3. We've come to understand the importance of mentoring for new teachers. What might a mentoring program for supporting teachers' transition into leadership look like?

6

How to Use Cases to Support Teacher Leadership

Case-by-Case Facilitation Guides

This final chapter is intended as a resource to further support you in learning to use case methods to strengthen teacher leadership in your district or community. We begin by providing facilitation guides for each of the 16 cases in this book. Each guide includes possible session goals, a case summary, and a brief account of the central leadership dilemmas that occur in the case. You will notice that other issues are present in these cases (see Figure 1.2, p. 22), so don't limit your focus to the dilemmas we've identified. They are simply intended to help you select cases and focus on a few ideas as you learn to facilitate case analysis. For each set of teacher leadership cases—school, district, and state and national—we include at least one suggested activity to extend participants' learning. We encourage you to use these activities as models to design case-based activities that specifically address your group's interests, priorities, and needs.

In all of the facilitation guides, we include connections to the Center for Strengthening the Teaching Profession's (CSTP's) Teacher Leadership Skills Framework (see Resource C1). The Teacher Leadership Skills Framework identifies the knowledge, skills, and dispositions needed by effective teacher leaders in a variety of roles within five main domains: working with adult learners, communication, collaborative work, knowledge of content and pedagogy, and systems thinking. Each of the domains in the Framework includes a short vignette and additional reflection questions that might give you more ideas to fuel your case discussions. To accompany the Teacher Leadership Skills Framework, CSTP has developed two companion tools. The Teacher Leader Self-Assessment (see Resource C2) helps teacher leaders examine the skills they possess in the Framework's five domains and determine the areas in which they can grow. The four-part tool we call School and District Capacity to Support Teacher Leadership (see Resource C3) helps teacher leaders think about systems-level resources that are available to them as well as identify resources that need to be developed to support teacher leaders' professional growth. Its four sections are entitled Establishing a Supportive Environment, System Vision and Alignment, Professional Development, and Access to Resources. School and district leaders can also use Resource C3 to prompt discussion about what systems-level supports are present and what is needed in order for teacher leaders to thrive. Again, we hope these ideas will stimulate your thinking about ways you can tailor any of these activities to the particular needs of your group.

SCHOOL-LEVEL LEADERSHIP

Facilitation Guide for *How Hard Do I Push?*

Possible Session Goals

- Strategize about how to use or create school structures to support teacher collaboration and professional learning.
- Consider the implications for developing and maintaining collaborative relationships among teachers.
- Discuss the purpose and potential of grade-level meetings and how to make them productive.

Case Summary

Debra, the teacher leader, initiates lesson study in her elementary school to increase teacher collaboration between the multiage and grade-level teachers and to improve fifth-grade math scores. The initial success of her lesson study group creates interest and support from the principal and other grade-level teachers and specialists and soon expands to include most of the staff. Debra secures funding to continue lesson study after the first two years of grant funding runs out and begins to promote professional reading to enhance teachers' knowledge base in other content areas. Her school's lesson study successes are shared across the district and start to spread.

In year four of the initiative, the district restructures the elementary schools and breaks up their now cohesive staff. A new curriculum adoption competes for teachers' limited professional development time. Overwhelmed, new teachers and grade-level teams without strong leadership or investment in lesson study threaten to undermine the initiative. Then the principal, who has championed the work, leaves the school. Debra has to try to win over a new principal while her staff support is dwindling. She wonders whether she has the strength, authority, or right to keep pushing.

Leadership Dilemmas

This case raises questions about how to keep a successful change initiative alive after a successful period of implementation, when new initiatives that demand teachers' time and attention and personnel changes disrupt the cohesiveness of the staff. The case presents different perspectives about the need to provide all teachers with professional learning that addresses their individual needs, which may conflict with more comprehensive school improvement goals.

This case provides opportunities to discuss the following dilemmas:

- *Building support among administrators:* How does a teacher leader build support from the school principal, especially someone new to the building who doesn't know the history of the school, the change in culture, or the teacher leader who spearheaded the work?
- *Sustaining commitment to change:* In light of too many initiatives competing for teachers' time and attention, how can a teacher leader continue to generate enthusiasm for the work so that it keeps producing visible results? In this case, what might it look like to "work smarter, not harder"?

Connections to Teacher Leadership Skills Framework

To go deeper into the challenge of building support among administrators, have participants work through the Collaborative Work (see pp. 163–164) and Systems Thinking (see pp. 169–170) sections of Resource C2, Teacher Leader Self-Assessment. You can extend your discussion about sustaining commitment to change by using the Establishing a Supportive Environment section (see pp. 172–173) of Resource C3, School and District Capacity to Support Teacher Leadership.

Facilitation Guide for *Navigating New Waters*

Possible Session Goals

- Investigate the knowledge and behaviors that give a teacher leader credibility.
- Compare how teacher leaders' connections to students translate into connections with colleagues.

Case Summary

Claudia, an established teacher leader in her school and small K–8 district, is moving to a new school in a new district. Having facilitated meetings of her professional learning community (PLC) for three years as part of her National Board Certification process, she is excited about the opportunity to help her new district launch PLCs and to develop the practices that transformed her old school. In fact, her experience with leading PLCs is one of the reasons she was selected for her new job.

Although confident in her ability to lead this work, Claudia is apprehensive about trying to lead a veteran staff to whom she is an unknown. She will be on a team of nine fourth-grade teachers, but she is the only National Board Certified Teacher (NBCT) in the school. She worries that her new colleagues may not share her passion for teaching, collaborating, or developing content expertise. In the past, she won over her colleagues because of the success of her students, and she wonders if a similar strategy would be best to adopt in her new school—take it slow, be patient, and wait for others to come to her, rather than offer her insights about what she knows works.

Leadership Dilemmas

Many teacher leaders wonder how they can share expertise without their colleagues perceiving them as being pushy. Some teacher leaders grapple with this concern when they, like Claudia, join a new school in a new district. Others face this challenge when they attempt to share new practices with their colleagues.

Use this case to help participants reflect upon the following issues:

- *Establishing credibility:* What are some constructive ways that a teacher leader can share knowledge and expertise without alienating new colleagues?
- *Building and sustaining commitment to change (implementing PLCs):* What can a teacher leader do to help others develop the knowledge and skills needed to make PLCs successful? What kind of support do teacher leaders need from administrators to institute new practices?

Connections to Teacher Leadership Skills Framework

You might use the Working With Adult Learners (see pp. 161–162) or Collaborative Work (see pp. 163–164) sections of Resource C2 to support teacher leaders' reflection on establishing credibility among their peers. Think about having participants work through the System Vision and

Alignment section (see pp. 174–175) of Resource C3 to generate additional ideas for building and sustaining commitment to change.

Facilitation Guide for *Out of the Closet . . . and Out the Door?*

Possible Session Goals

- Consider the challenges of leadership when advocating on behalf of students versus advocating for teachers.
- Learn to analyze the consequences of a teacher leader's actions.

Case Summary

This case opens with Christopher, a high school humanities teacher, listening to a student share his end-of-the-year advice to next year's class: "Don't ever use the phrase 'that's so gay,' because you will just be *destroyed.*" With mixed emotions, Christopher is pleased that his lessons about using respectful language have been learned. As an openly gay teacher, he led an effort to create a safe and supportive place for teenagers who question their sexual orientation. In his small progressive high school, staff and students are receptive, but the principal balks at establishing a gay-straight alliance (GSA), until Lisa, a district specialist, lobbies the principal.

After the GSA is formed, a verbal insult that goes undisciplined sparks student outrage and raises questions about the principal's commitment. Lisa helps Christopher and the GSA develop an antiharassment training for students and staff, which gradually builds awareness, and students' participation in the GSA swells. A schoolwide community meeting is held to discuss GLBT (gay, lesbian, bisexual, transgender) issues, and Christopher develops a curriculum to include GLBT rights in the humanities civil rights unit. A culminating oral history project proves to be a powerful learning experience for the whole school.

Having succeeded in transforming his small school into a safe haven for vulnerable young people, Christopher is motivated to take his cause to a larger forum—the district or national level—but he is torn. He wonders whether his accomplishments will survive without his hands-on leadership. He's also unsure whether he can expand support to GLBT students beyond the progressive climate of his unique school.

Leadership Dilemmas

This case highlights the difficulty of exercising leadership on behalf of those who lack status or power within a school. Maintaining a climate of acceptance and support requires an ongoing commitment. For this reason, the challenge of sustaining the work may be even more difficult if the original leaders are replaced with others who lack the same level of personal conviction.

This case offers participants the opportunity to investigate the following leadership challenges:

- *Building and sustaining a commitment to change:* What constitutes the "critical mass" needed to sustain lasting change? How can a teacher leader ensure that changes will endure once the primary advocate leaves? What structures need to be established to institutionalize new behaviors?
- *Advocating for others:* How might it be dangerous for a teacher leader to be seen as an ardent advocate for a cause? What criteria should be used to judge the effectiveness of advocacy work?

Connections to Teacher Leadership Skills Framework

The Communication (see pp. 165–166) and Systems Thinking (see pp. 169–170) sections of Resource C2 are good tools to help teacher leaders assess their capacity for building and sustaining a commitment to change. Resource C3 may assist participants in developing additional ideas to increase their effectiveness in advocating for others. In particular, take a look at the Establishing a Supportive Environment (see pp. 172–173) part of the tool.

Facilitation Guide for *Overwhelmed and Underappreciated*

Possible Session Goals

- Brainstorm strategies for engaging the principal in staff professional development and teacher leader meetings.
- Consider how to build leadership by sharing responsibility for setting the agenda and facilitating teacher meetings.

Case Summary

At Northside K–8 school, teacher leadership is an expectation. By design, the school is planned around shared leadership and has only a half-time principal. The instructional leadership team (ILT), composed of teacher leaders, does most of the planning for student learning. In theory, all teachers would rotate onto the ILT every few years, but the reality is that the same teachers do the work year after year, and they are starting to burn out.

Karen, the perpetual volunteer, ends up doing the lion's share of the work. In the opening of the case, Louise, a fellow ILT member, is shocked when Karen uncharacteristically erupts in frustration over a seemingly minor matter—the ILT loses its regular meeting place for one day. It turns out this is the proverbial "straw that broke the camel's back," signaling to Karen that the ILT's work is taken for granted and not valued. The principal's sporadic participation reinforces her feelings.

Louise is worried that Karen is reaching the breaking point but isn't sure what can be done. Does her school need to "require" all teachers to take on leadership roles? Would mandated ILT service undermine commitment and the quality of the work? Would rewarding Karen for her extra efforts make a difference?

Leadership Dilemmas

When classroom teachers take on leadership roles, time becomes an issue. Teaching is already a demanding job, so why do more than is required? Often, teachers do extra things to extend or enhance the effectiveness of what they do in their classroom. However gratifying the results may be, teachers need to be supported to make the extra effort. The challenge is to create a balance so that the investment produces both intrinsic rewards and the desired outcomes.

This case lends itself to discussing several persistent issues that teacher leaders face:

- *Handling the workload:* Why do teacher leaders go the extra mile? What are the intrinsic rewards of leadership work? Should there also be extrinsic rewards? If there is compensation, is it leadership, or just another job responsibility? What strategies or supports might help teachers manage the demands of leadership work?
- *Building support among administrators:* How do teacher leaders build support among administrators who are stretched too thin themselves? If the work is vital to the school's success, are there symbolic ways that principals can acknowledge and support the work that teacher leaders do?

Extension Activity

To help participants narrow down what is at the core of this case, ask them to generate an alternate title. Have each participant explain why she or he chose the title. Then, engage the whole group in debating the strengths of each proposed title, as well as the author's title. Try to reach consensus on which title best captures the essence of the case.

Connections to Teacher Leadership Skills Framework

You might use the Collaborative Work section (see pp. 163–164) of Resource C2 to further examine the issues involved in handling the workload and how to address them. Using the Professional Development section (see p. 176) of Resource C3 in a mixed group of teacher leaders and administrators might be an effective way to collaboratively problem-solve ways to build support among administrators.

Facilitation Guide for *Free Money?*

Possible Session Goals

- Identify strategies a teacher leader can use to cultivate partnerships and strengthen relationships to maintain support for student learning.
- Explore the pluses and minuses of dependence on temporary funding for cultivating teacher leadership.

Case Summary

Irene seizes upon a grant opportunity to create an engaging interdisciplinary service-learning project for her middle school students. Securing two colleagues' commitment to the project, Irene agrees to take the lead and do most of the grant writing. The $10,000 award pays for summer training and a trip to the national conference to present their work.

Even before they have the money in hand, both of Irene's partners experience medical issues that preclude their full participation. By now, she's committed to the grant and reaches out to two other teachers to fulfill the cross-disciplinary requirements of the grant. Irene pitches in to plan for two grade levels to make it easier for her ailing colleague's long-term substitute to participate. Even so, she feels forced to drop some of her language arts curriculum to cover some of the sub's science lessons.

To fulfill the 25 service hours requirement, each classroom has to come up with its own project that fits with the river ecology theme Irene and her colleagues chose. A host of snafus cause last minute improvising, and Irene keeps coming to the rescue—taking on more and more to fulfill the requirements of the grant. Her efforts pay off in the end with an impressive celebration. The community partners are grateful, and parents are thrilled with the students' accomplishments. They want service learning to become a yearly event! Irene is left wondering what the true cost of the $10,000 of "free money" really was. How did she end up carrying the load?

Leadership Dilemmas

Teacher leaders accomplish amazing things with small amounts of funding. The creative aspects of the grant work are energizing, but the administrative responsibilities add substantially to the workload. With limited resources, there are rarely funds to cover unforeseen circumstances that inevitably arise. Irene's sense of responsibility for the entire grant, whether real or perceived, led her to adopt heroic actions to "save" the project.

Analyzing this case gives participants the opportunity to examine the following ideas:

- *Handling the workload:* What are the dangers of overloading oneself in order to accomplish objectives, even if unusual circumstances arise? What strategies can teacher leaders use to place limits on the work they do?
- *Coping with isolation:* What are the dangers of "going it alone" on projects that involve others? How can teacher leaders develop their own support systems to combat the uncertainty that often accompanies working solo?

Connections to Teacher Leadership Skills Framework

The Communication (see pp. 165–166) and Collaborative Work (see pp. 163–164) sections of Resource C2 can help teacher leaders reflect on the tendency to take on too much and can serve as a springboard for participants to brainstorm ways that teacher leaders can handle their workloads more effectively. To expand your discussion on coping with isolation, take a look at the Establishing a Supportive Environment section (see pp. 172–173) of Resource C3.

Facilitation Guide for *When Do I Tell?*

Possible Session Goals

- Explore the relationship between a teacher leader's goal for colleagues and professional standards of practice.
- Analyze strategies a teacher leader might adopt to respond to a teacher's need for improvement.
- Examine the pluses and minuses of alternative approaches to support teacher development.

Case Summary

This case begins in the midst of a crisis. Ryan, a struggling second-year teacher, has a class that is out of control. In the middle of class, he sends an urgent SOS to his mentor Christy. She has invested significant time in working with Ryan—modeling, coplanning, and providing feedback—as she gradually releases responsibility to Ryan for teaching the science kits.

As Christy enters the novice teacher's room, she sees that the class is once again in chaos: Students are out of their seats, the noise level is deafening, and students are fooling around with the science equipment as Ryan yells reprimands. He pleads for Christy to get the class back on track. Christy knows that Ryan has to establish his authority, so rather than take charge, she quietly guides him to regroup. He tells the class that he will get fired if they don't behave.

During recess, Christy tries to debrief. She reviews conversations she has had with Ryan several times about professional standards and his word choices. In five months, he has made little progress, and his students are falling behind. Christy questions whether Ryan should be a teacher. It's not her decision to make, but she's not sure the principal (Ryan's evaluator) is aware of Ryan's troubling performance. She tries to decide if her responsibility for maintaining confidentiality outweighs the potential harm to students if Ryan is allowed to continue.

Leadership Dilemmas

Assuming a leadership role often raises questions about appropriate behavior and ethical choices that teacher leaders have to make. In this case, Christy is caught between breaking confidentiality, which could undermine her future ability to mentor other new teachers, and using her professional judgment to act on behalf of students. Either choice may have consequences for the teacher leader's relationships with other teachers and with administrators.

Use this case to engage participants in considering how they would deal with the following dilemmas:

- *Establishing and maintaining credibility:* How do teacher leaders establish credibility among their peers? What do they have to do to maintain credibility over time? What options do mentors have when they observe a protégé's disturbing behavior? What actions might jeopardize their ability to be credible leaders in the eyes of their peers? In the eyes of administrators?
- *Defining and straddling roles:* How do teachers assume leadership roles while still maintaining their membership in egalitarian ranks of fellow teachers? How does a teacher leader negotiate her relationships with other teachers versus her relationship with administrators? Is it necessary to sacrifice one for the other?

Connections to Teacher Leadership Skills Framework

The Working With Adult Learners section (see pp. 161–162) of Resource C2 may be useful for further examination of the challenges teacher leaders face in establishing and maintaining credibility. In addition, the Establishing a Supportive Environment section (see pp. 172–173) of Resource C3 will allow participants to identify the need to more clearly define teacher leadership positions, especially those that straddle more than one role.

DISTRICT-LEVEL LEADERSHIP

Facilitation Guide for *Filling a Leadership Vacuum*

Possible Session Goals

- Examine the role of an instructional coach and guidelines for effective practice.
- Consider strategies teacher leaders can use to engage reluctant teachers in examining their practice and its impact on student learning.
- Strategize possible moves to ameliorate complaints and fears about learning in public group settings.

Case Summary

As a district literacy coach, Joanna works one on one with high school English teachers in their classrooms to help them develop engaging student-centered instruction that supports students in learning at high levels. The goal is to create laboratory classrooms where others can observe skilled teaching practice. The teachers involved in this work are used to being observed by other teachers, consultants, and administrators, but only English teachers have been part of this intense professional development.

In the third year of this work, the English teachers' investment at one school seems to be waning. In an effort to revive their commitment, Joanna arranges a visit to another high school where schoolwide progress is evident. The English teachers are inspired by what they see and are especially impressed by the leadership of the principal. Their own principal is uninvolved, so the teachers ask Joanna to facilitate a whole staff meeting to get everyone to create a schoolwide vision of effective instruction.

The meeting has mixed results. The principal shows up for part of the meeting but doesn't participate. While the staff express consistent expectations for student learning and everyone engages in the discussion, any mention of observing each other's teaching immediately produces resistance. Joanna is left wondering why she, a district literacy coach who is not even based at the school, is running the meeting. Why isn't the principal running the meeting? Joanna has no authority to require teachers to be involved. She wants to support the English teachers, but questions whether they—even with her support—can influence the school culture without principal support.

Leadership Dilemmas

This case focuses on the role of a district-level instructional coach and surfaces the precarious position these teacher leaders occupy. District-level instructional coaches are not members of any school staff, and they must cultivate relationships across several schools. Although these coaches are responsible for helping staff implement reforms in all of the schools with which they work, they lack administrative authority to require action.

While a number of dilemmas are evident in this case, it presents an obvious opportunity to discuss the following issues with participants:

- *Defining and straddling roles:* When a teacher leader's role is not clearly defined, what criteria should be used to identify the limits of one's job? Who should be involved in clarifying job responsibilities?
- *Dealing with resistance:* How can a teacher leader determine the cause or source of resistance? How can teacher leaders respond to resistance they encounter, with and without administrative support? Where can they find allies to support their efforts?
- *Building and sustaining commitment to change:* What kind of experiences or information will help create teachers' investment in reforms? When fatigue sets in or frustrations threaten to stall the reform, what strategies can a teacher leader use to reinvigorate teachers' efforts?

Extension Activity

Form small groups and ask each group to create a job description for an instructional coach that will clarify the expectations and boundaries for the coach role. Ask participants to define the principal's role in facilitating the coaches' work. Then, bring the group back together and brainstorm a list of questions or concerns that may make it difficult to implement the coach's role as intended.

Connections to Teacher Leadership Skills Framework

The Communication (see pp. 165–166) and Systems Thinking (see pp. 169–170) sections of Resource C2 might be effective instruments for helping participants further reflect on how to deal with resistance and steps that might help sort out and define roles. The Establishing a Supportive Environment (see pp. 172–173) and System Vision and Alignment (see pp. 174–175) sections of Resource C3 could also be used to extend your conversation about dealing with resistance and building and sustaining commitment to change so reforms will last.

Facilitation Guide for *Considering All Voices*

Possible Session Goals

- Examine the differences between authority and credibility. (What role does each play in a teacher leader's work?)
- Compare the similarities and differences between a teacher leader's goals for and responsibilities to teachers and his or her goals for and responsibilities to district leaders; analyze the complications that arise from trying to serve two masters.
- Analyze the role of content expertise in promoting new approaches to teaching.

Case Summary

The scene opens in a tense meeting of the K–6 curriculum committee where the district curriculum director accuses Diane, the district elementary math specialist, of trying to derail the committee's work. The team is in the process of identifying power standards—the concepts and skills each student must master before advancing to the next grade. The issue for Diane is that she has spent years working to build the skills of teacher leaders for mathematics, who now have significant expertise in how children learn math. Many of these teacher leaders were not asked to serve on the committee. Instead, some novices and even some resisters have been included.

The curriculum director's priority is to consider input from all teachers to engender greater teacher buy-in. Diane is committed to increasing teachers' content knowledge so that they understand the progression of mathematical ideas. She supports the need to identify essential power standards to build consistency across the district, but Diane is concerned that many of her dedicated teacher leaders will feel snubbed. They have committed a great deal of time, and their exclusion from this important process will send a message that their expertise is not valued. Yet, these same teachers will be asked to lead their buildings in learning to use the power standards. Diane worries about the teacher leaders' willingness to carry out these new expectations.

Leadership Dilemmas

This case highlights the sensitive position teacher leaders occupy in leading reforms. They need validation from administrators, and they need to nurture relationships with the teachers who will implement new practices. Often, this places teacher leaders in an awkward spot without clear direction, trying to reconcile conflicting perspectives. This is an example of the difficulties that can arise when roles are not clearly delineated.

This case affords an opportunity to investigate the following concepts:

- *Building support among administrators:* Why is administrative support critical for enabling teacher leaders to be effective in carrying out reforms? What strategies can a teacher leader use to align conflicting priorities to achieve desired outcomes?
- *Advocating for others:* What is the appropriate role of a teacher leader in advocating for other teacher leaders? How can teacher leaders advocate for themselves?

Extension Activity

To extend your study of this case, consider bringing together a mixed group of teacher leaders and administrators. Have the teacher leaders read the case with the goal of understanding the perspectives of the administrators. Have the administrators read the case to understand the perspectives of the teacher leaders. Then, in mixed teams, devise a plan for moving the work described in the case forward in a way that satisfies the concerns of both groups.

Connections to Teacher Leadership Skills Framework

The Communication section (see pp. 165–166) or the Systems Thinking section (see pp. 169–170) of Resource C2 can help stimulate further thinking about the challenges of building support among administrators or advocating for others. If you want to extend participants' thinking to examine systemic obstacles, you might have them complete the Establishing a Supportive Environment (see pp. 172–173) or the System Vision and Alignment (see pp. 174–175) section of Resource C3.

Facilitation Guide for *Crossroads*

Possible Session Goals

- Examine the leadership challenges for teachers who work with special needs students.
- Explore the relationship between one's membership in a group (e.g., special education teacher) and maintaining credibility as a leader or advocate on behalf of the group.

Case Summary

As a veteran resource room teacher, Jean understands the isolation that specialists—particularly those who work with special needs students—often experience. Although she is committed to special education, she knows exactly why so many special education teachers burn out and move into regular education. The workload is overwhelming and there are few opportunities for professional growth. She completes the National Board Certification process, thinking it will fulfill her needs, and in some ways it does. It opens doors outside her district to pursue leadership roles, but within the district there are few calls for her expertise. Feeling torn, she leaves her resource room behind.

Still committed to supporting her special education colleagues, Jean secures a grant to create a networking opportunity for resource room teachers. The meetings provide much needed support and a venue to share ideas and curricula, answer questions, and develop relationships. When she tries to sell the idea to district administrators, however, she is rebuffed; people at the university are more receptive than those in her own district.

Now that Jean is teaching a professional certification class and leading other teachers through the National Board Certification process, she laments the fact that these new leadership roles are taking her farther away from the field she loves. She reflects on her experience and tries to understand why there are so few opportunities for leadership in special education and why her contributions are recognized elsewhere but not in her own district.

Leadership Dilemmas

In this case, opportunities for teacher leadership appear limited, and the status of a specialist tends to increase isolation. Establishing credibility seems to be particularly problematic when there are few chances to collaborate with colleagues across schools.

Use this case to engage participants in reflecting on structural barriers that intensify the following challenges:

- *Coping with isolation:* How does a teacher leader share her or his expertise when there are no structures that allow for teachers to work together? How can teacher leaders continue to nurture their own needs to grow as professionals when they occupy a "one of a kind" role within a school?
- *Establishing and maintaining credibility:* Without opportunities to collaborate, how do teacher leaders demonstrate the expertise they can contribute? What can a teacher leader do to demonstrate to administrators that he or she has the knowledge and skills to effectively lead change?

Connections to Teacher Leadership Skills Framework

To go deeper into the challenge of establishing and maintaining credibility, you might have participants complete the Collaborative Work section (see pp. 163–164) of Resource C2 to reflect on practices that enhance one's work with peers and in the eyes of administrators. The Establishing a Supportive Environment section (see pp. 172–173) of Resource C3 may be useful in identifying ways to help teacher leaders reduce the isolation.

Facilitation Guide for *Where Do I Stand? Leadership in a Culture of Us and Them*

Possible Session Goals

- Examine the difficulties that arise when job descriptions are incomplete or ambiguous.
- Compare the district's priorities for the coach and those of the teacher leaders. (How can a balance be achieved?)

Case Summary

In Molly's district, there's a lot of speculation swirling around concerning the restructuring and creation of new content specialist positions. With the district's history of constantly adopting new initiatives every few years, many teachers are cynical about how long the new changes will last. Linda, the coordinator of the peer-coaching program, is enthusiastic about the new leadership positions and encourages Molly to apply. Molly trusts Linda's assessment, but she is surrounded by colleagues who don't trust the district to follow through.

When Molly decides to apply to go to the district office, her peers immediately view her with suspicion. Once she gets the job, many of her colleagues and her school's principal make jokes about her going to work for the "enemy" that sometimes seem to have a serious undertone. All of the negative reactions make Molly uneasy. She was interested in the new position because it meant that she could do more to support teachers in their classrooms, but will they even want her help?

When Molly learns that the district has changed the role of instructional coaches to include evaluating teachers, she questions her decision. Linda, her mentor, resigns over the change, and Molly wonders whether she can work under policies she does not agree with. She holds out hope that there will be a way to moderate the division between her school's staff and the district administrators, but she's concerned she'll be forced to take sides.

Leadership Dilemmas

District administrators' expectations for teacher leaders often change as reforms are articulated. Like many teacher leaders who work at the district level, Molly feels torn between the school and the district, and she struggles to reconcile the responsibilities of a newly redefined role with strong beliefs about how to best support teachers. As their roles evolve, teacher leaders need to develop effective ways to generate support for themselves from both sides in order to be effective in their new roles.

This case will stimulate exploration of the following common dilemmas:

- *Defining and straddling roles:* As districts create new roles for teacher leaders, what perspectives can teacher leaders contribute in defining their roles? What policies might engender support for their work?
- *Establishing and maintaining credibility:* What strategies will help teacher leaders establish themselves as credible to other teachers? To administrators? Once they are viewed as leaders, what kind of strategies do they need to sustain their credibility?

Connections to Teacher Leadership Skills Framework

You might have participants complete the Working With Adult Learners (see pp. 161–162) and Systems Thinking (see pp. 169–170) sections of Resource C2 to engage them in thinking more deeply about the process of establishing and maintaining credibility as a leader. The Establishing a Supportive Environment section (see pp. 172–173) of Resource C3 could be used to generate ideas about how school and district leaders could help define teacher leader roles to avoid the ambiguity and confusion that often limits their effectiveness.

Facilitation Guide for *Preparing for the Future? Reliving the Past?*

Possible Session Goals

- Consider the steps a teacher leader can take to foster collaborative relationships within a group with divergent perspectives.
- Analyze the factors that contributed to the conflict; brainstorm strategies a teacher leader can use to create a shared focus and responsibility for solving the problem.

Case Summary

Matthew, a second-year high school AP (Advanced Placement) teacher, is still finding his way in his new school. His district has asked a team of middle school Highly Capable (HiCap) Program teachers and high school Advanced Placement (AP) Program language arts teachers to engage in joint planning to help ensure that the district has consistently high expectations, common text experiences, and shared terminology for all students who journey through the system. There is also a goal to move toward AP open enrollment; this will give students from groups that are underrepresented in AP classes because of grades, economics, and test scores a chance to participate in the classes. Matthew is the new chair of the team, and he is in the hot seat.

With the addition of a number of young teachers, progress slows, and many of the HiCap teachers stop attending meetings. Strong differences in perspective are evident between the HiCap teachers and the AP teachers. The HiCap teachers are under a lot of pressure. The middle schools have no consistent language arts curriculum; instruction differs from classroom to classroom within each school, as well as from school to school. Further, the middle schools must raise seventh graders' reading and writing scores on the state test. The high school's curriculum and standards are already more closely aligned and calibrated, and the AP teachers are convinced that if the middle schools adopt a rigorous language arts curriculum that aligns with the high school's challenging AP program, middle school students' state test scores will rise regardless of whether the curriculum precisely aligns with the state standards. Tensions build between the HiCap and AP teachers, and the team falls apart.

Once Matthew realizes that the most immediate goal is alignment, not rigor, he knows the team must seriously consider a HiCap teacher's recommendation to use a program by the AP test developers that meets—but does not exceed—the state standards. Even though AP teachers have vetoed the program as not rigorous enough, the program could bring consistency across the three middle schools that feed the high school, and it would raise the middle school standards. Matthew gets the AP teachers to reconsider. He knows there is still a lot of work to do to prepare all students for AP classes, but they now have a shared vision for beginning that work. Next up: In order to make real progress, Matthew knows they have to get *all* of the teachers on board, and he's not sure how to do that.

Leadership Dilemmas

Many teachers are asked to take on leadership roles without any training or support. Learning to facilitate often requires a leader to put aside his or her own point of view in order to advance the work of the group. In this case, Matthew has to figure out on his own what the obstacles are and develop a strategy to overcome them.

This case will spark a rich discussion of the following issues:

- *Developing new expertise:* What kinds of knowledge and skills do teachers need to be effective leaders? What professional development or mentoring is available to foster their development as leaders? Why are facilitation skills important leadership skills?
- *Dealing with resistance:* What strategies can teacher leaders use to uncover what motivates resistance to change? How can teacher leaders learn constructive ways to address resistance?

Connections to Teacher Leadership Skills Framework

One way to help teacher leaders identify strategies for dealing with resistance would be to have participants complete the Working With Adult Learners section (see pp. 161–162) of Resource C2. The Professional Development section (see p. 176) of Resource C3 could be a useful instrument for helping teacher leaders identify ways to develop new expertise.

Facilitation Guide for *Is It Just a Crazy Dream?*

Possible Session Goals

- Consider the steps a teacher leader can take to get a collaborative study process started. (What can the leader do to create and maintain a shared responsibility and authority for their work together?)
- Brainstorm strategies that might alleviate colleagues' fears about learning new ways of working.

Case Summary

Jane left teaching in order to help others be more effective teachers. She became a school counselor. With support from her principal, she transformed how discipline issues are handled throughout her elementary school. She runs a "Kid's Café" to teach restaurant manners, runs a peer mediation group, trains playground attendants in conflict resolution, and teaches social skills lessons in classrooms alongside teachers.

Jane explains this approach to a comprehensive counseling program, but her fellow elementary school counselors are quick to explain why it can't work at their schools: too many high-needs kids, overload with support groups, or their principal would never agree to it. Jane tries other approaches, including suggesting a book club to study the national association standards, but the elementary school counselors don't show up. When Jane signs up to become a National Board candidate, in hopes it will help her reflect on and resolve her leadership struggles, she finds that the National Board standards reinforce her conviction that she is on the right path with the changes she is trying to make in her district.

Armed with more evidence supporting her approach, Jane wants to keep trying to persuade her colleagues, but she's not sure she has the energy to carry on alone. She longs for support and acknowledgment.

Leadership Dilemma

Jane transforms herself into a leader in her school, but she runs into resistance when she tries to convince her colleagues at other schools of the benefits of a new approach. Expertise is intertwined in the dynamics; her colleagues feel that Jane possesses abilities they lack, and this adds to their apprehension.

The following challenges will be familiar to many of the teacher leaders with whom you share this case:

- *Dealing with resistance:* How can a teacher leader utilize existing supporters to win over resisters? How can a teacher leader address the lack of knowledge or skill that causes fear when teachers are asked to change?
- *Coping with isolation:* What supports do teacher leaders need to sustain them in leadership work? Collegial? Administrative? Expert advisers? Where might teacher leaders find the support they need?

Connections to Teacher Leadership Skills Framework

You might try using the Working With Adult Learners section (see pp. 161–162) or the Knowledge of Content and Pedagogy section (see pp. 167–168) from Resource C2 to further examine how to use expertise effectively to deal with resistance to change. The Establishing a Supportive Environment (see pp. 172–173) and Access to Resources (see p. 177) sections of Resource C3 may help participants develop insights about new structures or practices that will reduce isolation or at least help teacher leaders cope with working on their own.

STATE- AND NATIONAL-LEVEL LEADERSHIP

Facilitation Guide for *Truth and Power*

Possible Session Goals

- Consider the implications of advocating for colleagues within the hierarchy of a bureaucracy.
- Compare the status of teacher leaders in various roles and organizations that depend on their expertise.

Case Summary

Kate has just joined a national organization with a mission to promote teacher development. The organization has historically relied upon the expertise of teacher leaders to shape its programs. Under new leadership, the management team is turning more and more to noneducators with business and marketing acumen to expand the organization's reach. Veteran teachers whose contributions have built the organization's foundation are suddenly leaving—voluntarily or involuntarily. It puts everyone on edge.

New to the organization, Kate struggles to understand the changes that are underway. When asked for her input, she offers it, even though others are reticent to speak up. She senses that her ideas are not well received. Requests for her to run trainings drop off, and one long-time employee suddenly leaves the organization. When a nonteacher is hired to lead the trainings, it's clear to Kate that the leadership of this organization for teachers is being taken over by nonteachers and doesn't respect the contributions teachers make.

Kate wrestles with her feelings of betrayal and the advisability of "speaking truth to power." She knows that speaking out may be counterproductive. But her anger and the importance of the issue outweigh the costs, and she states her concerns. Immediately, she knows her comments are not welcome. Now Kate wonders if standing up for her beliefs has accomplished anything besides jeopardizing any future role she might have had in the organization.

Leadership Dilemmas

The dynamics between the teacher leader and administrators in this case present a clash of cultures. Each is committed to advancing the organization, but they have different perspectives about the best way to achieve that objective. Although they both want to raise the visibility and influence of the organization, it's not clear that their different visions are compatible.

This case is a particularly good one for delving into the following dilemmas:

- *Learning the politics:* How does a teacher leader learn the politics of an organization? How can teacher leaders identify allies who are politically savvy and who can guide them in negotiating new territory?
- *Advocating for others:* Does a teacher leader have to have power (perceived or real) in order to effectively advocate on behalf of others?

Connections to Teacher Leadership Skills Framework

To help participants continue to explore the skills needed to advocate for others, you might want to have them complete the Systems Thinking section (see pp. 169–170) of Resource C2. This instrument will help teacher leaders assess their progress in learning about political issues similar to those described in this case. Completing the Professional Development section (see p. 176) of Resource C3 will also be a useful exercise to help teacher leaders identify opportunities (or the lack thereof) to strengthen their skills in these challenge areas.

Facilitation Guide for *One Step Forward, Two Steps Back*

Possible Session Goals

- Consider the role and responsibility that teacher leaders can assume for raising standards of practice within their profession.
- Analyze the leadership skills required to influence policy. Explore what effective leadership preparation for engaging in policy work might include.

Case Summary

As a board member of the Washington Library Media Association (WLMA), Sarah is inundated with cries for help from school librarians across the state whose jobs are being eliminated due to budget cuts. To lobby for the survival of the profession, Sarah takes on several new activities: speaking to the state board of education; corresponding with university professors, legislators, and association members; convening statewide meetings to draft new guidelines for the profession of "teacher-librarian"; and establishing a new law to enforce the requirements.

Although the first hurdle is cleared when new guidelines for standards for the profession are approved by the state board of education, the governor strips the state board of its authority to oversee the library regulations. Now WLMA has to work to pass a new law.

Even after legislative victories, the e-mail pleas continue, and teacher-librarian positions continue to be cut and replaced by positions for paraprofessionals. A challenge for WLMA is that there are still some librarians who are not meeting standards. The new law does not specify who is responsible for enforcing the regulations. WLMA can offer mentoring and professional development, but it lacks the authority to compel compliance. Yet Sarah realizes that if the WLMA tackles this challenge, the librarians who don't meet the new standards threaten the security of all teacher-librarians.

Leadership Dilemmas

Learning to lead at the state level requires advocacy for policy changes. Teacher leaders must be effective public speakers, must be able to develop a carefully honed message, and must understand the workings of the legislative process. These skills are rarely taught as part of teacher preparation.

Use this case to engage participants in a discussion of the following challenges:

- *Developing new expertise:* What new knowledge and skills are needed to effectively influence policy? How does one go about acquiring the expertise required?
- *Learning the politics:* When several worthy programs compete for scarce resources, what kinds of data do you need to convince policymakers that your cause deserves priority? To make a strong case, which constituencies' support is essential to influence policy decisions? What strategies might help strengthen the voice of teacher leaders in influencing policy decisions?

Extension Activity

To expand participants' analysis of this case, consider having the group design an informational or professional development session to convince school and district administrators of the need to support the work of teacher leaders. Ask participants to figure out how they will engage administrators in collaborating to build their ownership of and commitment to shared goals for teacher leaders.

Connections to Teacher Leadership Skills Framework

The Systems Thinking section (see pp. 169–170) of Resource C2 will help teacher leaders sort out how politically savvy they currently are and what they still need to learn. Use of the Professional Development section (see p. 176) of Resource C3 might be a good way to evaluate the availability of specific learning opportunities in the state or district.

Facilitation Guide for *Hanging in the Balance*

Possible Session Goals

- Brainstorm strategies a teacher leader might adopt to establish a strong professional network among specialists who lack school or district support.
- Examine the personal and professional costs of voluntary leadership. (What benefits—real or potential—might offset the price paid?)

Case Summary

Krista, a National Board Certified Teacher, is passionate about world languages. As the only world language teacher in her school, she teaches six levels of Spanish. When she was a first-year teacher, she was eager to find more experienced colleagues who could share ideas. At the first district professional development day, she quickly learned that there were no sessions for world language teachers, but she found what she was looking for at the state conference for foreign language teachers. She was inspired by the awards ceremony as recipients expressed their gratitude to colleagues who helped and motivated them to "give back" to the profession.

Just a few years later, Krista has her first opportunity to start giving back when she accepts an invitation to serve as regional vice president for the American Association of Teachers of Spanish and Portuguese. In this capacity, she serves on the board, participates in planning the annual conference, raises funds, and works with legislators to preserve funding for world languages. She begins presenting at the conference each year; first one session, then two, then three sessions in one year.

To reach out to world language teachers in her district, Krista secures a grant to run a statewide competition for students. Fourteen teachers agree to help plan the event, and Krista enthusiastically prepares for the first planning meeting. When only three teachers show up, her enthusiasm fades. In the end, only two other teachers stick it out and help develop a plan, and without more help, the competition must be placed on hold. Krista is not just disappointed, she begins to feel used. She wonders if she is the problem— she doesn't know how to say no. Does she need to stop giving back altogether, or can she find a way to give back without feeling exploited?

Leadership Dilemmas

Although research stresses the need for widely distributed leadership, teachers who lead often find that once they step forward, others keep asking for more. This may be especially true among specialists, who constitute a smaller pool of potential leaders. However, since leadership is voluntary, the availability of willing and able candidates can be problematic.

The issues in this case offer a chance to examine the following difficulties:

- *Handling the workload:* What strategies can be used to nurture leadership development in others? How can leadership be distributed to make it less demanding on individual teacher leaders?
- *Building and sustaining commitment to change:* When reform initiatives span districts, what strategies can a professional organization adopt to encourage investment in the endeavor? What kind of resources might the organization secure in order to expand and sustain teacher leaders' investment in the cause?

Connections to Teacher Leadership Skills Framework

Try using the Collaborative Work section (see pp. 163–164) of Resource C2 to explore how working together can address the need to handle the workload. The System Vision and Alignment section (see pp. 174–175) of Resource C3 can help participants identify unifying strategies to build and sustain commitment to change efforts.

Facilitation Guide for *Transitions*

Possible Session Goals

- Examine the role that professional community plays in validating and supporting leadership work.
- Explore the relationship between teachers' goals for students and for the profession at large. How can teacher leaders maintain a focus on both priorities?

Case Summary

Achieving National Board Certification propels Terese into a range of teacher leadership opportunities created for NBCTs in the state. When the coordinator of the National Board initiative chooses Terese to succeed her, she nervously agrees; she is reassured that the succession will be gradual, and the coordinator will guide Terese through the transition.

Terese finds that the most challenging aspects of her new job are grasping the dynamics and the cultures of various groups that operate in the state's educational landscape and hierarchy. She also has to work with the media and the legislature, two areas she finds completely intimidating. Fortunately, a new speakers' training session is available just in the nick of time, and she learns the skills she needs to do the job.

Even as Terese gains confidence and competence in her new role, she experiences a loss of professional community. The more she does at the state level, the less teachers see her as one of their ranks, even though she still identifies herself as a teacher. Some of her former classroom colleagues even view her as a traitor. She wonders about the relative impact she can have on children by working indirectly through teachers rather than face to face with students.

Leadership Dilemmas

The transition from teacher to leader can be traumatic. Routines and responsibilities change. Professional relationships change, and ties to one's former professional community are often lost. Having a mentor to smooth the path and opportunities to acquire the professional skills needed to be successful in new roles helps tremendously. But developing a new professional community can be very problematic; many teacher leaders' positions are "one of a kind," with no peers with whom to compare notes.

This case offers participants the opportunity to examine the following challenges for teacher leaders:

- *Developing new expertise:* How does the expertise that a teacher leader needs differ from that of a principal or district administrator? What might an "internship" in teacher leadership entail?
- *Defining and straddling roles:* As a teacher leaves the classroom and transitions into a leadership role, what can the teacher do to maintain credibility among teachers? How does a teacher earn the respect of administrators at the same time?

Extension Activity

To further your group's investigation into this case, ask small groups of participants to create an internship for teacher leadership. Request that they describe the knowledge and skills that need to be learned, identify who should teach interns, and list the qualities they would want a pool of potential mentors to possess. Ask: Where might you find qualified mentors for interns?

Connections to Teacher Leadership Skills Framework

The Systems Thinking section (see p. pp. 169–170) of Resource C2 can help teacher leaders identify the new expertise they need to develop to be effective in leading at the state level. The Establishing a Supportive Environment (see pp. 172–173) and Professional Development (see p. 176) sections of Resource C3 can also be used to stimulate reflection about defining new roles and learning to straddle roles that blur the lines between teacher and leader.

SUMMING UP

Throughout this book, we have argued that case methods are powerful tools for fostering the professional growth of teacher leaders. To support you in using these methods, we have provided several kinds of resources for facilitators and anyone interested in exploring these dynamic learning processes. In Chapter 2, we offered an array of facilitation tips and ideas in our discussions of the case-analysis and case-writing processes. This chapter added case-by-case facilitation guides.

The cases themselves are the richest resource for facilitators and teacher leaders. By identifying the salient teacher leadership dilemmas contained in each case, we have sought to give you a head start in mining the cases that are most appropriate for your group and your purpose. We have also offered questions and activities to stimulate your thinking about how your group can get the most out of each case. Of course, use your own strategies and creativity to bring the processes to life for participants. Enjoy, and please share your successes with us.

GOING FORWARD: FROM WORDS TO ACTIONS

If we are to meet the challenges of helping all students achieve at high levels, we must tap the wealth of expertise that all teacher leaders possess. The cases in this volume highlight recurring dilemmas that teacher leaders confront as they take on new roles and lead reform. CSTP has successfully used case analysis and case writing to help teacher leaders learn to overcome these dilemmas and to make all educators aware of the roadblocks that limit the effectiveness of teacher leadership in supporting reform; we strongly advise others to do the same.

The overarching goal of cases is to stimulate reflection, discussion, case writing, and action by teacher leaders and those who can support and sustain their work. As Judy Shulman said of her work, the cases "exemplify the importance of learning from the accidents that occur when careful planning and design collide with the inevitable vagaries of lived experience" (2002, p. 17). Narrative cases are teachers' ways of leaving behind accounts of such collisions, and by recounting their stories here, they stimulate learning in both writers and readers. The hope is that these cases will help future teacher leaders and administrators avoid some of the "accidents"—and unproductive detours, u-turns, and dead ends—that these teacher leaders ran into, and simultaneously help them develop strategies for learning from the new accidents that will inevitably occur in their own leadership journeys.

We close with the words one of the case authors wrote as she looked back on the progression of her case—from a haunting memory of an "accident," to a dilemma, to a discussion, to a draft, to a published case that inspired her principal and colleagues to form a group to read all of these cases to better understand the needs of teacher leaders:

> I realized the importance of being a leader and that there are different capacities of leadership and that just writing about it wasn't enough—that I needed to continue it. Because in the conversations that we all had, people asked, well you are going to do something about it, aren't you? So I felt like I had to. I think that also helped me to realize that if it's important enough to write about it, I also need to act on it.

Resource A

Recommended Books, Websites, and Readings

FOR TEACHER LEADERS

Effective Teacher Leadership: Using Research to Inform and Reform, **edited by Mangin and Stoelinga (2008).** This edited volume of research on teacher leadership presents a conceptual framework readers can use to understand the function performed by teacher leaders. It also identifies the supports and barriers, as well as organizational contexts, that influence the effectiveness of teacher leaders.

How Teachers Become Leaders: Learning From Practice and Research **by Lieberman and Friedrich (2010).** This book includes vignettes of teachers' leadership development, and in teachers' own words, it describes how, in the process of becoming leaders, they construct a new identity, develop the skills and abilities to handle conflict, learn to facilitate learning communities, and learn new practices. It provides additional insights into many of the dilemmas at the heart of the cases in this book: dealing with resistance, establishing and maintaining credibility, defining and straddling roles, and developing new expertise.

Resources for Teacher Leadership **by Education Development Center (2010) (http://cse.edc.org/products/teacherleadership/).** This website provides links to a number of helpful resources for supporting colleagues, training mentors, developing the skills of master teachers, and providing professional development for teacher leaders (especially in mathematics and science).

How to Thrive As a Teacher Leader **by Gabriel (2005)** is a practical book offers strategies for becoming an effective teacher leader, including identifying leadership qualities in others, team building, improving communication and earning respect, overcoming obstacles to change, motivating colleagues, and increasing student achievement. The book contains a number of templates to help track data and survey colleagues, and it offers sample checklists and examples of department communications such as memos.

Teacher Leadership Skills Framework by The Center for Strengthening the Teaching Profession (CSTP) (2009) (www.cstp-wa.org). The *Teacher Leadership Skills Framework* helps clarify the specific professional development needs of teacher leaders in order to positively impact learning in schools. The skill sets are organized under five categories: working with adult learners, communication, collaborative work, knowledge of content and pedagogy, and systems thinking. A copy of this framework is included in Resource C1 of this book.

FOR PRINCIPALS AND ADMINISTRATORS

"Exploring New Approaches to Teacher Leadership for School Improvement," by Smylie, Conley, and Marks, in *The Educational Leadership Challenge: Redefining Leadership for the 21st Century,* edited by Murphy (2002). This chapter presents three approaches to teacher leadership that appear to be more effective than formal leadership roles in promoting school improvement. Principals can instead promote and facilitate the following:

- *Teacher research as leadership:* Teacher inquiry in collaborative contexts can create new opportunities for teachers to learn and to lead efforts to improve their schools.
- *New models of distributive leadership:* These models indicate that teachers can and do perform important leadership tasks inside and outside formal positions of authority.
- *Leadership of teams:* Self-managed teams promote teacher collaboration, improve teaching and learning, and address problems of school organization.

Success at the Core: How Teams and Teachers Transform Instruction by Vulcan Productions and Education Development Center (2010) (www.successatthecore.com/default.aspx). This online resource's video and print materials are designed to support teams of principals, teacher leaders, and other leaders in working together to drive schoolwide instructional improvement. Leadership development materials include seven modules, each structured as a group learning experience. Teacher development materials include 24 strategies.

Principals: Leaders of Leaders **by Childs-Bowen, Moller, and Scrivner (2000).** This article describes the areas in which principals can create opportunities for teachers to lead, build professional learning communities, provide quality results-driven professional development, and celebrate innovation and teacher expertise.

Leadership for Student Learning: Redefining the Teacher as Leader **by the Institute for Educational Leadership (2001) (www.iel.org/programs/21st/reports/teachlearn.pdf).** This report provides suggestions for principals and communities to enhance teacher leadership. It examines teacher leadership issues within the community's goals for education, and then moves on to analyze teacher leadership structures, with a view toward improving them if they fall short. The report suggests key questions to begin a self-study, such as the following:

- Do teachers have frequent and meaningful opportunities for peer networking and collaboration?
- Do schools encourage action research and the sharing of effective instructional approaches?
- Does the preparation and professional development for teachers expose them to policy issues and management and leadership skills?
- Is teaching in our community a "flat" career, or is there a ladder for professional advancement?

FOR FACILITATORS

A Guide to Facilitating Cases in Education **by Miller and Kantrov (1998)** and *Teacher Leadership in Mathematics and Science: Casebook and Facilitator's Guide* **by Miller, Moon, and Elko (2000).** The strength of these books is that they offer both specific strategies for effectively facilitating a case and a framework for purposeful facilitation. They also offer a wealth of suggestions for activities one might use to structure a case discussion, such as role playing, reflective writing, and ideas for small and large group discussions. Many of these activities could be easily adapted to use with the cases in this volume, depending on one's purpose and the needs of the participants.

Cultivating a Math Coaching Practice: A Guide for K–8 Math Educators **by Morse (2009)** offers extensive facilitation support for each of the 12 cases in the book. In the case discussions, the guide provides support for facilitators by integrating analysis of the math content with analysis of the coaching practice. The book includes detailed agendas, session goals, and facilitation support as well as anecdotes from the author's actual experience working with teachers and the cases.

How to Make Meetings Work **by Straus and Doyle (1976)** is a seminal resource that defines roles, tasks, and tools of facilitation.

The Skilled Facilitator **by Schwarz (1994)** builds on Straus and Doyle's foundation and provides a comprehensive reference for anyone charged with guiding groups to realize their potential as skilled and creative problem solvers. The book includes essential materials for facilitators, such as effective ground rules for governing group interaction, suggestions for keeping a group on track, practical strategies for handling emotions, models for solving problems, and a process for creating conditions for potent learning. Both of these books are excellent sources for help with general facilitation skills to make group work more productive.

Getting to Yes: Negotiating Agreement Without Giving In **by Fisher and Ury (1981).** This classic little handbook on negotiating personal and professional disputes may seem like an unlikely resource for facilitators, as facilitators do much more than moderate conflict. However, understanding how disagreements and differences of opinion arise gives facilitators valuable insight for recognizing and addressing emotions, deeply held values, and different viewpoints that will make guiding participants' analysis of cases easier.

The Adaptive School: A Sourcebook for Developing Collaborative Groups **by Garmston and Wellman (1998).** This book is designed as a problem-based user's guide for all of those who want to learn to develop and facilitate collaborative groups to improve student learning. The authors' seven norms of collaborative work help facilitators lead more productive groups, and the book provides practical tools for monitoring effectiveness in getting work done and running productive groups.

The Power of Protocols: An Educator's Guide to Better Practice **by McDonald, Mohr, Dichter, and McDonald (2007)** provides not only facilitation tips but also a host of protocols to use to design activities to deepen teacher leaders' investigation of the dilemmas in a case or to expand the lessons to be learned from the dilemmas.

Resource B

Just What Is Teacher Leadership?

Bass (1990): "Leaders are agents of change—persons whose acts affect other people more than other people's acts affect them. Leadership occurs when a group member modifies the motivation or competencies of others in the group" (pp. 19–20). Leadership thus is defined as a relationship of social influence.

Senge (1990): "It is impossible to reduce natural leadership to a set of skills or competencies. Ultimately people follow people who believe in something and have the abilities to achieve results in the service of those beliefs. . . . Who are the natural leaders of learning organizations? They are the learners" (p. 360).

Kouzes and Posner (1993, 1995, 2003) collected thousands of case studies of admired leaders. Their analysis revealed that leaders consistently employ the following five practices when accomplishing extraordinary things: "challenge the process, inspire a shared vision, enable others to act, model the way, and encourage the heart" (2003, p. xiii). They found that all five practices are essential to effective leadership and that all five practices contribute to explaining why certain leaders are successful.

Fullan (1994) extends the conception of teacher leadership by identifying six domains, and he hypothesizes that leadership can be fostered among teachers on a large scale only if all six of the following domains are developed as part of the professional work of teachers:

- Knowledge of teaching and learning
- Knowledge of collegiality
- Knowledge of educational context

- Opportunities for continuous learning
- Management of the change process
- A sense of moral purpose

Kouzes and Posner (1995) define leadership as "the art of mobilizing others to want to struggle for shared aspirations" (p. 30). It is an attitude that expresses a sense of responsibility for making a difference. When individuals are clear about their own personal values, they are motivated to act on their convictions, and this creates the passion that, for instance, drives teachers to serve their students and the profession. Ultimately, leadership comes from the heart—it is passion that drives teachers to serve their students and their colleagues. It is also passion, bolstered by their high level of expertise, that earns them the respect and commitment of their professional community.

Miller, Moon, and Elko (2000) observe that "Teacher leadership generally refers to actions by teachers outside their own classrooms that involve an explicit or implicit responsibility to provide professional development to their colleagues, to influence their communities' or districts' policies, or to act as adjunct district staff to support changes in classroom practices among teachers. . . . Leadership, like any other professional capacity, requires cultivation, practice, and reflection" (p. 4). They note, "Teacher leaders are those who hold a position or play a role that is identified by others as providing leadership for change" (p. 5).

Donaldson (2001): "School leadership is the ability to mobilize people to adapt a school's practices and beliefs so that it more fully achieves its mission with all children. It mobilizes members to think, believe, and behave in a manner that satisfies emerging organizational needs, not simply their individual needs" (p. 5).

Swanson (2001): Teacher leaders are those who have demonstrated a deep understanding of what it takes to translate high standards into effective classroom practices, and have assumed leadership roles in which they are helping other teachers learn to do the same. Being a teacher leader implies that teachers are committed to extending their influence beyond the classroom.

Five Dimensions of Teacher Leadership:

"1. *Empowerment:* Empowered teachers are confident in their ability to make a difference in student learning. They exhibit a high degree of agency through their willingness to take risks and their resourcefulness as problem solvers. Teachers who are empowered are characterized as optimistic, determined, and self-actualized. At the highest levels, these teachers are skilled in empowering others.

2. *Expertise:* Fueled by a passion for their subject area, expertise in teaching requires deep pedagogical content knowledge. Teachers with expertise have a keen understanding of their students' developmental cognitive capacities, and they are skilled at creating varied and rich curriculum to motivate and challenge their students. Expert teachers understand the goals or standards that must be met; they are able to analyze where their students are now and where they need to go. They can break their teaching down into manageable and well-sequenced mini-lessons to scaffold student learning toward meeting standards. These teachers hold high expectations for themselves and their students and continually seek ongoing opportunities to enhance and refine their craft.

3. *Reflection:* Reflective practitioners are able to discern what is happening in the classroom and adapt their efforts by understanding the perspectives of others, while, at the same time, being conscious of their own values, thoughts, and biases. Reflective teachers possess a high degree of agency and are willing to ask themselves, 'How can I change to improve the outcome?' and 'What can I do differently?'

4. *Collaboration:* Characterized by a high degree of collegiality and cooperation, collaborative teachers recognize that collective expertise offers the possibility of generating optimal solutions to the complex problems of teaching and learning. Such teachers are accessible and demonstrate strong communication skills.

5. *Flexibility:* Flexible teachers understand that teaching is an art and a science, requiring innovation and improvisation along with structure and planning. Flexibility requires a high tolerance for ambiguity, and flexible individuals respond and adapt as they go. They rely on their intuition as well as more formal analytic abilities" (p. 11).

Crowther, Kaagan, Ferguson, and Hann (2002): "Teacher leadership facilitates principled action to achieve whole school success. It applies the distinctive power of teaching to shape meaning for children, youth, and adults. And it contributes to long-term, enhanced quality of community life" (p. 10).

Knapp et al. (2003) define leadership (all leadership, including teacher leadership) as "the act of imparting purpose to an organization as well as motivating and sustaining effort in pursuit of that purpose" (p. 13).

Lambert (2003): [Teacher leadership] "is not a role but rather performing actions . . . that enable participants in a community to evoke potential in a trusting environment; to inquire into practice; to focus on constructing meaning; or to frame actions based on new behaviors and purposeful intention" (p. 6).

Lieberman and Miller (2004): Teacher leaders are those with the capacity to transform schools.

Danielson (2006) defines teacher leaders as those who informally and voluntarily lead activities that mobilize colleagues in efforts to increase student learning.

Krovetz and Arriaza (2006): "A teacher leader may be seen as a person in whom the dream of making a difference has been kept alive, or has been reawakened, by engaging colleagues in a true community of practice. Those who have managed to keep their sense of purpose alive and well are reflective, inquisitive, focused on improving their craft, and action oriented, and they accept responsibility for student learning" (p. 5).

Reeves (2006) identified dimensions of leadership that he suggests are necessary in every leadership team but rarely present in a single leader:

- Relationship leaders exhibit genuine passion for their mission and the people around them.
- Systems leaders know the key indicators to watch, how to leverage resources, and the warning signs that help them avoid catastrophes.
- Reflective leaders take time to think about the lessons learned, record the small wins and setbacks, document conflicts between values and practices, and notice trends that emerge over time.
- Collaborative leaders involve others in decision making, because implementation can only happen through collaboration.
- Analytical leaders ask good questions.
- Communicative leaders are both high tech and high touch—they make personal connections.

Spillane (2006): "Leadership refers to activities tied to the core work of the organization that are designed by its members to influence the motivation, knowledge, affect, or practices of other members of the organization" (p. 10). The term *leadership* is reserved for activities that either administrators or teachers design to influence others in the service of the organization's core work.

Mangin and Stoelinga (2008): Instructional teacher leadership roles are (a) nonsupervisory, (b) focused on instructional improvement, (c) aimed at building teachers' capacity to increase student learning, and (d) located at the school level. These teacher leaders can facilitate instructional improvement by providing teachers with effective professional development—sustained, supported, and school-embedded opportunities to learn about the core technologies of teaching. They bring specialized knowledge about teaching to the school setting.

CSTP (2009) includes the following definition of teacher leadership in its *Teacher Leadership Skills Framework* (see Resource C1): "Knowledge, skills, and dispositions demonstrated by teachers who positively impact student learning by influencing adults, formally and informally, beyond individual classrooms" (p. 1).

Katzenmeyer and Moller (2009): "Teacher Leaders lead within and beyond the classroom; identify with and contribute to a community of teacher learners and leaders; influence others toward improved educational practice; and accept responsibility for achieving the outcomes of leadership" (p. 6).

References for Resource B

Bass, B. M. (1990). *Bass & Stogdill's handbook of leadership: Theory, research, and managerial applications* (3rd ed.). New York, NY: The Free Press.

Center for Strengthening the Teaching Profession. (2009). *Teacher leadership skills framework.* Retrieved from http://www.cstp-wa.org

Crowther, F., Kaagan, S. S., Ferguson, M., & Hann, L. (2002). *Developing teacher leaders: How teacher leadership enhances school success.* Thousand Oaks, CA: Corwin.

Danielson, C. (2006). *Teacher leadership that strengthens professional practice.* Alexandria, VA: ASCD.

Donaldson, G. A. (2001). *Cultivating leadership in schools: Connecting people, purpose, and practice.* New York, NY: Teachers College Press.

Fullan, M. (1994). Teacher leadership: A failure to conceptualize. In D. R. Walling (Ed.), *Teachers as leaders: Perspectives on the professional development of teachers* (pp. 241–253). Bloomington, IN: Phi Delta Kappa Educational Foundation.

Katzenmeyer, M., & Moller, G. (2009). *Awakening a sleeping giant: Leadership development for teachers* (3rd ed.). Thousand Oaks, CA: Corwin.

Knapp, M. S., Copland, M. A., Ford, B., Markholt, A., McLaughlin, M. W., Milliken, M., & Talbert, J. E. (2003). *Leading for learning sourcebook: Concepts and examples.* Seattle: University of Washington, Center for the Study of Teaching and Policy.

Kouzes, J., & Posner, B. (1993). *Credibility: How leaders gain and lose it, why people demand it.* San Francisco, CA: Jossey-Bass.

Kouzes, J., & Posner, R. (1995). *The leadership challenge.* San Francisco, CA: Jossey-Bass.

Kouzes, J., & Posner, R. (2003). *Encouraging the heart: A leader's guide to rewarding and recognizing others.* San Francisco, CA: Jossey-Bass.

Krovetz, M. L., & Arriaza, G. (2006). *Collaborative teacher leadership: How teachers can foster equitable schools.* Thousand Oaks, CA: Corwin.

Lambert, L. (2003). Shifting conceptions of leadership: Towards a redefinition of leadership for the twenty-first century. In B. Davies & J. West-Burnham (Eds.), *Handbook of educational leadership and management* (pp. 5–15). London, England: Pearson Education.

Lieberman, A., & Miller, L. (2004). *Teacher leadership.* San Francisco, CA: Jossey-Bass.

Mangin, M. M., & Stoelinga, S. R. (2008). *Effective teacher leadership: Using research to inform and reform.* New York, NY: Teachers College Press.

Miller, B., Moon, J., & Elko, S. (2000). *Teacher leadership in mathematics and science: Casebook and facilitator's guide.* Portsmouth, NH: Heinemann.

Reeves, D. B. (2006). *Reframing teacher leadership to improve your school.* Alexandria, VA: ASCD.

Senge, P. M. (1990). *The fifth discipline: The art & practice of the learning organization.* New York, NY: Doubleday Currency.

Spillane, J. P. (2006). *Distributed leadership.* San Francisco, CA: Jossey-Bass.

Swanson, J. (2001). *The role of teacher leaders in scaling up standards-based reform.* Final report prepared for the U.S. Department of Education, National Institute for Student Achievement, Curriculum and Assessment, Office of Educational Research and Improvement. Grant #R305F970040–99. Retrieved from http://eric.ed.gov/PDFS/ED444947.pdf

Resource C1

Teacher Leadership
Skills Framework

TEACHER LEADERSHIP SKILLS FRAMEWORK

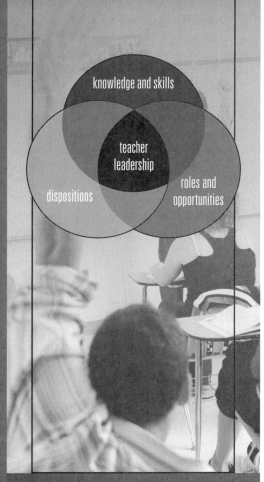

knowledge and skills

teacher leadership

dispositions

roles and opportunities

CSTP
Center for Strengthening
the Teaching Profession
2009

253-752-2082
www.cstp-wa.org

With the publication of this Teacher Leadership Skills Framework, the Center for Strengthening the Teaching Profession (CSTP) takes another step towards articulating and clarifying the specific professional development needs of teacher leaders that will positively impact learning for students in all of our schools.

This framework can be used to design professional development offerings, serve as a discussion tool to address the dilemmas that arise when leadership is shared, and contribute to the ongoing dialogue about the roles teacher leaders assume in efforts to improve student learning.

Special thanks to the many educators who gave their time and energy to this work, especially the following:

Bonnie Bless-Boenish .... Sequim School District
Jen Brotherton .... Olympia School District
Christina Carlson... Yakima School District
Jacqueline Coomes........................ Eastern Washington University
Betsy Cornell .... Moses Lake School District
Erin LaVerdiere .... Sumner School District
Barbara Lawson .... Consultant
Cindy Marum.. Edmonds School District
Beth McGibbon .... Spokane School District
Mindy Meyer... CSTP
Michaela Miller.. OSPI
Nancy Place.............................. University of Washington, Bothell
Vince Riccobene... Sequim School District
Cindy Rockholt... Yakima School District
Barbara Tibbits .... Everett School District
Tom White... Edmonds School District
Tracy Williams.. Spokane School District
Sue Yerian .... Consultant

Grant funding for the Teacher Leadership Skills Framework provided by WaMu, now a part of JP Morgan Chase.

January, 2009

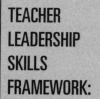

TEACHER LEADERSHIP SKILLS FRAMEWORK:

OVERVIEW

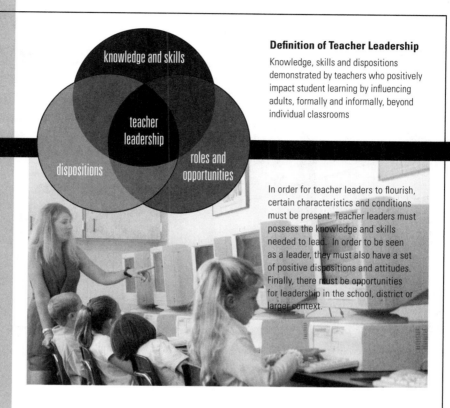

knowledge and skills

teacher leadership

dispositions

roles and opportunities

Definition of Teacher Leadership

Knowledge, skills and dispositions demonstrated by teachers who positively impact student learning by influencing adults, formally and informally, beyond individual classrooms

In order for teacher leaders to flourish, certain characteristics and conditions must be present. Teacher leaders must possess the knowledge and skills needed to lead. In order to be seen as a leader, they must also have a set of positive dispositions and attitudes. Finally, there must be opportunities for leadership in the school, district or larger context.

Knowledge and Skills Needed by Effective Teacher Leaders

The skills teacher leaders need to be effective in a variety of roles can be broken into five main categories. These skills sets are further defined on subsequent pages.

1. Working with adult learners
2. Communication
3. Collaborative work
4. Knowledge of content and pedagogy
5. Systems thinking

Dispositions of Effective Teacher Leaders

Effective teacher leaders share a set of dispositions and attitudes. They are energetic risk takers whose integrity, high efficacy, and content knowledge give them credibility with their colleagues. Their desire to work with adults is grounded in their belief that systems-level change will positively impact student learning, and that their contributions to the profession are important and needed. The natural curiosity of teacher leaders makes them life-long learners who are open to new experiences and challenges. Juggling many important professional and personal roles, they effectively prioritize their work to maintain a sense of balance. Teacher leaders often seek like-minded colleagues with similar positive intentions as allies, however they also value different ideas and approaches that move the work forward. Difficult challenges require teacher leaders to tap into their deep sense of courage, and their unwavering perseverance helps them to follow through. When best-laid plans have unexpected outcomes, teacher leaders are open to constructive criticism. They reflect on their experience, learn from it, and then with resilience move forward to the next challenge.

CSTP
Center for Strengthening
the Teaching Profession
2009

253-752-2082
www.cstp-wa.org

Grant funding for the Teacher
Leadership Skills Framework
provided by WaMu, now a part
of JP Morgan Chase.

TEACHER LEADERSHIP SKILLS FRAMEWORK:

OVERVIEW, continued

Roles of Teacher Leaders

Working to Strengthen Instruction:
Instructional/Curriculum Specialist
- Action researcher
- Assessment developer
- Assessment literacy
- Assessment specialist
- Content coach
- Instructional coach
- Data analyst
- Data coach
- Graduation expectation specialist
- Resource provider
- Teacher on Special Assignment
- Learning team leader
- Technology coach
- Technology expert

Advocate/Partner
- Association reps/leaders
- Advocate for teachers, students
- NCATE examiner
- OSPI committees
- Policy influence
- Publishing
- Partner with organizations
- Partner with universities (adjunct faculty, advisory boards)
- Professional content organization

Working to Strengthen Instruction:
Classroom Supporter
- Assessment leader
- Grade level/team leader
- Instructional coaches
- Teacher on Special Assignment

Mentor
- Mentor 1st or 2nd year teacher
- Mentor teachers new to the district
- Mentor student teachers

Learning Facilitator
- Advanced certification facilitator
- Group facilitation (large, small)
- Lab classrooms
- Teacher trainer (Professional Development)

Learner
- Book study facilitator
- Critical Friends Group facilitator
- Lesson study facilitator

School Leader
- Committee work
- Curriculum work
- Department head/chair
- School improvement work
- Team leader

The following pages

detail the five categories of knowledge, skills and dispositions that teacher leaders need to be effective in a variety of roles. Each category includes a vignette illustrating the dilemmas teacher leaders face, as well as reflective questions to prompt thinking and discussion. A resource list for each category is also included.

knowledge and skills

teacher leadership

dispositions

roles and opportunities

CSTP
Center for Strengthening
the Teaching Profession
2009

253-752-2082
www.cstp-wa.org

WORKING WITH ADULT LEARNERS

LINDA DARLING-HAMMOND

"If teachers are to prepare an ever more diverse group of students for much more challenging work — for framing problems; finding, integrating and synthesizing information; creating new solutions; learning on their own; and working cooperatively — they will need substantially more knowledge and radically different skills than most now have and most schools of education develop."

CSTP

Center for Strengthening the Teaching Profession
2009

253-752-2082
www.cstp-wa.org

Grant funding for the Teacher Leadership Skills Framework provided by WaMu, now a part of JP Morgan Chase.

Knowledge and Skills

Building trusting relationships

- Fostering group membership
- Listening intentionally
- Taking an ethical stance
- Taking a caring stance
- Creating a safe environment
- Developing cultural competency

Facilitating professional learning for teachers

- Using reflection strategically
- Structuring dialogue and discussion
- Disrupting assumptions
- Fostering learners' engagement
- Encouraging collegial inquiry
- Understanding development of teacher knowledge both in terms of content knowledge and pedagogical knowledge
- Foster responsibility for the group's learning by all group members

Dispositions

- Believe that teacher learning is interwoven with student learning
- Value the work of learners
- Accept and act on constructive feedback
- Possess courage to take risks
- Is reliable

Vignette

Jack will lead his first grade level team meeting in a few days. The task of the group will be to look at common assessment data. Jack confided to his building coach/principal that he knew one team member, Shane, was uncomfortable sharing his data with the team. Jack and Shane fish together on the weekends and go on an annual hunting trip. Asking Shane to share his students' results with the team makes Jack uncomfortable.

Reflection Questions

- What steps would you take if you were Jack?
- What advice would you give Jack if you were the coach or principal?
- How could the team meeting be structured to ease Shane into sharing data?
- What does this team need to address?
- What evidence of effective adult learning do you see in the vignette?

Resources

Bransford, J., Brown, A., & Cocking, R. (Eds.). (2000). *How people learn: Brain, mind, experience and school*. Washington, DC: National Academy Press.

Cave, J., LaMaster, C., & White, S. (1997, 2006). *Staff development: Adult characteristics*. Available from http://www-ed.fnal.gov/lincon/staff_adult.html

Edmunds, C., Lowe, K., Murray, M., & Seymour, A. (2002). *The ultimate educator: Achieving maximum adult learning through training and instruction*. National Victims Assistance Academy Advanced Topic Series. Washington, DC: U.S. Department of Justice. Available from http://www.ncjrs.gov/ovc_archives/educator/welcome.html

Zemke, R., & Zemke, S. (1984, March 9). 30 things we know for sure about adult learning. *Innovation Abstracts, 6*(8).

COMMUNICATION

HENRY DAVID THOREAU

"The greatest
compliment
that was ever
paid me was
when someone
asked me what
I thought,
and attended
to my answer."

Knowledge and Skills

Building relationships through communication

- Maintains objectivity
- Develops cultural competency
- Understands adults as learners
- Risks inviting and honoring diverse views
- Comfortable with healthy, productive discussion

Technical skills

- Facilitate learning focused conversations
- Give and receive feedback
- Deep listening skills (i.e. paraphrasing, asking clarifying questions)
- Questioning strategies
- Lead data driven dialogue
- Know the difference between conversation, dialogue and discussion
- Synthesize and summarize, use mediation skills
- Facilitate large and small groups
- Effectively use technology to enhance communication (i.e. Powerpoint presentations)
- Written communication (e.g., memos, minutes, email)
- Strategies for setting up spaces, materials and pacing

Dispositions

- Honors all perspectives
- Holds a positive presupposition that all are working in the best interests of students
- Values professional expertise
- Fosters community

Vignette

Clare is a grade level team leader. At the last team meeting the discussion went badly and two of the team members left with hurt feelings. The disagreement centered on the creation of a common formative assessment. One team member thought the assessment should be multiple-choice to match the state assessment format, while another was invested in short answer response to get at student thinking. Clare met with them the following day. She spent the first part of the meeting objectively restating the issue and had the team find where there was common ground. The team members then focused on how to compromise and agree to disagree on the assessment format.

Reflection Questions

- What questions do you think Clare asked to find common ground?
- What presuppositions did Clare make about her teammates?
- What would happen if the teammates would not compromise or agree to disagree?
- Are there other strategies that might have worked for Clare and her team?
- What evidence of or possibilities for effective communication do you see in the vignette?

Resources

Garmston, R., & Wellman, B. (1999). *The adaptive school: A sourcebook for developing collaborative groups.* Norwood, MA: Christopher-Gordon.

Lipton, L., & Wellman, B. (1998). *Pathways to understanding: Patterns and practices in the learning-focused classroom* (3rd ed.). Arlington, MA: MiraVia.

McDonald, J. (2007). *The power of protocols: An educator's guide to better practice.* New York, NY: Teachers College Press.

CSTP
Center for Strengthening
the Teaching Profession
2009

253-752-2082
www.cstp-wa.org

Grant funding for the Teacher
Leadership Skills Framework
provided by WaMu, now a part
of JP Morgan Chase.

COLLABORATIVE WORK

AFRICAN PROVERB

"If you want to go quickly, go alone. If you want to go far, go together."

Knowledge and Skills

Collaborative skills

- Teaching, developing, and using norms of collaboration
- Conflict resolution/mediation skills
- Using protocols or other strategies
- Modeling/valuing diverse opinions
- Matching language to the situation
- Sharing responsibility and leadership
- Holding yourself accountable to the group's goals and outcomes

Organizational skills

- Facilitating a meeting
- Documenting a meeting
- Moving a group to task completion
- Knowing resources and how to access resources
- Delegating responsibility to group members

Dispositions

- Knows when to compromise
- Able to read the group
- Admitting when wrong/don't know
- Honest courageous communication
- Desire to work with adults
- Passion for topic motivates others

Vignette

An ESD in rural Washington State has received a three-year math and science grant. The purpose of the grant is to improve student learning by improving instructional practices in math and science. At one elementary school, K-5 teachers are using the "Teaching and Learning Cycle" to collaboratively plan and implement lessons, analyze student work and make adjustments to their instruction. However, one grade level group is having difficulty collaborating. Sarah, a teacher leader on the team, shares the group's challenges with the principal. The principal responds by asking Sarah to assume leadership of the group to ensure success.

Reflection Questions

- How should Sarah approach her new role as team leader?
- Where should Sarah begin to help the group collaborate?
- What tools might Sarah use to help the group 'own' the work?
- What evidence of or possibilities for effective collaboration do you see in the vignette?

CSTP
Center for Strengthening the Teaching Profession
2009

253-752-2082
www.cstp-wa.org

Grant funding for the Teacher Leadership Skills Framework provided by WaMu, now a part of JP Morgan Chase.

Resources

Dufour, R., Dufour, R., & Eaker, R. (2008). *Revisiting professional learning communities that work: New insights for improving schools.* Bloomington, IN: Solution Tree.
Dufour, R., Dufour, R., Eaker, R., & Many, T. (2006). *Learning by doing: A handbook for professional learning communities at work.* Bloomington, IN: Solution Tree.
McDonald, J. (2007). *The power of protocols: An educator's guide to better practice.* New York, NY: Teachers College Press.
Tobia, E. (2007, April). The professional teaching and learning cycle: Implementing a standards-based approach to professional development. *Southwest Education Development Laboratory Letter,* 19(1).

KNOWLEDGE OF CONTENT AND PEDAGOGY

DIANA RIGDEN

"Research demonstrates that there is a strong reliable relationship between teachers' content knowledge and the quality of their instruction. Teachers with a deep conceptual understanding of their subject ask a greater number of high-level questions, encourage students to apply and transfer knowledge, help students see and understand relationships between and among ideas and concepts, and make other choices in their instruction that engage students and challenge them to learn"

knowledge and skills

teacher leadership

dispositions

roles and opportunities

CSTP

Center for Strengthening the Teaching Profession 2009

253-752-2082
www.cstp-wa.org

Grant funding for the Teacher Leadership Skills Framework provided by WaMu, now a part of JP Morgan Chase.

Knowledge and Skills

- Strong subject matter knowledge including assessment strategies
- The ability to analyze both subject matter concepts and pedagogical strategies
- Personal experience using effective pedagogical strategies in the classroom
- Ability to assist colleagues at multiple entry points to increase content knowledge and classroom application

Dispositions

- Life-long learner
- Reflective
- Committed to supporting growth of others
- Enjoys challenges

Vignette

As an experienced middle school teacher with a math minor, Bill has built a good relationship with a colleague, Sally. It was 4:00 on a Thursday when Sally approached him for help on her next day's math lesson. Bill really wanted to go home but knew he needed to nurture this relationship, and deep down knew it would be valuable to share with her the reflective strategies he uses to deepen content knowledge and support students' conceptual understanding. He thought he could give her a lesson plan on the concepts, but felt it was more important to help her own the math so she could develop the lesson. So, Bill invited her into his room and asked a series of questions to find an entry point. What ideas do you have? Have you taught these concepts before? What do your students already know? Together they looked at recent student work so they could make connections. He also shared strategies he had used in the past and detailed the ways students thought about the concepts in response to these strategies, and how he revised his plans after analyzing their misconceptions. Finally, they looked at Sally's students' work and brainstormed a plan together. Bill pulled some of his resources and Sally added some of hers. They agreed to come back Friday during planning to talk about how the lesson went.

Reflection Questions

- In what ways does Bill's response to Sally acknowledge her content knowledge? How does Bill demonstrate his own?
- How does Sally receive the pedagogical strategies modeled and suggested by Bill?
- What skills and dispositions demonstrated by Bill and Sally align with your leadership/learning experiences?
- What evidence of or possibilities for effective content/pedagogy leadership do you see in the vignette?

Resources

Association of Supervision and Curriculum Development, http://www.ascd.org
National Staff Development Council, http://www.nsdc.org
National Board for Professional Teaching Standards, http://www.nbpts.org
National content standards
Content practitioner journals

SYSTEMS THINKING

Knowledge and Skills

Working effectively within system
- Recognize layers of system(s)
- Understand power structure and decision making in context
- Understand and work within rules of hierarchy (formal and informal)
- Garner support from and work with stakeholders
- Deal effectively with resistance
- Facilitate collective inquiry practices
- Understand and leverage finances/resource allocation
- Ask the right questions at the right time

Skills of advocacy
- Set achievable goals
- Create and implement plan to meet goals
- Build capacity for sustainability
- Identify decision makers
- Craft and deliver an effective message
- Mobilize people into action

Dispositions
- Interested in larger/bigger picture
- Attuned to relationships
- Ability to "read" people and situations
- Embraces the opportunity to work with those with diverse views

Vignette

Two teachers come back from a conference energized about a new initiative to implement in their district that will cost a small amount of money and meets a stated need. They meet to draft the proposal, inform and garner support from other staff and then present the idea to the person who they think is the decision-maker. To their dismay and disappointment, they get a no. After careful thought and analysis of the situation, they wonder if the person who turned down their proposal was actually the person who makes such a decision. They ask a lot of questions and find the proposal actually needs to be approved by a professional development advisory group, and they get permission to present the idea to this group. They know from past experience that this group has one person who will likely not be supportive.

Reflection Questions
- How common do you think it is for teacher leaders to initially misidentify the decision maker for new ideas? How often do ideas stop there?
- After their proposal was turned down initially, how did the teacher leaders determine next steps?
- Knowing there will be an unsupportive member of the PD group, what might the teacher leaders do in advance of their presentation?
- What evidence of or possibilities for system thinking/learning do you see in the vignette?

Resources
Fullan, M. (2005). *Leadership and sustainability: System thinkers in action.* Thousand Oaks, California: Corwin.
Katzenmeyer, M., & Moller, G. (2001). *Awakening the sleeping giant.* Thousand Oaks, CA: Corwin.
National Board for Professional Teaching Standards Advocacy Link, http://capwiz.com/nbpts/home
Officer of Superintendent of Public Instruction. (2009). *National board policy symposium: A final report to the Quality Education Council.* Available from http://www.cstp-wa.org/sites/default/files/QEC_Final_Symposium_Report.pdf

Resource C2

Teacher Leader Self-Assessment

WORKING WITH ADULT LEARNERS

Teacher leaders who successfully work with adult learners build trusting relationships and facilitate professional learning environments in order to empower their colleagues. They understand the development and inter-relationship of teacher knowledge and practice and believe that teacher learning is grounded in student learning.

CONTEXT: Think about a leadership role in your work with adult learners, such as teaching colleagues, mentoring, coaching, or facilitating collaborative groups, or a role that you would like to assume in the future. Keep that context in mind as you complete the *Working With Adult Learners* self-assessment.

Knowledge and Skills: Building Trusting Relationships	Consistently	Usually	Occasionally	Rarely	Evidence/experience used to determine ratings.
I foster group membership for all participants so that all perspectives are valued.					
I listen intentionally to all participants to fully understand what is communicated.					
I take an ethical stance and support others in operating from an ethical perspective.					
I take a caring stance to ensure that all participants feel valued.					
I create a safe environment so that each participant feels safe to risk, learn and share.					
I am aware of and act on the cultural needs and interests of my participants.					

What does this tell me about my strengths when working with adult learners? What knowledge and skills do I need to develop to be more effective when working with adult learners?

Knowledge and Skills: Facilitating Professional Learning for Adults	Consistently	Usually	Occasionally	Rarely	Evidence/experience used to determine ratings.
I use reflection strategically as a tool to inform my practice and improve adults' learning.					
I intentionally structure dialogue and discussion to further specific learning goals.					
I create environments and activities that encourage adult learners to question their assumptions.					
I foster adult learners' engagement in order to maximize opportunities to learn.					
I encourage collegial inquiry so that participants can transform their practice.					
I consider the spectrum of content knowledge and understanding of pedagogy as I plan professional learning opportunities.					
I foster mutual responsibility for all group members' learning.					

What does this assessment tell me about my strengths in facilitating professional learning? What knowledge and skills do I need to develop to be more effective in facilitating professional learning?

Dispositions	Consistently	Usually	Occasionally	Rarely	Evidence/experience used to determine ratings.
I frame my work on the belief that adult learning is interwoven with student learning.					
I take the time to notice and appreciate the work of adult learning and convey this to participants.					
I accept and act on constructive feedback in order to model an open mind and improve my practice.					
I demonstrate the courage to take risks in order to support the participants' learning.					
I am reliable and follow through on my commitments to participants and to the work.					

What does this assessment tell me about my strengths in developing dispositions in working with adult learners? What dispositions do I need to develop to be more effective in working with adult learners?

Given all of my strengths and areas of need in *working with adult learners*, where do I fall on this continuum?

Refining	Proficient	Developing	Emerging
I motivate others to build trusting relationships that promote collaborative inquiry, disrupt existing assumptions, value diversity of opinion, and foster mutual responsibility for the group's learning. I affect teacher change by planning and implementing powerful instruction based on knowledge of adult learners' needs and grounded in reflective practice. I help others to create an environment that encourages risk taking and innovative thinking.	I build trusting relationships that promote collaborative inquiry, disrupt existing assumptions, value diversity of opinion, and foster mutual responsibility for the group's learning. I plan and implement intentional instruction that engages adult learners and is grounded in reflective practice. I create an environment that supports risk taking.	I promote friendly relationships that encourage group conversations and create a cooperative environment. I plan appropriate instruction that engages adult learners and moves some to reflective practice. I act on constructive feedback in order to model risk taking in my own practice.	I understand the need for building trusting relationships in teacher learning groups. I have participated in cooperative learning activities. I understand the need to value my colleagues' ideas and the power of reflection on my own practice.

What patterns do I see in my *Working With Adult Learners* self-assessment? What are my next steps?

Additional questions to ponder:
1. Who are the adult learners in my instructional context and what strategies might be most effective in working with them?
2. What fears do I have about working with adult learners? What might I do about confronting or challenging my fears?
3. To what degree do I hold the same patience with adult learners as I do with my students?

CSTP
Center for Strengthening the
Teaching Profession
253-752-2082
www.cstp-wa.org

Funding for the
Teacher Leader Self-Assessment
provided by the
Office of Superintendent
of Public Instruction.
2009

COLLABORATIVE WORK

TEACHER LEADER SELF-ASSESSMENT

Teacher leaders use skills and strategies to work with a variety of people to achieve multiple goals. Tools such as norm setting and protocols allow leaders to facilitate groups in reaching agreement even while working with diverse points of view. Leaders document meetings, access appropriate resources and delegate responsibility to help the group move toward solutions. Teacher leaders adjust their facilitation based upon the size of the group, the familiarity the group members have with one another, and the length of time they will work together.

CONTEXT: Think about a collaborative leadership role such as grade level chair, department head, building, district, state or federal work, association work, professional organizations or a role that you would like to assume in the future. Keep that context in mind as you complete the *Collaborative Work* self-assessment.

Collaborative Skills	Consistently	Usually	Occasionally	Rarely	Evidence/experience used to determine ratings.
I develop, teach, and effectively use norms of collaboration to ensure collaborative and organizational skills are embedded in all meetings.					
I use conflict and mediation skills to ensure that groups collaborate to achieve common outcomes.					
I use strategies including protocols as tools for collaborative processes.					
I show that I value diverse opinions as an important element of problem solving.					
I match my language to the situation.					
I share responsibility and leadership to enhance the collaborative work process.					
I hold myself accountable to the group's goals and outcomes so that the group is successful.					

What does this assessment tell me about my collaborative skill strengths? What skills do I need to deepen my collaborative expertise?

Organizational Skills	Consistently	Usually	Occasionally	Rarely	Evidence/experience used to determine ratings.
I successfully facilitate meetings that actively engage participants.					
I document meetings to record the work and thinking of the group.					
I move the group to task completion using appropriate processes.					
I know multiple resources and access them when appropriate.					
I delegate responsibility to enhance efficiency.					

What does this assessment tell me about my strengths in organizational skills? What organizational skills do I need to deepen?

Dispositions	Consistently	Usually	Occasionally	Rarely	Evidence/experience used to determine ratings.
I know what to compromise and when, in order to move the work forward.					
I read the group using verbal and non-verbal cues to successfully adjust facilitation.					
I am willing to admit when I'm wrong or don't know.					
I communicate honestly and courageously.					
It is my desire to work with adults.					
My passion motivates others.					

What does this assessment tell me about how the strengths of my dispositions enhance collaborative work? What dispositions do I need to develop to be more effective in collaborating?

Given all of my strengths and areas of need in *collaborative work*, where do I fall on this continuum?

Refining	Proficient	Developing	Emerging
I share responsibility in order to develop collaborative leadership and empower others. I actively seek new tools that help groups function effectively and introduce them when appropriate. I believe in the power of collaboration and model that belief in ways that motivate others.	I consistently use a wide variety of skills and strategies such as norm setting and protocols to achieve goals with groups representing diverse points of view. I document meetings, access appropriate resources and delegate responsibility to help the group move toward solutions. I am flexible in facilitation and open to compromise in order to move toward common goals.	The skills and strategies I use with groups meet with some success. I strive to master the organizational skills needed to help groups move toward solutions. I am actively working to demonstrate my commitment to collaborative work processes.	I recognize the power of collaboration and seek to increase my skills in working with colleagues. I have observed effective organizational strategies that I will work to develop. I desire to work with adults but face challenges in facilitating collaboration.

What patterns do I see in my *Collaborative Work* self-assessment? What are my next steps?

Additional questions to ponder:
1. Who do I know with exceptional collaborative skills? Specifically how do they model collaboration?
2. How could I gain more experience facilitating collaborative groups?
3. Where does collaboration work the best? Are there situations in which collaboration is not helpful?

CSTP
Center for Strengthening the
Teaching Profession
253-752-2082
www.cstp-wa.org

Funding for the
Teacher Leader Self-Assessment
provided by the
Office of Superintendent
of Public Instruction.
2009

COMMUNICATION

Teacher leaders use effective communication strategies to build relationships and help working groups accomplish tasks. They are expert listeners who use their technical skills to facilitate large and small groups. They understand the culture and contributions of group members and honor all perspectives.

CONTEXT: Think about a current leadership role in which communication is key to your success, such as department chair, coach, mentor, or a role that you would like to assume in the future. Keep that context in mind as you complete the *Communication* self-assessment.

Building Relationships	Consistently	Usually	Occasionally	Rarely	Evidence/experience used to determine ratings.
I maintain an open mind while building positive relationships.					
I use the diversity of the group as a strength to promote cultural competency.					
I adapt my communication skills for the unique needs of adult learners in a group.					
I invite and honor diverse views.					
I embrace healthy, productive discussions.					

What does this assessment tell me about my strengths in building relationship through communication? What knowledge and skills do I need to develop to be more effective in building relationships through communication?

Technical Skills	Consistently	Usually	Occasionally	Rarely	Evidence/experience used to determine ratings.
I facilitate learning-focused discussions in a way that involves all stakeholders.					
I give and receive feedback honestly, openly and constructively.					
I understand and demonstrate deep listening skills, such as paraphrasing and asking clarifying questions.					
I ask the right question to get the feedback necessary to complete the assigned task.					
I lead data-driven dialogue in a manner that facilitates informed decisions and appropriate actions.					
I use conversation, dialogue and/or discussion based on the context and task.					
I synthesize, summarize and use mediation to move large or small groups to decisions.					
I effectively use technology to enhance communication.					
My written communication (i.e. memos, minutes, email) effectively supports goals/purposes.					
I use effective strategies for setting up spaces, organizing materials and pacing activities to enhance communication.					

What does this assessment tell me about my strengths in technical communication skills? What knowledge and skills do I need to deepen my technical communication expertise?

Dispositions	Consistently	Usually	Occasionally	Rarely	Evidence/experience used to determine ratings.
I honor and welcome all perspectives.					
I presume positive intentions that all group members are working in the best interest of student learning.					
I value the professional expertise and experience of group members.					
I foster a sense of community.					

What does this assessment tell me about how the strength of my dispositions enhances my communication? What dispositions do I need to develop to be more effective in communicating?

Given all of my strengths and areas of need in *communication*, where do I fall on this continuum?

Refining	Proficient	Developing	Emerging
I empower others to build relationships through effective communication. I help others develop technical communication skills and hone their ability to facilitate group discussion and dialogue. I model inclusive practices that support the contributions of every group member toward a common goal.	I build relationships through effective communication in order to help working groups accomplish tasks. I use my technical skills to effectively facilitate large and small groups, learning-focused conversations and data-driven dialogue. I value the professional experience and expertise of others and foster a sense of community.	I have some success using effective communication to build relationships. My technical skills are effective in some contexts but not all. I am actively working to demonstrate that I value the professional experience and expertise of others.	I am aware of the importance of effective communication in building relationships. I intend to increase my technical skills in order to become a more effective communicator. I strive to approach this work with an open mind in order to build community.

What patterns do I see in my *Communication* self-assessment? What are my next steps?

Additional questions to ponder:
1. Who in my professional context exemplifies effective communication? What do I admire about his/her competence in communicating?
2. What fears do I have about communicating with adults? What might I do about confronting or challenging my fears?

CSTP
Center for Strengthening the Teaching Profession
253-752-2082
www.cstp-wa.org

Funding for the Teacher Leader Self-Assessment provided by the Office of Superintendent of Public Instruction.
2009

KNOWLEDGE OF CONTENT AND PEDAGOGY

TEACHER LEADER SELF-ASSESSMENT

Teacher leadership builds on the foundation of accomplished teaching. Teacher leaders initially demonstrate excellence in instructional contexts and continue to grow as they take on leadership positions in other contexts within the larger system. Content, instruction and assessment expertise is crucial to credible teacher leaders. Knowledge of content and pedagogy is developed in formal and informal roles and settings, with the expectation that learning in collaboration with colleagues is critical to both developing and refining teacher leadership.

CONTEXT: Think about a current leadership role, such as team leader, department chair, content specialist or coach, or a role that you would like to assume in the future. Keep that context in mind as you complete the *Knowledge of Content and Pedagogy* self-assessment.

Knowledge and Skills	Consistently	Usually	Occasionally	Rarely	Evidence/experience used to determine ratings.
I actively engage in studying and applying current professional literature and pursue professional learning opportunities focused on content, instruction and assessment.					
I understand how the curriculum standards and expectations in my classroom build on what comes before and contributes to what students will experience next.					
I understand how to build my instruction based on my knowledge of students.					
I am confident in my core values, balance my views with other's perspectives and continually reexamine my practices.					
I understand the linkages between content expectations, instructional materials and various assessments -- formative and summative; classroom, district and state.					
I use student work to inform my instruction and regularly adjust my plan based on student strengths and needs.					
I interpret multiple sources of data and use implications to improve teaching and learning in my classroom, school and district.					
I apply my knowledge of cultural competency to engage my students with appropriate content and supporting materials.					
While teaching, I select from a repertoire of effective instructional strategies to engage students in learning.					
I capitalize on multiple entry points to increase teacher content knowledge and classroom application.					
I use data to improve instruction in my classroom and facilitate colleagues' skills to do the same.					

What does this assessment tell me about the strengths of my knowledge of content and pedagogy? What content knowledge and skills do I need to deepen my expertise?

Dispositions	Consistently	Usually	Occasionally	Rarely	Evidence/experience used to determine ratings.
I exhibit a belief in life-long learning as a foundation for education.					
I demonstrate reflective practice, believing the improvement of teaching and learning begins with the teacher.					
I am committed to supporting the growth of colleagues.					
I enjoy the complexity of problem-solving instructional opportunity gaps, welcoming and honoring the contributions of others (parents, students, colleagues).					

What does this assessment tell me about how the strength of my dispositions enhances my understanding of content and pedagogy? What dispositions do I need to develop to deepen my instructional practice?

Given all of my strengths and areas of need in *Knowledge of content and pedagogy, where do I fall on this continuum?*

Refining	Proficient	Developing	Emerging
I consistently and fluently apply my expert knowledge of content, pedagogy and assessment with my students and frequently find myself leading colleagues in this area in both formal and informal roles. I constantly seek new learning challenges and opportunities for deep professional reflection.	I consistently and fluently apply my expert knowledge of content, pedagogy and assessment with my students and I am regularly invited to share my practices with colleagues in order to improve teaching and learning. I thrive on new learning challenges and continuously reflect on my practice.	I am increasing my expert use of the content, pedagogy and assessment skills needed to be effective with my students and learn from and with my colleagues. I accept learning opportunities with enthusiasm and am working to develop reflective practices.	I reflect on my own practice and solicit and value the input of others in order to build my personal capacity in content, pedagogy and assessment.

What patterns do I see in my *Knowledge of Content and Pedagogy* self-assessment? What are my next steps?

Additional questions to ponder:
1. What strategies keep me aware of research findings, a variety of perspectives and thought leaders in my content area?
2. How do I contribute to my learning community and to the broader profession at large?
3. How do I build a community that keeps me professionally relevant?

CSTP
Center for Strengthening the
Teaching Profession
253-752-2082
www.cstp-wa.org

Funding for the
Teacher Leader Self-Assessment
provided by the
Office of Superintendent
of Public Instruction,
2009

SYSTEMS THINKING

TEACHER LEADER SELF-ASSESSMENT

Effective teacher leaders understand that all decisions are made within the context of a larger system. Each decision made affects the system as a whole. Accountability and credibility is shared.

CONTEXT: Think about a goal, plan or project you have completed or want to complete. Think about how the decisions about your project affect the systems within your classroom, team, building, district or state. Keep that context in mind as you complete the *Systems Thinking* self-assessment.

Working Effectively Within a System	Consistently	Usually	Occasionally	Rarely	Evidence/experience used to determine ratings.
I recognize multiple layers of organization within a system as a whole.					
I understand the power structure and how decisions are made in various contexts within a system.					
I understand and work within the rules of formal and informal established hierarchies to complete the task(s).					
I understand and value the importance of garnering stakeholder support.					
I understand and manage resistance as a legitimate element of working within a system.					
I facilitate collective or collaborative inquiry processes and practices within a system.					
I pose the right questions at the right time to the right people.					
I understand how finances and resources are allocated (e.g., projects, schools, system wide) and can access resources when necessary.					

What does this assessment tell me about my strengths when working effectively within a system? What knowledge and skills do I need to develop to be more effective to work within a system?

Skills of Advocacy	Consistently	Usually	Occasionally	Rarely	Evidence/experience used to determine ratings.
I set achievable goals considering system constraints.					
I create and implement plans to meet goals.					
I consider capacity for sustainability when creating goals and implementing plans.					
I identify and influence key decision makers.					
I craft and deliver effective messages to stakeholders and key decision makers.					
I mobilize the right people into action.					

What does this assessment tell me about strengths in my advocacy skills within systems thinking? What advocacy skills do I need to develop to become more effective in systems thinking?

Dispositions	Consistently	Usually	Occasionally	Rarely	Evidence/experience used to determine ratings.
I am keenly interested in the larger/bigger picture of how decisions impact a system.					
I am attuned to relationships and how they influence decisions.					
I have the ability to "read" people and situations.					
I embrace the opportunity to work with those who hold dissenting views.					

What does this assessment tell me about my dispositions related to systems thinking? What dispositions do I need to develop to become a more effective systems thinker?

Given all of my strengths and areas of need in *systems thinking*, where do I fall on this continuum?

Refining	Proficient	Developing	Emerging
I affect change through finding new and effective ways to work as a systems leader and empowering others to do the same.	I effectively negotiate the inner-workings of a system, involving key decision makers and stakeholders along the way.	I exhibit some knowledge, skills, and dispositions necessary for being an effective systems thinker both alone and with others.	I participate in and am aware of effective systems thinking. I can identify observable skills, knowledge and dispositions in others.

What patterns do I notice in my *Systems Thinking* self-assessment? What are my next steps for developing knowledge, skills and/or dispositions in systems thinking?

Additional questions to ponder:
1. How does my school/district communicate the stakeholders involved in decision-making?
2. What evidence of effective systems thinking/learning do I see in my school or district?
3. What would I do when confronted with a dissenting view of my proposal?
4. How would I determine next steps after an initial proposal was rejected?

CSTP
Center for Strengthening the
Teaching Profession
253-752-2082
www.cstp-wa.org

Funding for the
Teacher Leader Self-Assessment
provided by the
Office of Superintendent
of Public Instruction.
2009

Resource C3

School and District Capacity to Support Teacher Leadership

ESTABLISHING A SUPPORTIVE ENVIRONMENT

School and District Capacity to Support Teacher Leadership

For teacher leaders to thrive and effectively impact colleagues' practice, school and district leaders must create an environment that provides credibility for their work and supports opportunities for professional growth and collaboration.

NOTE: *Assessment refers to "school or district leaders," but this tool can be modified to assess capacity in other levels of the system.*

CONTEXT: This assessment for system capacity for teacher leadership focuses on the _____ school _____ district _____ other _____ .

Clear Goals, Roles, Expectations	Consistently	Usually	Occasionally	Rarely	Evidence/experience used to determine ratings.
School or district leaders build coherence and continuity across the system with flexibility to utilize teacher leaders according to their talents and school needs.					
School or district leaders ensure clarity of roles by providing sample job descriptions, task contracts, expectations agreements, and common commitments.					
School or district leaders adjust workload, match duties with expertise and prioritize within resource limits.					

What does this indicate about the clarity of teacher leaders' roles and responsibilities in our system?

What resources and practices would make our system more effective at providing clarity for teacher leadership?

Professional Culture	Consistently	Usually	Occasionally	Rarely	Evidence/experience used to determine ratings.
School or district leaders emphasize collaborative team learning practices in the school/district culture.					
School or district leaders maintain focus on teaching and learning through data driven decisions.					
School or district leaders provide teacher leaders with regular feedback on instructional practice.					
School or district leaders safeguard the teacher leaders' relationships with peers.					
School or district leaders ensure appropriate confidentiality.					
School or district leaders provide opportunities to lead that advance both personal expertise and systems goals.					
School or district leaders examine evidence of teacher leader impact and collect data on performance measures in order to plan next steps in professional development.					

What does this assessment indicate about how our system's professional culture provides a supportive environment for teacher leaders?

What resources and practices would improve our professional culture for supporting teacher leaders?

WORKING WITH ADULT LEARNERS • COMMUNICATION • COLLABORATIVE WORK • KNOWLEDGE OF CONTENT AND PEDAGOGY • SYSTEMS THINKING

Leadership Collaboration	Consistently	Usually	Occasionally	Rarely	Evidence/experience used to determine ratings.
School or district leaders regularly convene teacher leaders to share successes, challenges and best practices.					
School or district leaders regularly convene principals and teacher leaders to collaborate, review and plan strategic approaches.					
School or district leaders provide timely access to needed information, resources and school personnel (i.e. leadership, curriculum, instruction, school improvement).					

What does this assessment indicate about collaborative opportunities for teacher leaders in our system?

What resources and practices would improve collaborative opportunities for teacher leaders in our system?

Human Relations/Personnel	Consistently	Usually	Occasionally	Rarely	Evidence/experience used to determine ratings.
School or district leaders facilitate recruitment of new leaders.					
School or district leaders connect teacher leaders to mentor, job coach or peer network for support.					
School or district leaders ensure teacher leaders are compensated for additional workload (salary, release time or stipend).					
School or district leaders ensure that clock hours or credits are offered for professional learning opportunities for teacher leaders.					

What does this assessment indicate about HR practices that create a supportive environment for teacher leaders?

What practices would improve the effectiveness of HR practices for supporting the work of teacher leaders?

Given all of our strengths and areas of need in *Establishing a Supportive Environment*, where do we fall on this continuum?

LOW CAPACITY		PARTIAL CAPACITY		HIGH CAPACITY	
Consistently low capacity	Low but beginning to grow; some evidence of developing key resources	Medium or high capacity in some areas, low in others	Processes/resources in place to move toward increased capacity	Consistent application, established mastery achieved	Consistently high capacity with processes/resources in place to sustain high levels

What patterns are evident in our capacity to *Establish a Supportive Environment*?

What are our next steps?

Additional questions to ponder:
1. Are the systems we have developed sustainable?
2. What data or evidence can we look at to continually assess our effectiveness?

CSTP
Center for Strengthening the Teaching Profession
253-752-2082
www.cstp-wa.org

Funding for the School and District Capacity Tool to Support Teacher Leadership provided by the Office of Superintendent of Public Instruction.
2010

WORKING WITH ADULT LEARNERS ● COMMUNICATION ● COLLABORATIVE WORK ● KNOWLEDGE OF CONTENT AND PEDAGOGY ● SYSTEMS THINKING

SYSTEM VISION AND ALIGNMENT

School and District Capacity to Support Teacher Leadership

For teacher leaders to effectively understand their role, district and building leaders must support them by clearly communicating the vision, rationale, and purpose for their work.

CONTEXT: This assessment for system capacity for teacher leadership focuses on the _____ school _____ district _____ other _____ .

NOTE: *Assessment refers to "school or district leaders," but this tool can be modified to assess capacity in other levels of the system.*

School and District Leadership	Consistently	Usually	Occasionally	Rarely	Evidence/experience used to determine ratings.
School or district leaders provide a clear vision, rationale, and moral purpose for teacher leadership.					
School or district leaders develop a culture of adult learning that supports teacher leaders' growth.					
School or district leaders identify criteria for success for teacher leadership using multiple measures and performance indicators.					
School or district leaders provide credibility, public recognition, and authority for teacher leaders.					
School or district leaders build trust and maintain problem-solving focus.					
School or district leaders practice effective communication to ensure information is shared across the system.					

What does this indicate about our system's strengths in communicating the importance of teacher leadership?

What areas should be developed to be more effective in communicating and promoting teacher leadership?

District Alignment	Consistently	Usually	Occasionally	Rarely	Evidence/experience used to determine ratings.
District leaders support the utilization of teacher leaders.					
District leaders provide School Board orientation and information to generate support.					
District leaders communicate with teacher union about roles, workload, and impact.					
District leaders support opportunities for local, regional and statewide committee work with a plan to bring learning back to school and district.					
District leaders ensure other system leaders understand necessary teacher leader supports.					
District leaders align teacher leadership with district initiatives and school improvement efforts.					

What does this assessment indicate about our strengths in aligning teacher leadership with district support?

What areas should be developed to be more effective in aligning district initiatives with teacher leadership?

WORKING WITH ADULT LEARNERS • COMMUNICATION • COLLABORATIVE WORK • KNOWLEDGE OF CONTENT AND PEDAGOGY • SYSTEMS THINKING

School Level Implementation	Consistently	Usually	Occasionally	Rarely	Evidence/experience used to determine ratings.
School leaders demonstrate support for and effective utilization of teacher leaders.					
School leaders articulate clear understanding of necessary teacher leader supports.					
School leaders align teacher leadership with school improvement efforts.					

What does this assessment indicate about our strengths in aligning teacher leadership with school and principal support?

What areas should be developed to be more effective in aligning school improvement with teacher leadership?

Given our strengths and areas of need in *System Vision and Alignment*, where do we fall on this continuum?

LOW CAPACITY		PARTIAL CAPACITY		HIGH CAPACITY	
Consistently low capacity	Low but beginning to grow; some evidence of developing key resources	Medium or high capacity in some areas, low in others	Processes/resources in place to move toward increased capacity	Consistent application, established mastery achieved	Consistently high capacity with processes/resources in place to sustain high levels

What patterns are evident in our *System Vision and Alignment*?

What are our next steps?

Additional questions to ponder:
1. What positive and negative experiences has the district/system had that help us to reflect on working with teacher leaders?
2. Who are the teacher leaders in our instructional context and what strategies might be most effective in supporting them?
3. What barriers and constraints have we experienced while working with teacher leaders? What might we do about confronting or overcoming these barriers?

CSTP
Center for Strengthening the Teaching Profession
253-752-2082
www.cstp-wa.org

Funding for the School and District Capacity Tool to Support Teacher Leadership provided by the Office of Superintendent of Public Instruction.
2010

WORKING WITH ADULT LEARNERS • COMMUNICATION • COLLABORATIVE WORK • KNOWLEDGE OF CONTENT AND PEDAGOGY • SYSTEMS THINKING

PROFESSIONAL DEVELOPMENT

A professional learning community promotes continuous learning and supports teacher leaders' development in working with adult learners. Opportunities are provided for teacher leaders in order to develop skills in effective communication, collaboration, content and pedagogy, and systems thinking.

NOTE: *Assessment refers to "school or district leaders," but this tool can be modified to assess capacity in other levels of the system.*

CONTEXT: This assessment for system capacity for teacher leadership focuses on the ____ school ____ district ____ other _____ .

Knowledge, Skills and Opportunities	Consistently	Usually	Occasionally	Rarely	Evidence/experience used to determine ratings.
School and district leaders provide opportunities for skill development in working with adult learners.					
School and district leaders provide opportunities for skill development in communications.					
School and district leaders provide opportunities for skill development in collaborative work.					
School and district leaders provide opportunities for skill development in content, pedagogy and assessment.					
School and district leaders provide opportunities for skill development in systems thinking.					

What does this indicate about our strengths in providing professional development for teacher leaders?

What knowledge, skills and opportunities should be developed to be more effective in providing professional development for teacher leaders?

Given our strengths and areas of need in *Professional Development*, where do we fall on this continuum?

LOW CAPACITY		PARTIAL CAPACITY		HIGH CAPACITY	
Consistently low capacity	Low but beginning to grow; some evidence of developing key resources	Medium or high capacity in some areas, low in others	Processes/resources in place to move toward increased capacity	Consistent application, established mastery achieved	Consistently high capacity with processes/resources in place to sustain high levels

What patterns are evident in our *Professional Development* to support teacher leaders?

What are our next steps?

Additional questions to ponder:
1. How will we know what teacher leaders don't know so the appropriate professional development can be provided?
2. How can we assess the effectiveness of the professional development provided?

CSTP
Center for Strengthening the
Teaching Profession
253-752-2082
www.cstp-wa.org

Funding for the School and District Capacity Tool to Support Teacher Leadership provided by the Office of Superintendent of Public Instruction.
2010

WORKING WITH ADULT LEARNERS • COMMUNICATION • COLLABORATIVE WORK • KNOWLEDGE OF CONTENT AND PEDAGOGY • SYSTEMS THINKING

ACCESS TO RESOURCES

School and District Capacity to Support Teacher Leadership

School leaders who successfully work with teacher leaders build their professional capacity by providing equitable access to a variety of resources.

CONTEXT: This assessment for system capacity for teacher leadership focuses on the _____ school _____ district _____ other _____ .

NOTE: *Assessment refers to "school or district leaders," but this tool can be modified to assess capacity in other levels of the system.*

Resources: Data/Technology Support	Consistently	Usually	Occasionally	Rarely	Evidence/experience used to determine ratings.
Teacher leaders have access to data systems (e.g., attendance, achievement, demographics).					
Teacher leaders have access to training in use of data systems, web-based information and data analysis (e.g., district information and student achievement).					
Teacher leaders have access to needed technology (e.g., interactive whiteboard, document viewer, and online collaborative tools).					

What does this indicate about how our school or district provides data and technology support for teacher leaders' work?

What additional data/technology supports are needed to support teacher leaders' work?

Resources: Collaboration	Consistently	Usually	Occasionally	Rarely	Evidence/experience used to determine ratings.
School or district leaders ensure that teacher leaders have access to training in how to effectively facilitate collaborative learning teams.					
School or district leaders provide varied opportunities for teacher leadership (e.g., district, school, community).					
School or district leaders provide time for effective planning and collaboration outside of the teaching assignment (e.g., building team and teacher leadership meetings).					

How much time is allocated for teacher leaders to collaborate by the building/district?

What additional opportunities would enhance teacher leaders' ability to collaborate?

WORKING WITH ADULT LEARNERS • COMMUNICATION • COLLABORATIVE WORK • KNOWLEDGE OF CONTENT AND PEDAGOGY • SYSTEMS THINKING

Resources: Materials	Consistently	Usually	Occasionally	Rarely	Evidence/experience used to determine ratings.
Teacher leaders have access to protocols and tools for adult learning (e.g., planning, facilitation).					
Teacher leadership materials are made available (e.g., books, videos, professional journals).					
Teacher leaders have access to record-keeping tools.					

How are teacher leaders provided with needed materials and resources?

What additional materials might support teacher leaders' work? What systems will keep resources up-to-date?

Given the strengths and areas of need in *Access to Resources*, where does our system fall on this continuum?

LOW CAPACITY		PARTIAL CAPACITY		HIGH CAPACITY	
Consistently low capacity	Low but beginning to grow; some evidence of developing key resources	Medium or high capacity in some areas, low in others	Processes/resources in place to move toward increased capacity	Consistent application, established mastery achieved	Consistently high capacity with processes/resources in place to sustain high levels

What patterns are evident in the *Access to Resources* we provide to support teacher leadership?

What are our next steps?

Additional question to ponder: 1. What system can we develop to continually assess needed resources?	CSTP Center for Strengthening the Teaching Profession 253-752-2082 www.cstp-wa.org	Funding for the School and District Capacity Tool to Support Teacher Leadership provided by the Office of Superintendent of Public Instruction. 2010

WORKING WITH ADULT LEARNERS • COMMUNICATION • COLLABORATIVE WORK • KNOWLEDGE OF CONTENT AND PEDAGOGY • SYSTEMS THINKING

Resource D

Case-Writing Seminar Part 1: Sample Agenda

Participants are asked to bring a laptop computer and flash drive. Facilitator provides casebooks and teacher leadership references, printer and paper, extension cord, surge protector, chart paper and easel, markers, sticky notes, highlighters, dictionary, thesaurus, and snacks! (All times are estimates. It's important to be flexible!)

1. Welcome and Introductions (15 minutes)

2. Establishing Norms for Our Work (15 minutes)
   a. Discuss the importance of confidentiality.
   b. Talk about warm and cool feedback.

3. Introduction to Case Methods (15 minutes)
   a. Explore the purpose of the case-writing seminar: to develop a set of cases that can be tools for inquiry into the dilemmas teacher leaders face.
   b. Discuss the following benefits of using cases:
      (1) Create models of teachers as leaders who can teach others.
      (2) Engage in collaborative analysis, reflection, and dialogue on teacher leadership.
      (3) Explore complex, messy challenges that don't have easy answers.
      (4) Help teacher leaders develop effective communication and problem-solving skills.
      (5) Learn to examine different points of view.

(6) Look at a situation, pursue ideas, and test hypotheses, while using the case to reflect on experience.

(7) Give teacher leaders an opportunity, through writing their stories, to reflect and dig deeper in analyzing their experience.

4. So What Is Teacher Leadership? (1 hour)

   a. Read the definitions handout.

   b. Work with a partner to identify themes or attributes that are common to many of the definitions.

   c. Reach agreement on a definition.

5. Review the Assigned Case (homework) (2 hours)

   a. Make notes in the margins and highlight key passages.

   b. Raise questions about the case.

6. Format of a Case Discussion—What Is the Case About?

   a. What happened? Who are the characters?

   b. What are the leadership dilemmas?

7. What Makes a Good Case? (30 minutes)

   a. What writing techniques make the case engaging?

   b. What does the case tell you about the author? How did you learn this?

8. Not All Stories Are Cases (30 minutes)

   a. To call something a case, one is making "a theoretical claim that it is a 'case of something' or an instance of a larger class" (Shulman, 1986, p. 11).

   b. What class or type of dilemma do teacher leaders frequently encounter in their work?

   c. What is this a case of? Is it complex? Is it a case of more than one thing?

9. Getting Started! (2 hours)

   a. Choose a recent leadership issue you've experienced.

   b. Write freely describing your dilemma for 10 minutes.

   c. Share your dilemma with a partner.

   d. Answer your partner's questions; clarify events.

   e. Share with the group—is this a leadership dilemma?

10. Writing Tips (15 minutes)

11. Draft Your Case! (2 hours)

12. Partners Review Drafts and Offer Feedback (1 hour)

13. Share Drafts with the Group—What Is This a Case Of? (2 hours)

14. Wrap-Up (30 minutes)

    a. Commit to keep writing and come to Part 2 of the seminar with a complete rough draft.

Resource E

Case-Writing Seminar Part 2: Sample Agenda

All participants are asked to bring two copies of their current draft to the retreat. Facilitator provides casebooks and teacher leadership references, printer and paper, extension cord, surge protector, chart paper and easel, markers, sticky notes, highlighters, dictionary, thesaurus, and snacks! (All times are estimates. It's important to be flexible!)

1. Progress Reports and Status Check on Drafts (1 hour)
   - What kind of support do you need now?

2. Group Analysis and Discussion of One Case Writer's Draft Case (Author's Chair) (1 hour)
   - Any volunteers?

3. Review Writing Tips—Q & A About Our Work (30 minutes)
   - Sign up for a one-on-one writing conference with facilitator.

4. Continued Revision (2 hours)
   - Partners read and share feedback on each other's drafts and offer suggestions.

5. Group Analysis and Discussion of Second Case Writer's Draft Case (Author's Chair) (1 hour)

6. Writing Time (2 hours)

7. Review Openings of Cases (1 hour)

8. Group Analysis and Discussion of Third Case Writer's Draft Case (Author's Chair) (1 hour)

9. Status Check on Drafts (1 hour)
   • What kind of support do you need now?

10. Group Analysis and Discussion of Fourth Case Writer's Draft Case (Author's Chair) (1 hour)

11. Review Titles (30 minutes)
    • Brainstorm alternate possible titles.

12. Group Analysis and Discussion of Fifth Case Writer's Draft Case (Author's Chair) (1 hour)

13. Group Analysis and Discussion of Sixth Case Writer's Draft Case (Author's Chair) (1 hour)

14. What Are These Cases Of? (1 hour)
    • Generate matrix.

15. Identify Discussion Questions (1 hour)
    • What questions does each draft case raise?

16. Work Commitments—Guidelines Leading to Publication (10 minutes)

17. Evaluation of the Case-Writing Seminar (10 minutes)

18. Wrap-Up (10 Minutes)

References

Bonoma, T. V. (1981). Questions and answers about case learning. *Harvard Business School, Note 9–582–059.* Cambridge, MA: President and Fellows of Harvard College.

Carpenter, T. P., Fennema, E., Peterson, P. L., Chiang, C., & Loef, M. (1989). Using knowledge of children's mathematics thinking in classroom teaching: An experimental study. *American Educational Research Journal, 26*(4), 499–531.

Childress, S., Elmore, R. F., Grossman, A. S., & Johnson, S. M. (2007). *Managing school districts for high performance: Cases in public education leadership.* Cambridge, MA: Harvard Education Press.

Childs-Bowen, D., Moller, G., & Scrivner, J. (2000). Principals: Leaders of leaders. *National Association of Secondary School Principals (NASSP) Bulletin, 84*(616), 27–34.

Chrislip, D. D. (2002). *The collaborative leadership fieldbook: A guide for citizens and civic leaders.* San Francisco, CA: Jossey-Bass.

Cohen, D. K., & Hill, H. C. (2001). *Learning policy: When state education reform works.* New Haven, CT: Yale University Press.

Desimone, L. M. (2009). Improving impact studies of teachers' professional development: Toward better conceptualizations and measures. *Educational Researcher, 38*(3), 181–199.

Dozier, T. K. (2007). Turning good teachers into great leaders. *Educational Leadership, 65*(1), 54–59. Available from http://www.ascd.org/publications/educational-leadership

Elmore, R. (2000). *Building a new structure for school leadership.* Washington, DC: Albert Shanker Institute.

Elmore, R. F. (2002). *Bridging the gap between standards and achievement: The imperative for professional development in education.* Washington, DC: Albert Shanker Institute.

Elmore, R. F., & Burney, D. (1997). *Investing in teacher learning: Staff development and instructional improvement: Community District 2, New York City.* Philadelphia, PA: Consortium for Policy Research in Education.

Fisher, R., & Ury, W. (1981). *Getting to yes: Negotiating agreement without giving in.* New York, NY: Penguin Books.

Fullan, M. (1993). *Change forces: Probing the depth of education reform.* New York, NY: Falmer.

Fullan, M. (1994). Teacher leadership: A failure to conceptualize. In D. R. Walling (Ed.), *Teachers as leaders: Perspectives on the professional development of teachers* (pp. 241–253). Bloomington, IN: Phi Delta Kappan Educational Foundation.

Fullan, M. (1999). *Change forces: The sequel.* Philadelphia, PA: Falmer Press.

Fullan, M., Hill, P., & Crévola, C. (2006). *Breakthrough.* Thousand Oaks, CA: Corwin.

Gabriel, J. G. (2005). *How to thrive as a teacher leader.* Alexandria, VA: ASCD.

Garet, M. S., Porter, A. C., Desimone, L. M., Birman, B., & Yoon, K. S. (2001). What makes professional development effective? Analysis of a national sample of teachers. *American Educational Research Journal, 38*(3), 915–945.

Garmston, R. J., & Wellman, B. M. (1998). *The adaptive school: A sourcebook for developing collaborative groups.* Norwood, MA: Christopher-Gordon.

Goldenstein, D., Barnett-Clarke, C., & Jackson, B. (1994). *Mathematics teaching cases: Fractions, decimals, ratios, and percents. Hard to teach and hard to learn?* Portsmouth, NH: Heinemann.

Golich, V. L., Boyer, M., Franko, P., & Lamy, S. (2000). *The ABCs of case teaching: Pew case studies in international affairs.* Washington, DC: Institute for the Study of Diplomacy.

Greenwood, G. E., & Parkay, F. W. (1989). *Case studies in teacher decision making.* New York, NY: Random House.

Guskey, T. R. (1994). Results-oriented professional development: In search of an optimal mix of effective practices. *Journal of Staff Development, 15*(4), 42–50.

Harrington, H. L., Quinn-Leering, K., & Hodson, L. (1996). Written case analyses and critical reflection. *Teaching and Teacher Education, 11,* 203–214.

Heifitz, R. (1994). *Leadership without easy answers.* Cambridge, MA: Belknap Press.

Johnson, S. M., & Donaldson, M. L. (2007). Overcoming the obstacles to leadership. *Educational Leadership, 65*(1), 8–13.

Katzenmeyer, M., & Moller, G. (2009). *Awakening a sleeping giant: Leadership development for teachers* (3rd ed.). Thousand Oaks, CA: Corwin.

Kennedy, M. M. (1998). *Form and substance in in-service teacher education* (Research Monograph No. 13). Arlington, VA: National Science Foundation.

Kouzes, J. M., & Posner, B. Z. (1999). *Encouraging the heart: A leader's guide to rewarding and recognizing others.* San Francisco, CA: Jossey-Bass.

Kowalski, T. J., Weaver, R. A., & Hensen, K. T. (1990). *Case studies in teaching.* New York, NY: Longman.

Lambert, L. (2003). *Leadership capacity for lasting school improvement.* Alexandria, VA: ASCD.

Leinhardt, G., & Green, J. G. (1986). The cognitive skill of teaching. *Journal of Educational Psychology, 78,* 75–95.

Levin, B. (1999). The role of discussion in case pedagogy: Who learns what? And how? In M. A. Lundberg, B. B. Levin, & H. L. Harrington (Eds.), *Who learns what from cases and how? The research base for teaching and learning with cases* (pp. 139–163). Mahwah, NJ: Lawrence Erlbaum.

Lieberman, A., & Friedrich, L. (2007). Teachers, writers, leaders. *Educational Leadership, 65*(1), 42–47.

Lieberman, A., & Friedrich, L. (2010). *How teachers become leaders: Learning for practice and research.* New York, NY: Teachers College Press.

Lieberman, A., & Wood, D. R. (2003). *Inside the National Writing Project: Connecting network learning and classroom teaching.* New York, NY: Teachers College Press.

Lord, B., Cress, K., & Miller, B. (2008). Teacher leadership in support of large scale mathematics and science education reform. In M. M. Mangin & S. R. Stoelinga (Eds.), *Effective teacher leadership: Using research to inform and reform* (pp. 55–76). New York, NY: Teachers College Press.

Loucks-Horsley, S. (1998). Foreword. In B. Miller, J. Moon, & S. Elko. *Teacher leadership in mathematics and science: Casebook and facilitator's guide* (pp. iv–v). Portsmouth, NH: Heinemann.

Lundeberg, M. A., Levin, B. B., & Harrington, H. L. (1999). *Who learns what from cases and how? The research base for teaching with cases.* Mahwah, NJ: Lawrence Erlbaum.

Mangin, M. M. (2008). The influence of organizational design on instructional teacher leadership. In M. M. Mangin & S. R. Stoelinga (Eds.), *Effective teacher leadership: Using research to inform and reform* (pp. 77–98). New York, NY: Teachers College Press.

Mangin, M. M., & Stoelinga, S. R. (2008). *Effective teacher leadership: Using research to inform and reform.* New York, NY: Teachers College Press.

Manno, C. M., & Firestone, W. A. (2008). Content is the subject: How teacher leaders with different subject knowledge interact with teachers. In M. M. Mangin & S. R. Stoelinga (Eds.), *Effective teacher leadership: Using research to inform and reform* (pp. 36–54). New York, NY: Teachers College Press.

Mattingly, C. (1991). Normative reflections on practical actions: Two learning experiments in reflective storytelling. In D. Schon (Ed.), *The reflective turn: Case studies in and on educational practice* (pp. 235–257). New York, NY: Teachers College Press.

McDonald, J. P., Mohr, N., Dichter, A., & McDonald, E. C. (2007). *The power of protocols: An educator's guide to better practice* (2nd ed.). New York, NY: Teachers College Press.

McLaughlin, M. W., & Talbert, J. E. (2006). *Building school-based teacher learning communities: Professional strategies to improve student achievement.* New York, NY: Teachers College Press.

Merseth, K. (1991). *The case for cases in teacher education.* Washington, DC: American Association for Higher Education.

Merseth, K. (1997). *Case studies in educational administration.* New York, NY: Longman/Addison Wesley.

Merseth, K. (2003). *Windows on teaching mathematics: Cases of secondary mathematics.* New York, NY: Teachers College Press.

Merseth, K. R. (2007). Introduction. In Metlife Fellows in the Teachers Network Leadership Institute, *Making the case* (pp. 2–5). Retrieved from http://www .teachersnetwork.org/tnli/cases/makingthecase.pdf

Miller, B., & Kantrov, I. (1998). *A guide to facilitating cases in education.* Portsmouth, NH: Heinemann.

Miller, B., Moon, J., & Elko, S. (2000). *Teacher leadership in mathematics and science: Casebook and facilitator's guide.* Portsmouth, NH: Heinemann.

Morse, A. (2009). *Cultivating a math coaching practice: A guide for K–8 math educators.* Thousand Oaks, CA: Corwin.

National Writing Project & Nagin, C. (2006). *Because writing matters: Improving student writing in our schools* (2nd ed.). San Francisco, CA: Jossey-Bass.

Naumes, W., & Naumes, M. J. (1999). *The art and craft of case writing.* Thousand Oaks, CA: SAGE.

Olson, L. (2007, May 9). Leadership by teachers gains notice. *Education Week, 26*(36). Retrieved from http://www.edweek.org/ew/arthicles/2007/05/09/36teachlead.h26.html

Penuel, W. R., Fishman, B., Yamaguchi, R., & Gallagher, L. P. (2007). What makes professional development effective? Strategies that foster curriculum implementation. *American Educational Research Journal, 44*(4), 921–958.

Portin, B. S., Knapp, M. S., Dareff, S., Feldman, S., Russell, F. A., Samuelson, C., & Yeh, T. L. (2009, October). *Leadership for learning improvement in urban schools.* Seattle: University of Washington, Center for the Study of Teaching and Policy, University of Washington. Retrieved from http://www.wallacefoundation.org/KnowledgeCenter

Reeves, D. B. (2008). *Reframing teacher leadership to improve your school.* Alexandria, VA: ASCD.

Schmoker, M. (2006). *Results now: How we can achieve unprecedented improvements in teaching and learning.* Alexandria, VA: ASCD.

Schwarz, R. (1994). *The skilled facilitator.* San Francisco, CA: Jossey-Bass.

Shulman, J. H. (1992). *Case methods in teacher education.* New York, NY: Teachers College Press.

Shulman, J. H. (1996). Tender feelings, hidden thoughts: Confronting bias, innocence, and racism through case discussions. In J. Colbert, K. Trimble, & P. Desberg (Eds.), *The case for education: Contemporary approaches for using case methods* (pp. 137–158). Needham Heights, MA: Allyn & Bacon.

Shulman, J. H., & Colbert, J. A. (Eds.) (1987). *The mentor teacher casebook.* San Francisco, CA: Far West Laboratory for Educational Research and Development.

Shulman, J. H., & Colbert, J. A. (Eds.). (1988). *The intern teacher casebook.* San Francisco, CA: Far West Laboratory for Educational Research and Development.

Shulman, J., Lotan, R. A., & Whitcomb, J. A. (Eds.). (1998). *Groupwork in diverse classrooms: A casebook for educators.* New York, NY: Teachers College Press.

Shulman, J. H., Whittaker, A., & Lew, M. (Eds.). (2002). *Using assessments to teach for understanding: A casebook for educators.* New York, NY: Teachers College Press.

Shulman, L. S. (1986). Those who understand: Knowledge growth in teaching. *Educational Researcher, 15*(4), 4–14.

Shulman, L. S. (1996). Just in case: Reflections on learning from experience. In J. Colbert, K. Trimble, & P. Desberg (Eds.), *The case for education: Contemporary approaches for using case methods* (pp. 197–217). Needham Heights, MA: Allyn & Bacon.

Simon, H. A. (1957). *Models of man—Social and rational.* New York, NY: John Wiley.

Small, R., & Strzepek, J. E. (1988). *A casebook for English teachers: Dilemmas and decisions.* Belmont, CA: Wadsworth.

Smith, M. S., Silver, E. A., & Stein, M. K. (2005a). *Improving instruction in algebra: Using cases to transform mathematics teaching and learning* (Vol. 2). New York, NY: Teachers College Press.

Smith, M. S., Silver, E. A., & Stein, M. K. (2005b). *Improving instruction in geometry and measurement: Using cases to transform mathematics teaching and learning* (Vol. 3). New York, NY: Teachers College Press.

Smylie, M. A. (2008). Foreword. In M. M. Mangin & S. R. Stoelinga (Eds.), *Effective teacher leadership* (pp. ix–x). New York, NY: Teachers College Press.

Smylie, M., Conley, S., & Marks, H. M. (2002). Exploring new approaches to teacher leadership for school improvement. In J. Murphy (Ed.), *The educational leadership challenge: Redefining leadership for the 21st century* (pp. 162–188). Chicago, IL: University of Chicago Press.

Smylie, M. A., & Hart, A. W. (2000). School leadership for teacher learning and change: A human and social capital development perspective. In J. Murphy & K. S. Louis (Eds.), *Handbook of research on educational administration* (2nd ed., pp. 421–441). San Francisco, CA: Jossey-Bass.

Spillane, J. P. (2006). *Distributed leadership.* San Francisco, CA: Jossey-Bass.

Spillane, J. P., Hallett, T., & Diamond, J. B. (2003). Forms of capital and the construction of leadership in urban elementary schools. *Sociology of Education, 76*(1), 1–7.

Stein, M. K., Smith, M. S., Henningsen, M. A., & Silver, E. S. (2000). *Implementing standards-based mathematics instruction: A casebook for professional development.* New York, NY: Teachers College Press.

Stoelinga, S. R. (2008). Leading from above and below: Formal and informal teacher leadership. In M. M. Mangin & S. R. Stoelinga (Eds.), *Effective teacher leadership: Using research to inform and reform* (pp. 99–119). New York, NY: Teachers College Press.

Straus, D., & Doyle, M. (1976). *How to make meetings work.* New York, NY: Jove Press.

Swanson, J. (2001). *The role of teacher leaders in scaling up standards-based reform.* Final Report prepared for the U.S. Department of Education, National Institute for Student Achievement, Curriculum and Assessment, Office of Educational Research and Improvement. Grant #R305F970040–99. Retrieved from http://eric.ed.gov/PDFS/ED444947.pdf

Sykes, G., & Bird, T. (1992). Teacher education and the case idea. *Review of Research in Education, 18,* 457–521.

Tippins, D. J., Koballa, T. R., & Payne, B. D. (2002). *Learning from cases: Unraveling the complexities of elementary science teaching.* Boston, MA: Allyn & Bacon.

Wenglinsky, H. (2000). *How teaching matters: Bringing the classroom back into discussions of teacher quality.* Policy Information Center Report. Princeton, NJ: Educational Testing Service.

Wheatley, M. J. (2002). *Turning to one another: Simple conversations to restore hope to the future.* San Francisco, CA: Berrett-Koehler.

York-Barr, J., & Duke, K. (2004). What do we know about teacher leadership? Findings from two decades of scholarship. *Review of Educational Research, 74*(3), 255–316.

Index

CORWIN
A SAGE Company

The Corwin logo—a raven striding across an open book—represents the union of courage and learning. Corwin is committed to improving education for all learners by publishing books and other professional development resources for those serving the field of PreK–12 education. By providing practical, hands-on materials, Corwin continues to carry out the promise of its motto: **"Helping Educators Do Their Work Better."**